PN
2881
Y3
1970

Yajnik, Ramanlal
Kanaiyalal.

The Indian theatre

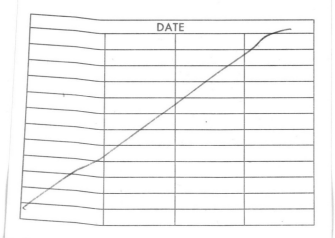

DATE

THE INDIAN THEATRE

THE INDIAN THEATRE

ITS ORIGINS
AND ITS LATER DEVELOPMENTS UNDER
EUROPEAN INFLUENCE

WITH
SPECIAL REFERENCE TO WESTERN INDIA

by

R. K. YAJNIK

M.A.(BOMBAY), PH.D.(LONDON)

*Professor of English Literature,
Samaldas College,
Bhavnagar, India*

HASKELL HOUSE PUBLISHERS LTD.

Publishers of Scarce Scholarly Books

NEW YORK. N. Y. 10012

1970

First Published 1934

HASKELL HOUSE PUBLISHERS Ltd.
Publishers of Scarce Scholarly Books
280 LAFAYETTE STREET
NEW YORK, N. Y. 10012

Library of Congress Catalog Card Number: 74-92995

Standard Book Number 8383-1214-4

Printed in the United States of America

THIS VOLUME

IS

GRATEFULLY INSCRIBED

TO

PROFESSOR

ALLARDYCE NICOLL

PREFACE

PART II of this book was a thesis approved for the Degree of Ph.D. in the University of London, in July 1931, and its publication was aided by a grant from the Publication Fund of the University. Its full title was *The Influence of British Drama on the Indian Stage, with special reference to Western India*. Obviously, the aim of the present writer has been to concentrate mainly on the theatres in Western India. He is fully conscious of the fact that, even more than the problem of direct borrowings by way of translations and adaptations, the question of assimilation of Western ideas and of general inspiration derived from Western models in original vernacular plays, especially Bengali, is of great importance. For this purpose one full chapter is devoted to this type of subtle influence, though a detailed study of individual Indian dramatists of note would require a companion volume. For the moment, a greater emphasis is sought to be laid on the earlier type of British influence in all its theatrical bearings.

In accordance with the advice of eminent Indian scholars, Mr. P. V. Kane and Dr. S. K. De, Part I of this work is retained after a thorough revision. Mr. P. V. Kane writes: "The first part dealing with Sanskrit dramaturgy is meant to give an ordinary reader an idea, however imperfect, of what Sanskrit dramatic theory and practice was. The scholar may, no doubt, say that that part is rather meagre; but Dr. Yajnik has not written the first part for the scholar. In my opinion Part I may be kept as it is, with slight abridgment here and there, particularly because most English readers as well as modern educated men in India are not familiar with the theory and practice of Sanskrit drama."

The present writer has attempted to present in Part II as wide a survey as possible of the activities of the vernacular theatres of India. Both because of an intimate personal knowledge of the existing conditions and of a detailed study of all relevant material, it may be claimed that nothing of importance has been omitted. As part of the subject has been dealt with already by Dr. Gupta, in an unpublished thesis, it may be explained that the present work adds to his valuable dissertation in several directions: (1) by treating the theme from the point of view of the theatre and not from that of the study; (2) by providing analysis of many other adaptations of Shakespeare—unknown to Dr. Gupta; (3) by dealing with the adaptations of a number of Western plays not by Shakespeare; and (4) by devoting a chapter to the general influence of Western drama on original Indian productions. In a word, Dr. Gupta's aim was to consider the literary quality of the vernacular versions, mainly Bengali, of Shakespeare's works; the purpose of this volume is to present a survey, from the theatrical point of view, of the general influence on India of the Western stage.

In the course of a long tour especially undertaken for the purpose of studying the conditions at first hand, the writer visited most of the important theatres in Bombay, Poona, Madras, Calcutta, and Delhi. He was also given facilities for examining some of the MS. copies of plays preserved in the Police Commissioner's office at Bombay, and also of seeing several prompt-copies in the various theatres. Moreover, he was allowed to make his own notes from the unpublished diary of Mr. Joseph David Penkar, a well-known Bombay producer. During this tour he was able to gather together many rare copies of plays, "opera-books", critical articles in periodicals, playbills, and photographs, which were carefully studied.

The writer wishes to express indebtedness to many students and scholars, such as Messrs. C. R. Shah (who kindly permitted him to read his excellent notes based on the "opera-books" of about seven Urdu adaptations of Shakespeare's plays), G. L. Pandya, K. B. Mehta, T. N. Dave, R. J. Jani, I. V. Trivedi, N. V. Thakkur, N. R. Pathak, V. N. Naik,

S. B. Mazmudar, and Rao Bahadur P. Sambanda; and various friends, play-wrights, managers, producers, and actors for helping him in many ways. He also thanks Mr. Clifford Leech for his valuable assistance; and Dr. Bailey of the School of Oriental Studies, Dr. Randall of the India Office Library, and Mr. G. Whitworth of the British Drama League, for their uniform kindness and courtesy. Above all he is deeply indebted to Professor Allardyce Nicoll for his constant sympathy and able guidance.

After this thesis was written Professor C. J. Sisson, Professor C. R. Shah, Mr. P. V. Kane, and Dr. S. K. De have been kind enough to go through the work carefully and give the writer the benefit of their very valuable suggestions and excellent notes. To all these scholars the writer owes a deep debt of gratitude.

Finally, hearty thanks are due to the University of London and to the Bhavnagar State for their financial aid in the publication of this volume. Messrs. George Allen & Unwin Ltd. deserve all possible credit for their uniform courtesy and whole-hearted co-operation.

R. K. YAJNIK

SAMALDAS COLLEGE
BHAVNAGAR, INDIA

January 21, 1933

CONTENTS

A NOTE ON TRANSLITERATION AND ABBREVIATIONS

(1) The system followed in the transliteration of Sanskrit and Urdu words is that approved by the Royal Asiatic Society. The same system has also been observed in transliterating Marathi, Gujarati and Bengali words, with the exception of many conventional words and proper names which are spelt in the popular manner.

(2) The following abbreviations have been used in the footnotes and Appendix C:

- (i) Western India: M. for Marathi; U. for Urdu or Hindustani; G. for Gujarati.
- (ii) Eastern India: B. for Bengali.
- (iii) Northern India: H. for Hindi; P. for Punjabi.
- (iv) Southern India: Ta. for Tamil; Te. for Telegu; K. for Kanarese.

(3) Versions marked with a star (*) are either not published or are out of print.

PART I

THE EARLY INDIAN STAGE

CHAPTER I

THE DRAMATIC THEORY OF THE HINDUS

UNDOUBTEDLY the Indian drama of to-day is profoundly influenced by contact with the West; but it is not to be forgotten that for centuries before the European drama was introduced to its audiences, India had a great national theatre of its own. To study, therefore, in proper perspective the epoch-making influence of British drama on the Indian stage, it is necessary first to take a preliminary panoramic view of the evolution of the early Indian drama itself. There is a distinct line of continuity from the Gupta golden age (often compared to the age of Pericles, A.D. 320 to 480),[1] when Kālidāsa wrote plays for the Gupta royal court theatre and the Sanskrit drama reached its zenith, through its decline and ruin after the Mohammedan conquest in the twelfth century and the cultivation of the medieval "Mystery and Morality" popular stage in the villages, where this type of play still lingers, down to the most modern performances on the Indian stage. In fact, the Indian theatre of to-day marks the meeting-point of three main streams, viz. the ancient Indian classical drama, the medieval popular stage and the powerful British influence. In order to grasp the full significance of the last, it is desirable in the first place, by way of a general background, to take a rapid survey of the dramatic theory and practice of the Hindus and of the character of the medieval performances and then to sum up the position of the Indian stage till the year 1756 (the year before the battle of Plassey), when the first English theatre was established in Calcutta.[2]

1. Vincent Smith: *The Oxford History of India*, 1920, p. 156.
2. Binoy Krishna Deb: *The Early History and Growth of Calcutta*, 1905.

A. SOURCES AND FIRST PRINCIPLES

All true study of this type of literature[3] must start with a
careful reading of the *Nāṭyaśāstra*[4] (*Science of Dramaturgy*)
of Bharata, who is believed to have flourished about the
beginning of the Christian era.[5] Since he mentions many
types of Sanskrit drama, it is obvious that the ancient
Indian drama must have been cultivated many years
previous to the time of Kālidāsa As, however, most of
those plays seem to have perished, there is a peculiar
difficulty in making a just appreciation of Bharata.

Ancient tradition, based on his work, gives a curious
mythical account of the origin of the Indian dramatic art.
A play, styled *Lakṣmīswayaṁvara* (*The Choice Marriage of
Lakṣmī*), was being produced at the celestial theatre of
Indra (the Indian Jupiter). The principal nymph, Urvaśī, in
the rôle of Lakṣmī, the consort of Viṣṇu, was now dancing
and singing, now displaying her skill in clever pantomime
and now giving vent to her erotic emotions by means of
appropriate gesture and vocal expression. Losing herself in
a momentary reverie concerning her earthly paramour, she
blundered in the midst of her dialogue, whereat Great Jove
frowned and cursed her to descend to earth. Good, however,
came out of this evil, for Urvaśī brought her theatrical art
to the world.

This popular legend has, at least, the advantage of
emphasizing the original nature of drama, for here the
services of music, dancing, gesture and dramatic expression
were all utilized in the same representation. The truth of
this inherent theatrical unity is illustrated by the fact that
the Sanskrit word for a play (*nāṭaka*) has for its root *nṛt*,
= to dance. The four cognate words, *nṛtya* (dance), *nṛtta*

3. For a list of Sanskrit plays, cf. *A Bibliography of the Sanskrit
    Drama*, New York, 1906, p. 13 fn.
4. See the Benares Edition of 1929.
5. P. V. Kane: Introduction to *Sāhityadarpaṇa*, p. viii.

(pantomime), *nāṭya* (drama) and *naṭa* (a dancer, an acrobat or an actor), throw a flood of light on the evolution of the theatrical art from dance and music to studied gesture and dramatic expression.

To realize the implications of the dramatic theory of the Hindus, it is essential to start with the above derivative meaning of the important terms. For the development of the study it will be necessary to refer to *Bharata Nāṭyaśāstra, Daśarūpa* of Dhanañjaya[6] (*c.* 975) and *Sāhityadarpaṇa* of Viśvanātha (*c.* 1300),[7] "a triumvirate in the domain of Sanskrit dramatic criticism" (P. V. Kane). A reference has already been made to the first, an ancient encyclopædic work which aims at embracing most of the departments of dramatic art. As it saw light only recently, earlier critics like Wilson failed to grasp the full significance of the drama of India. The second is a treatise on Hindu Dramaturgy concerned mainly with the ten types of drama; and the third, in the sixth chapter, deals with dramatic theory in all its details.

Raja S. M. Tagore[8] starts his valuable collection, in English, from the standard authorities on the ancient Indian theatre, with the quotation: "Sages have divided Music (or Poetry) into two classes, viz. *Dṛśya Saṅgīta* (Visible Music), and *Śrāvya Saṅgīta* (Audible Music), by reference to the organs of sight and hearing, by which it is apprehended by the mind. . . . Personation or representation by an assumed character being essential to the 'Visible Music', it is called *Rūpaka* (from *Rūpa* = Form). *Abhinaya* or Acting is the representation of high and low characters on the stage under suitable guises." It is clear that, being an important division of the art of poetry, the drama ought to be truly suggestive to conform to the highly cultivated *Dhvani* (Art of Suggestion) theory of the Sanskrit

6. Translated by Dr. C. O. Haas, New York, 1912.
7. Translated by Ballantyne and Mitra, Calcutta, 1875.
8. *The Hindu Drama*, Calcutta, 1880.

critics. The finer the suggestion, the higher the enjoyment. Again, the position of spectacle on the stage, with that of the various assumed rôles, is equally clear.

A representation is 'to reflect the life of the world as if in a mirror' (Tagore). As H. H. Dhruva[9] quotes from Bharata: "all arts and sciences are to be met with there". The purpose of the drama, like that of all poetry, is to please and teach at the same time, or "to instruct in a very pleasing manner in the style of a loving wife", as the art-critic Mammaṭa would put it. But how is this aim of combined pleasure and instruction to be achieved? By means of inspiring various sentiments (*rasas*) in the audience, in the course of an imitation by actors of the different states of life in the midst of diverse action.

B. MAIN CHARACTERISTICS OF HINDU DRAMA

The first thing, perhaps, which strikes a student of Sanskrit literature is the fundamental religious basis of the entire edifice. The characteristic Hindu attitude to life may be judged from certain deeply rooted national beliefs. The doctrines of *Karma* (Action or Deeds) and of 'rebirth' go hand in hand. Deeds of the past life are held more or less responsible for birth in a high or low caste and family, and also for happiness and misery falling to the human lot. However, since God is supposed to hold the scales of justice even, it is open to a human soul, by means of meritorious deeds, to rise to the summit of evolution and experience, the consummation of pure joy, i.e. *Mokṣa* (Absolution).

It is not difficult to trace the influence of this great doctrine on the Hindu Drama. Human suffering was thus easily accounted for. Śakuntalā, by a deed of omission, offended a fiery sage, who pronounced the curse of conjugal separation on the erring damsel. Similarly, Sītā holds the sins of her past birth mostly responsible for her tragic situation.

9. *Asiatic Quarterly Review*, vol. 4, 1896, p. 359.

Consequently, the problem of their intense suffering does not deeply agitate the soul of the great Hindu dramatists.

If one takes the special point of the attitude to death, it may be observed that in the West death overshadows everything, whereas the Indian artist, while not denying decay, sees in it a condition of renewal. Still, the Hindu playwrights admit that death is a terrible thing to witness on the stage and they agree that the great mythological heroes should rather inspire in the minds of the audience feelings of reverence than of agony by an undignified spectacle of their death, which would resemble that of ordinary mortals. If they swoon, they always recover. Thus there was no question of a tragic *dénouement*.[10]

This philosophical attitude was supported by a general moral purpose[11] to encourage virtue and condemn vice or sin. Partly to achieve this end and partly to preserve the usual romantic atmosphere, there were presented on the stage ideal heroic characters strongly contrasted with vicious antagonists. Poetic justice, as practised by Western poets, is almost unknown, for, while good characters are ultimately rewarded, the villains, such as Saṁsthānaka in *The Toy Cart*, are forgiven that the hero's virtue may shine the more.[12]

In order to maintain an idealistic atmosphere, not only was a tragic end forbidden, but other important and far-reaching restrictions were also imposed. Propriety and decorum were emphasized and the dramatist had to observe the 'decencies' of the stage. Grim realism was not to be practised, for this could not exalt the human mind. Painful, disgusting and debasing things were to be avoided on the stage. "One should not visibly represent a long journey, murder, fighting, revolt of a kingdom or province, a siege,

10. For the views of Dr. De and Dr. Belvelkar, see Appendix A.
11. For Dr. De's view, see Appendix A.
12. It is interesting to compare the similar treatment of Angelo and of Iachimo in Shakespeare.

eating, bathing, intercourse, anointing the body, putting on clothes, or the like." This tendency towards refinement progressed more and more as rhetorician succeeded rhetorician, and one can easily perceive that in urging their point, stage limitations largely influenced their judgment. A long journey cannot be made convincing on the stage; nor can the representation of a great revolt or siege or battle. Attempts to reproduce these would prove merely ridiculous.

In that age of royal patronage the Brahmin author, with his serene and complacent attitude to life, pleased the king by paying him a compliment and at the same time by placing a striking model before him. A great Brahmin minister, like Cāṇakya (often styled 'the Indian Machiavel'), was depicted as above all temptations. He was wedded to learning. Poverty pleased him. He had no axe of his own to grind; therefore he could give the right advice fearlessly to the King. It is this religious attitude of doing one's duty without caring for reward which marks a striking contrast between this author of *Arthaśāstra* and the ambitious author of the *Prince*. The ideal of renunciation of the world after the object is achieved is constantly present in the Sanskrit drama, even in relation to kings.

The religious basis also in its attitude to external nature is likewise a marked characteristic of the Hindu drama. Possibly the influence of Buddhism and of Jainism had something to do with it. "The heart and essence of the Indian experience is to be found in a constant intuition of the unity of all life".[13] This pantheistic conception lends a unique colour and charm to the Hindu drama, for not only the birds and the beasts, but even the plants, the flowers, the sky and the hills express divine sympathy towards Śakuntalā and towards Sītā.

The second outstanding quality in the ancient Hindu drama is its all-pervading poetry and its peculiar dramatic

13. A. Coomarswamy: *Dance of Śiva and Other Essays*, New York, 1918, p. 1.

form. A great number of distinct types of verses are interspersed in the prose dialogue. These lyrical pieces might be
either recited on the stage or sung to the accompaniment
of varied stringed instruments. The science of *Alaṅkāras*
(Flowers of Speech) being most assiduously cultivated in
ancient India and deeply appreciated at the royal courts,
poets vied with each other in excelling in this particular
art even in their plays. Often, the cadence was subtly
varied to harmonize with the mood of a particular character.
All scholars agree that this fascinating poetry and infinite
subtlety of music cannot be translated into any other
language and may be fully enjoyed only in the original
Sanskrit.

The third characteristic—and here the Sanskrit drama may
be contrasted with the Greek—is the great variety of
characters, male and female, introduced into the plays.
There is no attempt here to keep to certain classes or persons.
Undoubtedly, in accordance with the monarchical tradition,
kings, ministers, high officials and attendants often figured
very prominently; but all other persons, high and low, are
here provided with parts. The Sanskrit critics noted in
detail several attributes of many dramatic stock types,
particular emphasis being laid on the nobler qualities with
a view to placing good models before the audience; although
human follies and foibles, of course, are allowed to creep in,
lest the characters should become mere wooden figures. The
most interesting of the 'lower' stock types, perhaps, are the
comic characters of *Vidūṣaka*, the polished wit (*viṭa*) and
the foolish villain (*Śakāra*).

With reference to the women characters, it is worthy of
notice that unmarried women of high birth, like Mālatī and
Sāgarikā, were introduced into lighter scenes of comic life,
"an accession to which ancient comedy was a stranger, for
it is never found in Plautus and Terence".[14] An intrigue
with a married woman was not permitted to be the theme

14. Cf. Wilson: Introduction to *The Theatre of the Hindus*.

of a play. Again, as the Hindu youths (e.g. Cārudatta), like the Greek youths, sought intellectual company outside their homes, amidst a distinct class of most accomplished females, *vārānganās* or courtesans, the dancing-girl (e.g. Vasantasenā) could figure as an accomplished heroine endowed with an admirable character.[15]

The fourth distinguishing quality is the romantic setting of the Sanskrit drama, due to the presence of celestial machinery on the Indian stage. Along with the variety of male and female characters just mentioned, the inhabitants of the other world constantly figure. The playwrights not only made the fullest use of all available mythological and historical material and of religious tradition, but they also gave the fullest latitude to the imagination. In the world of the theatre, therefore, gods and nymphs could be seen on the stage, side by side with kings and clowns. The romantic atmosphere, say, of *Uttara-rāma-carita*, is thus not unlike that of *A Midsummer Night's Dream*.

Fifthly, in this romantic atmosphere, there is a curious element of realism introduced by the use of many dialects according to the status of the various characters. Only gods, most of the Brahmins and princes talk in pure Sanskrit. The women characters generally speak Prakrit. Other inferior characters hold their conversation in different dialects of their supposed provinces. It is noteworthy that the audience, gifted with the knowledge of the slight variations of dialect, enjoyed this impression of reality as much as the Elizabethans appreciated the Welsh dialect or the French accent in Shakespeare. These dialects are classified by the critics in detail. In fact, elaborate classification as regards plot, construction, characters, modes of speech, etc., is the keynote of the Sanskrit dramatic criticism. At this stage it may be useful to glance at some of the important points of this detailed classification.

15. Cf. S. K. De: *Treatment of Love in Sanskrit Literature*, Calcutta, 1929, p. 83.

C. CLASSIFICATION IN HINDU DRAMATIC THEORY

The relation of the main plot to the under-plot, it was said, should be organic, for the latter represents an important 'limb' of the main 'body' of the former. Here the emphasis is laid on the prime necessity of concentrated dramatic appeal. In the conduct of the plot, the primary aim should be to direct all efforts to reach ultimately *phalaprāpti* ('object of the business of drama'), i.e. the catastrophe. This aim is secured by keeping a fivefold object in view.[16] Even more important than this classification are the five main *sandhis* (junctures or links of the plot) of a drama *par excellence*. These are: (1) *mukham* (Opening or Protasis); (2) *pratimukham* (Progression or Epitasis); (3) *garbha* (Development or Catastasis); (4) *vimarśa* (Pause or Peripateia); and (5) *nirvahaṇa* (Conclusion or Catastrophe).[17]

Speaking broadly, this fivefold evolution of plot is easily illustrated from *Ratnāvalī*, a play which had a great theatrical success: (1) In Act I, the minister is preparing the ground for the princess of Ceylon, incognita, by introducing her to the harem of the king; (2) in Act II, the discovery by a girl and the clown that the king is in love with her and the suspicion of the queen; (3) in Act III, the 'discovery' of the truth by the king that he is making love to the queen and not to the princess, due to a confusion of costume; (4) the obstacle arising from the queen's withholding her consent; and (5) in the fourth and last Act, the disappearance of all the clouds, the clearing of the mystery of birth, the consent to union and the king's victories.

Dr. Wilson[18] has cleverly applied this Hindu classification

16. (a) *prārambha* (Beginning); (b) *prayatna* (Promotion); (c) *prāptyāśā* (Prospect of Attainment); (d) *niyataprāpti* (Certainty of Attainment); and (e) *phalāgama* (Attainment of the Fruit or Object).
17. Dr. De suggests these English equivalents.
18. *Select Specimens of the Theatre of the Hindus*, London, 1827, Vol. I, p. xl.

to *Romeo and Juliet*: "The ball at the house of Capulet may be considered the *mukha* (*sandhi*): the *pratimukha* is the interview with Juliet in the garden: the *garbha* is Juliet's apparent assent to the marriage with Paris; the *vimarśa* is the despair of Romeo, consequent on a contrivance intended to preserve Juliet's faith. The catastrophe needs no elucidation." This fivefold division is to be discovered also in *Twelfth Night* or *Cymbeline*, as indeed in most Shakespearean plays; an evolution through five stages— "The Introduction and Beginning of Conflict", "The Development of Conflict", "The Crisis", "The Disentanglement" and "The Catastrophe"—is generally acknowledged.

So far as the characters are concerned, this formal classification marks out numbers of types commonly represented on the stage. The gods belong to the *dhīroddhata* (jealous, haughty, boastful and powerful) class; the kings to the *dhīralalita* (loving fine arts and of sweet disposition) class; ministers and generals to the *dhīrodātta* (serious and magnanimous) class; and the Brahmins and merchants to the *dhīraprasānta* (calm and dignified) class. A Richard III, a Macbeth, and a Lear have many qualities of the first; an Orsino and an Antony have some of the second; an Antonio and an Othello not a few of the third; and a Brutus has something which may fall in the last class.

The women characters, too, are classified according to their types. They may be self-controlled (*dhīrā*) like a Helena, gay and pleasure-loving (*lalitā*) like a Cleopatra and high-spirited (*udāttā*) like a Portia. Moreover, married women devoted to their husbands (*svīyā*) may be either in the freshness of budding youth (*mugdhā*) like a Viola, or grown up and slightly rude in speech (*madhyā*) like a Lady Percy or a full mature woman (*pragalbhā*) like a Hermione.[19]

There are, too, many points of interest in the critical divisions and arrangement of plot material. The play opens

19. For an elaborate classification of the heroine, see S. K. De: *Sanskrit Poetics*, Vol. II, p. 339 f.

with a prelude (*pūrvaraṅga*) containing a prayer, a reverential address to the assembly (*sabhā*), on behalf of the author of the piece, and an introduction of the subject proper (*prastāvanā*). The play is divided into acts (*aṅka*); and often scene-divisions within an act (*garbhāṅka*) are implied. Short scenes, subdivided according to the status of characters, are to be introduced between acts, to give the necessary information. There may be similar intimations, also, from 'within', i.e. from behind the curtain or from 'above'. The play ends with an epilogue, verses of prayer to God, invoking blessings.

The critics, too, have discussed several tricks of speech and various dramatic devices. One of the most interesting of these dramatic devices is the use of the play within a play, which is so replete with pathetic irony in *Uttara-rāma-carita* and which reminds one of the similar examples in *The Spanish Tragedy, A Midsummer Night's Dream, Hamlet* and other Elizabethan dramas.

Of all the subtle classifications, however, the minute analysis of the dramatic sentiments (*rasas*) has appealed most to European scholars. The *rasa* theory is considered as the principal original contribution made by Sanskrit criticism to the dramatic theory of the world.

D. THE *RASA* THEORY

"On mature consideration it will clearly appear that sentiment (*rasa*) is the corner-stone of theatrical representations; since it is their avowed object to awaken sentiments in the minds of the audience similar to those which they body forth."[20] "*Rasa* or poetic sentiment is a peculiar affection of the mind giving rise to the well-known emotions such as those of love, heroism," etc.[21] As Mr. P. V. Kane[22] neatly

20. Raja S. M. Tagore: *The Eight Principal Rasas of the Hindus*, Calcutta, 1879, p. 1.
21. Dr. S. K. Belvelkar: Notes to *Kāvyādarśa* (1–18).
22. Introduction to *Sāhityadarpaṇa*, p. cxlvii.

sums up the position of the *rasa* school in relation to the
dramatic art, "the central pivot round which the whole
rasa system revolves is a statement by Bharata, which
declares that '*rasa* results from the combination of determi-
nants, the consequents and the secondary or accessory
moods (with the permanent or dominant moods)' ". This
pithy statement has given scope to a great controversy.
The generally accepted interpretation of Abhinavagupta is
on the following lines:

The principal aim of a stage representation, with the aid
of all theatrical accessories, is to appeal to and to rouse
the latent emotions in the audience. Thus the spectators
witness on the stage certain characters, say Rāma and
Sītā. These are expressing their feelings by appropriate
words and gestures. If it is the sentiment of love which is
sought to be exhibited, such excitants as the beauty of
spring and the charm of the moon are suggested by the
necessary stage effects. The characters reveal by means of
several physiological external manifestations the influence
of the season, etc. Moreover, certain fleeting psychological
moods, such as despondency in the case of the dominant
passion of love, go to develop the permanent mood. All
these combine to rouse a certain dominant mood in the
spectator, say of love;[23] and the cumulative effect of all
these is to develop to perfection the æsthetic enjoyment of
the erotic sentiment (*śṛṅgāra rasa*). "What is manifested is
not the *rasa* itself, but its relish; not the mood itself but
its reflection in the form of a subjective condition of æsthetic
enjoyment in the reader or the spectator."[24]

In a word, there is a certain dominant or permanent
mood (*sthāyi-bhāva*) latent in a spectator. This gradually
develops, stage by stage, till it reaches the point of complete

23. The permanent or dominant moods that poetry or drama may
    call forth are eight: Love, Gaiety, Sorrow, Anger, Energy or
    Vigour, Fear, Repugnance, and Wonder.
24. S. K. De: *Sanskrit Poetics*, Vol. II, p. 165.

æsthetic enjoyment or *rasa*. Such a consummation is achieved by (1) the presence of actors on the stage in the rôles of certain characters (*ālambana-vibhāvas*); (2) by the appropriate acting (*abhinaya*), i.e. by "certain tokens of mental feelings, delineated in the dramatic representation by an imitation of human nature through steady concentration of the mind" (Bharata's *sattvābhinaya*);[25] (3) by the exciting causes, such as the moon, flowers, etc., in love (*uddīpana-vibhāvas*); (4) by certain external manifestations, e.g. movement of eyes, etc., in love (*anu-bhāvas*); and (5) by certain passing or secondary moods which serve the purpose of completely manifesting the permanent mood, e.g. despondency in love (*vyabhicāri-bhāvas*). All these act on the latent dominant moods (*sthāyi-bhāvas*) of the human mind and rouse them to the complete æsthetic enjoyment or *rasa*.[26]

Critics classify the *rasas* into eight or nine species, viz. (1) The First or the Erotic; (2) the Heroic; (3) the Pathetic or Tragic; (4) the Terrific; (5) the Comic or Farcical; (6) the Horrible; (7) the Odious; (8) the Wonderful; and (9) the Quiescent.

25. S. K. De: *Sanskrit Poetics*, Vol. II, p. 31.
26. Apart from the above popular view, three other important interpretations of the *rasa* theory of Bharata are interesting:
(a) According to Lollaṭa, *rasa*, in the primary sense, belongs to the hero, Rāma, etc.; it is the actor, who throws himself completely into a particular rôle, who then transfers it to the spectator.
(b) According to Śaṅkuka, the *rasa* is not transferred from the actor to the spectator, but is inferred by the audience on account of the illusion produced by the actor in cleverly imitating the original action.
(c) Finally, according to Bhaṭṭa Nāyaka, "the *rasa* consists in the permanent mood, experienced in a generalized form in poetry and drama, and enjoyed by a blissful process, till it is raised to a state of pleasurable relish, which is not worldly but disinterested, and which is akin to the philosophic meditation of Brahma" (S. K. De). (For an excellent, exhaustive treatment of the *rasa* theory, see S. K. De: *Studies in the History of Sanskrit Poetics*, Vol. II, p. 147 f.)

The ancient critics anticipated the modern theory of the 'Unity of Impression' by laying down a rule that each play must have only one dominant sentiment or *rasa*. Love is the outstanding passion of Kālidāsa's masterpiece. The prevailing note of Bhavabhūti's great drama is tragic; the principal flavour resulting from *Veṇīsaṁhāra* is terrific, and so on.

Along with the principal *rasa*, however, other subsidiary sentiments might and even should be experienced in the same play. Consequently, it must not be assumed that it was the object of the dramatist to produce a play with a monotonous emphasis on one emotion. One *rasa* must be predominant, but the introduction of others, it is recognized, will add to the beauty and richness of the whole. The Sanskrit rhetoricians, of course, insist on the necessity of subordinating these subsidiary *rasas* to the major *rasa* of the play, the dominant sentiment having to retain its hold on the mind of the audience from start to finish, the other sentiments merely contributing to the enjoyment of the play by appealing to diverse human tastes and moods. *Mālatī-mādhava* may be used as an illustration. The principal sentiment here is erotic, but almost all subordinate sentiments, even those radically different, are experienced in the witnessing of the piece. The Heroic is felt at the bold fight of the hero with the devilish priest of the goddess; the Pathetic sends a shudder through the body when the heroine, on the point of death, makes her touching confessions; the Farcical makes all laugh whole-heartedly as they hear of the sorry plight of the fool Nandana bewitched by a boy-wife. The Odious and the Terrible are experienced in the crematorium of Ujjayinī. Still the erotic sentiment predominates; and the final impression is of Love with its youth, beauty and joy. The idea seems to be that the most contradictory sentiments, properly grouped, may lead to the highest harmony, just as the riot of colours or the discordant notes controlled by a master painter or a gifted musician.

E. ROMANTIC FREEDOM

The Sanskrit drama was not really 'cabin'd, cribb'd, confined' by rules as such critics as Sheldon Cheney[27] have
alleged. Indeed, Sanskrit criticism itself, in spite of the
tendency towards detailed classification, indicates the
enormous variety of types of plays. It is of course true that
the minutest analysis of every type of play in relation to
the plot, characters and situations or incidents is trying to
the patience of modern scholars; but it must be realized
that this minute critical analysis did not mean a fettering
of the creative dramatists in their work. The subject matter,
the hero and the sentiment provide, in their combinations,
a wide field of varied forms. There is scope for a playlet of
only one act in monologue with the aid of ventriloquism,
styled *bhāṇa*, and also for a full-dress serious play, in five
to ten acts, as in the works of Kālidāsa and Bhavabhūti,
called *nāṭaka* or 'drama' proper. There is scope for a purely
farcical realistic satire, a *prahasana*, for a gloomy type
representing terrible events, portents, incantations, etc., a
ḍima, and also for a most spectacular piece, based on mythological fable, staging tempests and combats and displaying
the full pride and pomp of war (not permitted in standard
plays) such as is represented in *Samudramathana* (*The
Churning of the Ocean*). This type is styled *samavakāra*.
There are sparkling comedies of intrigue like *Ratnāvalī*,
which is styled a 'small play' (*nāṭikā*), for it consists of
four acts only. There are revenge plays like *Veṇīsaṁhāra*
mentioned above. There are great masterpieces possessing
neither love sentiment, nor any feminine characters of note,
such as *Mudrārākṣasa*, wherein the awe-inspiring Cāṇakya
stands in tragic isolation.

Apart from the freedom of these diverse forms, the
whole atmosphere is completely romantic. The so-called

27. *The Theatre*, London, 1929, p. 109.

c

Unities of Time, Place and Action are not observed. So far as action is concerned, it may be noted that Sanskrit criticism welcomes, beside the major plot, the development of subsidiary incidents and situations. The fundamental 'Unity of Action' is to be observed, it is true, but only in the Shakespearean sense.

The 'Unity of Time' was ignored both in theory and practice, so far as the drama as a whole was concerned; although a sense of dramatic propriety demanded that "an Act should be arranged with a single purpose exemplified by the doings of a single day". Accordingly, an act by itself creates its own illusion during which one may suppose that at the most a whole day is spent. But between the acts many years may roll away, as in *Śākuntala*, when Bharata grows from birth to boyhood, or in *Uttara-rāma-carita*, when similarly Lava and Kuśa grow, exactly as Perdita grows to maidenhood between the third and the fourth acts of *A Winter's Tale*. Time may slide over twelve or sixteen years, as the audience may learn from the chorus or by means of a short dialogue.

Similarly, the 'Unity of Place' is not observed. Within the same act the place is practically the same, except for small distances which are suggested by means of some brisk movement on the stage. In the following act, however, the scene may open at any other place, even in a celestial region. The concluding stages of a long journey are symbolically represented, so that the audience travels and reaches the destination imaginatively and then stays for the act in that locality. The idea of the locality is often picturesquely suggested by means of exquisite poetic descriptions. In certain plays, it is true, such as *Ratnāvalī*, where a royal intrigue is presented, all the acts are confined to the several chambers or gardens of the palace itself, just as in *The Tempest* the whole action is confined to the enchanted island. But such a restriction is voluntary on the part of the dramatist and is not imposed on him by theory.

F. SIDE-LIGHTS FROM EUROPEAN THEORY

Considering the Sanskrit dramatic theory as a whole, it is clear that the general tendency of the Hindu drama is supremely romantic, although a few important parallels between the Indian and the European dramatic theories noted by Professor A. B. Keith[28] are worthy of careful perusal. Apart from some ideas which run parallel with others in Aristotle's *Poetics*, there are several features of Western criticism which find similar expression in the theory of the East. Thus, the division of a play into five acts by Horace and the observation of the stage 'Decencies' prescribed by him have been anticipated by the Hindu drama. Similarly, Sidney and the Renaissance theorists are anticipated in their judgment that the playwright should teach delightfully in order to reach 'the very end of poetry'. Sidney's ridicule of the attempts made to represent two armies on the stage with four swords and bucklers is reflected there, as is his forbidding of laughter at sinful and execrable or at miserable and pitiable things. Pope's constant advice to follow the ancient models has its counterpart in the Sanskrit reverence for the past masters. Finally, Bharata anticipates, in a certain sense, Coleridge's theory of dramatic illusion.

From the above brief discussion of the Hindu dramatic theory, it would appear that the Sanskrit drama occupies a very peculiar position, for it is classical in form and romantic in spirit. Its romantic tragi-comedy clearly anticipated the Elizabethan drama in many respects and thus made it possible for the latter to take a firm root on Indian soil in the nineteenth century. Now, turning to the obscure region of the ancient Indian stage and to the medieval practice, one may perhaps be able to view correctly the evolution of the theatre in India.

28. *The Sanskrit Drama*, Oxford, 1924, p. 355.

CHAPTER II

THE ANCIENT HINDU STAGE

THE drama is not a part of literature alone. It is always dependent on the theatre. In considering, therefore, the Sanskrit dramatic art, not only must a picture of the ancient theatre be continually present in one's mind, but one must also attempt to visualize in some vague manner the audience, the actors who played the parts and the actual mode of production. Unfortunately, the evidence available in this particular field is very meagre and, despite the valuable services of Professors Sylvain Lèvi[1] and A. B. Keith,[2] especially in their sections on *mise-en-scène*, the results are far from complete. Thus, the subject bristles to-day with extraordinary difficulties.

The initial difficulty lies in too much attention being paid by Bharata to the forms and ceremonies of religious worship in connection with the presiding deities of the theatre. Apart from many other allusions, Bharata devotes one whole chapter (No. 3) to the detailed worship of the stage gods. He even gives the correct invocation to be used when laying the foundation of the theatre building; this, because of its interest, may be quoted here: "Oh Pillar! as the Himalaya Mountains are immovably fixed on the ground, be Thou even like them." This attention devoted to devotional ceremonies naturally leaves little space for the treatment of many important matters. Secondly, the marked indifference of the Hindu race towards mundane realities seems to have precluded it from the preservation of historical records of facts and figures, in the manner of the archives published by Aristotle in *Didascalia* "chronicling the choregi,

1. Lèvi: *Le Théâtre Indien*, Paris, 1890, pp. 367–392.
2. Keith: *The Sanskrit Drama*, pp. 358–373.

tribes, poet-didascali, actors, plays and victors".3 In India, some important events are found narrated in the *Purāṇas*; but the writers so often soared on the wings of imagination that it becomes difficult to distinguish between imaginative ideas and the reality. Thus, for example, in *Harivaṁśa*, a production of the play *Bhānumatīharaṇa*4 is described, but even here mythological romance intrudes and confuses the historical account.

The third difficulty arises from the works of some of the later dramatic critics (mentioned in Chapter I) themselves. Valuable as they are in this sphere of theory, these critics become pedantic and only of academic interest when they approach the stage, for they are sadly lacking in enthusiasm for actual theatrical practice. Fourthly, as the drama, as a rule, made the fullest use of its accessories of dance, music and pantomime, the play as such could not develop on its own lines independently, whereas the others could.

Lastly, perhaps the most noteworthy difficulty proceeds from the theatre on its physical side. The kings being the greatest patrons of playwrights and actors, theatrical buildings and great music halls were often incorporated in the royal palaces. As Vincent Smith points out (p. 111), the palace of Chandragupta surpassed the royal abodes of Persia: and "splendid architecture necessarily involves the successful cultivation of sculpture, painting and all the decorative arts". But the whole has perished; and modern excavations can hardly reveal much art, for the great edifices were constructed mainly of perishable wood.

In these circumstances, Bharata and the commentary of Abhinavagupta remain the sole great authorities on the ancient stage. To this, of course, may be added the valuable assistance given by the plays themselves, which are singularly rich in minute, almost Shavian, stage directions. Besides

3. Dr. R. C. Flickinger: *The Greek Theatre and Its Drama*, Chicago, 1918, p. 319.
4. Part II of *Viṣṇu Purāṇa*, Chaps. 88–93.

these, there are a few other miscellaneous documents, such as *Kuṭṭanīmata*[5] and others,[6] which occasionally prove of assistance in the elucidation of obscure points. Sometimes, too, medieval paintings serve a useful purpose in giving pictures of particular postures and expressions as well as indicating the general background.[7]

To grasp the arrangement of the ancient Indian theatre, it is essential, on the one hand, to disengage the mind from all modern conceptions and to travel imaginatively into distant times and climes where, in spite of a distinctly high civilization, life was yet primitive, highly religious, credulous and fixed in the mould of the caste-system. It is essential, too, to realize that this Indian civilization and the theatre which flourished in its midst presents at almost every point a sharp contrast to the civilization and the theatre of ancient Greece. The Greek state was democratic, whereas the Hindu state was autocratic. This was the root of all the difference between the two. Thus, all the familiar surroundings of the Athenian performances—the great crowd of citizens, the selection of judges and the prize-giving—were generally absent in the Hindu theatre. The Greek theatre, at Athens, in the fifth century B.C., consisted of an orchestral circle, with an auditorium arranged partly about it on the slope of the Acropolis; the Hindu theatre was mostly a part and parcel of the Emperor's palace itself.[8] The one was built of stone; the other was constructed of wood and bricks. The former could accommodate many thousands of spectators; the latter aimed at an appeal to a more or less select audience. The Greek tragic actors, with cothurnus and mask, aimed

---

5. By Dāmodaragupta: Description of an actual representation of *Ratnāvalī*, Act I.
6. E.g. *Mātṛguptācārya; Śilparatna; Saṅgītaratnākara.*
7. Cf. *Rūpam*, a Calcutta periodical, No. 4, October 1920: "Notes on Hindu Erotics"; No. 6, April 1921: "Dole-Leela," etc.
8. It is noteworthy that, apart from the royal theatres in palaces, many plays were also produced during *yātrā* festivals or fairs (cf. Bhavabhūti's plays).

at creating an impression of awe and grandeur; the Hindu actors aimed at a more intimate and vivid impression by means of studied facial gestures and movements. In a word, the Greek theatre was statuesque and the Indian theatre picturesque.[9]

Bharata devotes his second chapter to the discussion of the theatre building itself. Emphasis is laid on the selection of hard land, on its purification from bones, bushes, etc., and on fixing definite boundaries with a thread, so that exact prescribed measurements may be preserved. Laying the foundation of the theatre was to be an impressive religious ceremony, with the accompaniment of music, evening feasting of Brahmins, etc. The Director of the Company was prescribed a fast of three days before the ceremony. Regarding the four main pillars of the building, it is noteworthy that no pillar was to be in the centre and that the four were dedicated to the four castes, the lowest included. This reveals, curiously enough, a partially democratic basis of Hindu theatrical art, four colours being associated with the four castes, white, red, yellow and blue respectively. The explanation appears to be that all orders of society were represented in the king's retinue.

The father of the Hindu theatre starts his account by dividing the theatres into three groups according to their size.[10] The Commentator Abhinavagupta argues that in the

9. The latest edition of the *Encyclopædia Britannica* (Vol. 19, p. 964) refers to the obsolete theory of possible Greek influence on the Hindu drama; but dismisses it. Here is an important chain of arguments, not usually noticed, if more proof were needed, to prove the absurdity of the theory. The term *yavanikā* (a curtain), to which undue weight is attached by some, simply means that it was made of foreign material and nothing more, as Professor Keith also agrees. Even to-day the Sanskrit word for a foreigner is *yavana*. Dr. S. K. De is, however, of opinion that the right word may be *yamanikā*, which would mean "a covering or a curtain," from the root *yam*, to restrain.

10. (a) The large size had to be 128 × 64 cubits (192 × 96 ft.); (b) the medium size 64 × 32 cubits (96 × 48 ft.); (c) the small size 32 × 16 cubits (48 × 24 ft.).

first, where gods and angels figured, there ought to be frequent use of large musical instruments together with much movement on the stage. The medium size is that which is recommended specially and is, therefore, discussed in greater detail.

The standard theatre (*nāṭyaveśman*) was a rectangular building, 96 ft. in length and 48 ft. in breadth, subdivided into two equal divisions, viz. (*a*) the auditorium (*prekṣāgṛha*, i.e. 'the Spectacular Mansion') and (*b*) the stage (*raṅgabhūmi*). The construction of the theatre can be best explained with the aid of a diagram.[11]

It is clear at a glance that the auditorium is thus 48 ft. square; the front stage 12 by 24 ft.; the back stage 12 by 48 ft.; and the green room 24 by 48 ft. The front stage and the back stage together form the full stage. Portions of the back stage (X) seem to have been reserved for a threefold purpose, as the commentator points out: (*a*) for the resting actors; (*b*) for preserving the secrecy of entrance and exit; and (*c*) for artistic purposes (i.e. for the prompter's use and for securing some stage effects or storing stage properties). An interesting feature of the scene-building is a set of two side-buildings or wings (*mattavāraṇīs*) or 'Parascenia' (12 by 12 ft. each).[12] These wings were intended to give facilities to the actors to come on the stage from and go directly to the Green Room when they chose to do so. As these out-

11. (*a*) "It is interesting to note that a few years ago the late Dr. Bloch unearthed an ancient theatrical stage in a cave in Ramgarh, the ruins being proved 2,300 years old. The description of this stage substantiates the account in Bharat." S. Mookerjee: *The Calcutta Review*, January 1924, p. 109.
    (*b*) Cf. two Gujarati periodicals: (*a*) Mr. G. V. Pathak in *Prasthāna*, IV, 5, p. 361; and (*b*) Mr. D. R. Mankad in *Nāgarika*, VI, 2, p. 118.
    (*c*) After this was written, a valuable article on "Hindu Theatre" by Mr. D. R. Mankad has appeared in the *Indian Historical Quarterly*, September 1932, p. 480 f.
12. Mr. Mankad's view that they were special portions of the main stage does not appear to be correct.

buildings were spacious, the Orchestra also could be easily accommodated there or in portions of the back stage. The statement that these wings should be higher by 3 ft. than the stage proper might presumably imply that use of some sort of machinery was contemplated.

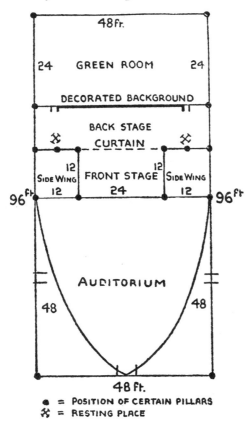

● = POSITION OF CERTAIN PILLARS
✿ = RESTING PLACE

The height of the theatre was designed in accordance with particular requirements. It would naturally depend on the type of plays to be presented and the use of celestial machinery. The question of height is complicated by the fact that a 'strong wall of thick bricks' was prescribed for the theatre and a central 'dome resting on ten circling

pillars' near the wall. Moreover, there was to be a gallery in
the theatre, for it is expressly stated that (II, 84), "The
theatre should be constructed with two stories having the
shape of a mountain den with only a few windows to
ensure excellent acoustic properties." Even in a play within
a play[13] the buffoon is seen dozing in the gallery when his
king-companion is playing the assumed rôle of a lover to
his sweetheart. Whether the stage itself had an upper
building ('Episcenium') remains a difficult problem. The
'terrace' in *Ratnāvalī* suggests that it had one. It is characteristic of the Hindu mind that even after prescribing so many
details, the utmost latitude is allowed to the architect to
meet particular requirements.

The Green Room (*nepathyagṛha*), it is stated, ought to
be a part of the main building. It ought to be fairly spacious
to give room to the several characters for their 'make-up'.
As the Sanskrit term implies, it 'led down' several feet from
the 'stage-head'. Thus it was lower than the stage proper.
After the characters were ready for the stage they could wait
in the intermediate space between or in the 'wings' if necessary.

The decorations of the theatre, we are told, should be in
harmony with Oriental splendour and love of colour and
brilliance. The front part of the stage (the Proscenium)
ought to be built of wood and should be richly decorated
with wooden carvings of water-pots (*kalaśas*), flags (*patākās*)
and images of damsels (*puttalikās*). It should also be hung
with garlands and furnished with ornamented arches. "The
lower end of the stage must be white-plastered and rendered
smooth, and the platform must on no account be slippery."
For the background of the stage, six wooden blocks were
to be erected. The intermediate space was to be filled up
with very fine black earth, in 'the shape of the back of a
tortoise'. This earth should have the lustre of a pure mirror
and it should be studded with emeralds, sapphires, corals
and other jewels arranged in various designs on all the four

13. Cf. *Priyadarśikā* of Harṣa.

sides. In the centre of this back-wall and on all the walls of the theatre 'pictures of lions, elephants, caves, mountains, cities, flower-groves, etc.', were to be painted.

The seats in the auditorium were to be arranged 'in the manner of a ladder, to ensure visibility'. They were to be made of wood and bricks 1½ ft. higher than the ground; on these seats people squatted. The arrangement of the seats is thus quoted from an authority by S. M. Tagore:[14] "The grounds to the east of the stage should be set apart for the king, or for the head of the assembly who must be well versed in the elegant arts, etc. Brahmins should be seated on the south and boys and persons belonging to the royal staff on the north and close to the stage. At the extremities are to be seated the heralds, eulogists, connoisseurs and guards in attendance. Armed strangers, heretics, etc., are not to be admitted." Generally, on the right side of the king sat the ministers, poets, critics, astrologers and merchants; and on his left the ladies of the harem (mostly veiled).

The full seating capacity provided for about a thousand persons. Great emphasis is laid on the high qualities of the fit audience. The dramatists often pay compliments to critical and experienced spectators. This audience was expected to share the feelings of the characters by the usual outward signs of 'laughter, tears, cries, hair standing on end, jumping from seats, clapping with hands, etc.'

As regards scenery, apart from the gorgeous and picturesque background to serve a general purpose, there seems to have been the common use of only one curtain between the front and the back stage. Although S. M. Tagore devotes some space to a 'drop-curtain',[15] it is generally acknowledged that the Hindu theatre had an open stage. Possibly, the central curtain was parted in the middle. Occasionally, an actor rushed forth on the stage from behind, in excitement, with

14. *Hindu Drama*, p. 6.
15. *Eight Principal Sentiments of Hindu Drama*, p. 58.

a toss of this curtain. Wilson believes that there was in some
cases a clever use of transverse curtains, when two rooms
or an outer court and an inner apartment were to be presented
at the same time on the stage; but this is doubtful.

Some sort of scene-building and stage-machinery are
contemplated by Bharata, for he carefully notices the process
of stage-carpentry (*dārukarma*) and mentions machines
(*yantras*) in relation to movements to and fro on the stage.
Mechanical lattices and windows are mentioned. Minute
stage directions become extremely useful in this study. The
presence of several deities in the sky is a noteworthy feature
of some plays like *Uttara-rāma-carita*. Now when these
celestial characters were actually on the stage but merely
imitating aerial motions, the direction is precise, viz. "Thus
they act" (*nāṭayanti*). Otherwise, this specific term is absent.
From Bharata it is easy to understand that some sort of
mechanical contrivance, probably a sort of crane and pulley
arrangement worked from the side wings (*mattavāraṇī*) did
exist. Of course, there is no reason to believe that any heavy
or elaborate device for turning a number of actors round
like the 'Eccyclema' existed. Nor was the use of the *deus
ex machina* a marked feature of the Hindu stage.[16] No doubt,
much was left to the imagination of the audience.

The stage-properties are classed under the generic style
of model work (*pusta*). "The *Nāṭyaśāstra* distinguishes three
forms of such objects; they may be made (*sandhimā*) with
the help of bamboos covered with skins or cloths; or they
may be made to work by certain mechanical means (*vyājimā*);
or prepared out of cloth only (*veṣṭita*). We hear of the making
of an elephant in *Udayanacarita*; the *Mṛcchakaṭika* owes its
name to the toy cart which appears in it; the *Bālarāmāyaṇa*
has mechanical dolls, and doubtless there were represented
houses, caves, chariots, rocks, horses and so on; monsters
with animal heads and many arms could be made of clay

16. It is unfortunate that neither Professor Lèvi nor Professor Keith
    has given full attention to this problem.

and bamboos and covered with cloths; we are expressly told that weapons must not be made of hard material, but that stocks of grass, bamboos and lac may be made to serve, and naturally gestures served in lieu of hard blows. It must be remembered, also, that their light properties were handy and convenient for being carried over from one court theatre to another by a company of actors and that the basic conception was to create an illusion (māyā) rather than to present real things. Professor Lèvi makes an interesting list of articles needed in Śākuntala and a Gujarati scholar[17] does the same with regard to a single act of Vikramorvaśīya.

The richness of colouring is noted as a characteristic of the costumes of classical Athenian performances;[18] but even a keener appreciation of colours was a marked feature of the Oriental drama; for in the representation of great legendary heroes, divinities, myths, etc., the dominant 'consideration of place, time, age, rank and profession was never to be lost sight of'. The eastern splendour of life was thus reflected on the stage not only by the use of the jewellery of variegated colours, but also by a combined effect of costumes of all hues set in a picturesque background. The fullest possible use seems to have been made of the regal paraphernalia with its luxurious apparel. No doubt there was a certain conventionalized stage-costume prescribed, but it was in keeping with the dresses of ordinary life. In the case of kings, and specially of ladies of distinction, ornaments of all sorts for head, ear, nose, neck, waist, wrist and ankle were freely utilized, but here again, they were not genuine, but of copper, mica or wax, sparkling from a distance and giving the effect of verisimilitude.

17. J. A. Patel in *The Gujarati* periodical, July 24, 1910 f. (a) Mountain enveloped by clouds; (b) dancing peacock; (c) cuckoo sitting on a branch of a *jambu* tree; (d) swans floating in waters; (e) pair of *cakravāka* birds; (f) bee in a lotus; (g) an elephant facing his mate; (h) a river-bank, etc., etc.
18. Professor Nicoll: *The Development of the Theatre*, London, 1927, p. 38.

As a contrast to the use of "the Greek mask, which rendered in conventional forms an indication of age, station and prevalent mood", for the Hindu actor, the manner of 'make-up' for particular parts is clearly prescribed. Paint of hues appropriate to several rôles are mentioned; and various mixtures suggested. People belonging to diverse provinces and professions and grades of society have appropriate distinguishing colours. Naturally the hair also attracts attention. Madmen and ghosts wear it loose; "the buffoon is bald; boys have three tufts of hair", and so on.

The highest contribution, however, to the art of the theatre, perhaps, lies in the Hindu actor's duty of representation (*abhinaya*) of the states or conditions of the personage for whom he stands. The art of gesticulation was most assiduously cultivated. At the special request of the gifted producer, Mr. Gordon Craig, the eminent Indian scholar, Dr. A. Coomaraswamy[19] published *The Mirror of Gesture*. This work makes interesting reading for it reveals how each member of the body is singled out for description. "Deep significance lies in the mode in which the head is shaken, the eyes glance, the brows move; cheek, nose, lip, chin and neck can all be used to convey subtle senses. An audience of unsparing critics witnessed with admiration the different manœuvres with the fingers, particular postures and the gait. Creation of illusion in the mind of a trained and experienced audience by the art of suggestion was the keynote in gesticulation. Accordingly, a set of movements of hands and feet would suggest characters groping in the dark. Mounting of a chariot or climbing up to the top of a palace would be indicated by another set of movements. If the garments are pulled up, the crossing of a river is plainly shown; if the motions of swimming are mimicked, clearly the river is too deep to wade." Thus, in the absence of pictorial scenery,

19. A translation of *Abhinayadarpaṇa* of Nandikeśvara, Cambridge, 1917.

this type of symbolic acting[20] created a desired effect and at the same time helped the economy of the stage.[21]

One or two illustrations will help to explain this mode of acting. In *Śākuntala* 'showing fear of a bee' is to be acted thus: "Move the head quickly to and fro (*vidhūtam*), the lips quivering, while (*patākā*) hands are held unsteadily against the face, palms inward." 'Gathering of flowers' is to be acted as follows: "Hold the left hand horizontally in *Aralā*, the right hand in *Haṁsāsya*, extended forward at the side. The left hand here represents a basket, and imaginary flowers are picked with the right hand and transferred to the left."

On the actual mode of production a partial record of the acting of *Ratnāvalī* in the eighth century throws a flood of light. The following points in it deserve close attention: (*a*) At the conclusion of the overture played by the flutes, etc., the director comes upon the stage. (*b*) After a piece of music, he calls the actress and speaks with her of domestic details. He departs with a song. (*c*) The minister enters and discloses his plan. Then he sees the King Vatsa ascend to the terrace to enjoy the festivities of Love. (*d*) The King describes the merriment of his subjects below. (*e*) Then the two girls sent by the Queen enter dancing. Later they approach the King and communicate the message. (*f*) They disappear behind the curtain. (*g*) Then the curtain is drawn aside and the Queen is seen with a serving girl, who happens to be Ratnāvalī. (*h*) In order that this beauteous damsel may not be seen by the King, the Queen dismisses her. (*i*) But she watches the rites of the Worship of Love from behind an arbour. (*j*) She falls desperately in love, and taking her eyes with great difficulty from the hero, she

20. Bharata enumerates four agencies of representation, viz.: (*a*) presenting the condition of the personage; (*b*) representing peculiar speech; (*c*) exhibiting appropriate emotions; and (*d*) appropriate gestures.

21. It is interesting to note that some modern experiments in acting also do the same, e.g. try to give an impression of smoking, without any cigar or matches, by means of gesticulation.

leaves the stage; and (k) when the songs and music are over the act is finished.[22]

From a comparison of the above summary of points regarding production with the text itself, it is safe to argue that every minute stage direction was faithfully followed. Consequently, critics who argue that these stage directions were intended for the benefit of the readers have failed to grasp the fundamental fact that the plays were written for production and that the directions were for the guidance of the producer and actors. After all, the reading public was bound to be limited and manuscript copies could not have been many.

From a study of the internal evidence relating to the Indian drama, Professor Horrwitz[23] has drawn a charming imaginative pen-picture of the première of *Śākuntala*. A critic has taken exception to this picture on the ground of its being fanciful; but he forgets the keen interest of the Gupta Emperor and the advance in theatrical art after Bharata.

Similarly, Mantzius, emphasizing the striking effect of pantomime (along with the deeply cultivated accessories of music and dancing) has drawn a fascinating picture of an ancient Hindu production, with the eye of a gifted actor. The staging of Śakuntalā's bee episode is thus described:[24] "While King Duṣyanta is hidden among the bushes observing Śakuntalā and her friends, she discovers a bee flying after her, and in her fright she exclaims: 'Ah! a bee . . . has left the young jasmine, and is trying to settle on my face' (her movements indicate that she is pursued by a bee). The King, meanwhile, looks at her lovingly, and says 'Beautiful! There is something charming even in her terror.' Then he sings:

'Where'er the bee his eager onset plies,
Now here, now there, she darts her kindling eyes,'

---

22. Cf. Sylvain Lèvi: *Le Théâtre Indien*, Paris, 1890, p. 389.
23. *The Indian Theatre*, London, 1912, p. 1.
24. *A History of Theatrical Art*, Vol. I, p. 25.

etc. We may suppose that while the King was singing with admiration, Śakuntalā performed a kind of dance or mimic scene, in which she expressed her childlike and graceful terror of the bee." In *Mālavikāgnimitra* also, the heroine sings and gives pantomime expressive of the sentiment. Such mimic intermezzi formed a chief attraction of the plays and were often introduced for their own sake.

The mode of production was facilitated by a series of accepted conventions. For instance, as there was no drop curtain, sometimes the King used to enter and sit on a throne, placed by a servant in the presence of the audience.[25] This business was described, as in Elizabethan plays, by the stage-direction, 'the King enters seated.' On other occasions. the central curtain could be parted and a scene disclosed.

Plays were generally produced on festive occasions, public or private. A vernal festival was the occasion of the staging of *Ratnāvalī*. The *Mudrārākṣasa* refers to the celebration of an autumn festival. In several plays the festival of *Kāma* (Cupid) is mentioned; this took place in Spring. Apart from these festivals, when a son was born to the King, on the occasion of a national triumph or of a religious fair, or when a new house was occupied by a prince or landlord, plays were produced. They belonged to the repertory of actors and were reproduced at many places.

The time of production was generally in the afternoon and lasted for nearly four or even five hours. It must be remembered that while in the Greek theatre, often three tragedies and a comedy were produced on the same day, in India one single, well-sustained and systematically evolved drama was produced. The Indian climatic condition would give the necessary light throughout the day, for as a rule few plays were produced during the rainy season, although the use of torches on the stage was not unknown.

The actors and actresses belonged generally to the Brahmin

25. Similarly, in China, even to-day, a number of persons are constantly present on the stage to help the actors.

caste and occupied a peculiar position in society. On the one hand they enjoyed the friendship and love of great kings and eminent dramatists (cf. Bhavabhūti's tribute in the Prologue to *Mahāvīracarita*) and on the other they were despised as 'low and degraded' and were denied some of the privileges of the highest caste. Most of the female rôles were played by women who belonged often to the family of the first actor. Sometimes the parts of old women were acted by male actors, as one can learn from the interesting division of work in the Prologue to *Mālatīmādhava*. Bharata even permits, when necessary, the acting of male rôles by women and *vice versa*.

If one may judge from the production of Sanskrit classical pieces in the presence of a highly critical audience and from the fact that they possessed a set of minute rules for histrionics, one may easily conclude that the level of acting must have been very high. Unity was maintained by the ability and accomplishments of the leader of the company, also the actor-manager and producer (*sūtradhāra*, i.e. one who controls all the threads), who was supposed to be a perfect master of many arts and sciences, especially music, dancing and gesticulation. All the actors, however, had to possess manifold qualifications and had to pass through a severe school of theatrical training.

The above general survey of ancient Indian theatrical practice may serve a useful purpose if it is carefully compared on the one hand with the medieval and modern theatrical practice in India, and on the other with the Elizabethan stage, which has influenced profoundly the Indian theatre of to-day. The first part may be reserved for later treatment, in the course of which it will be possible to trace fully the ancient Hindu tradition preserved in several respects even to-day, thus clearing the way for the proper understanding of the exact nature of the Western influence.

The Elizabethan stage has, curiously enough, many striking points of affinity with the ancient Hindu stage. This inherent affinity paved the way for a pronounced influence of the one theatre on the other. Indeed, most of the points noted by Sir E. K. Chambers[26] on 'The Structure and Conduct of Theatres' suit also the Hindu stage, with, of course, a certain number of modifications.

The Elizabethan stage, like the Hindu stage, was unlocalized. By the recitation of a minute description the audience could conjure up an imaginative picture of a supposed locality. Both used only one back curtain with an occasional employment of the 'back stage'. Stage properties were limited and were not so heavy as to need many stage hands. Some sort of use of primitive 'machines' on the stage has been noted also with regard to the Hindu theatre. Love of magnificent colour in costume was similarly a marked feature of the Elizabethan wardrobe. 'Alarms' were sounded at the 'entry' and 'exit' of kings. Various drum-beats were conventional on both stages, as the presence of stage hands, in the full view of the audience, was the accepted convention too. Use of animal masks is sanctioned by Bharata, presumably in the manner of Bottom's putting on the ass-mask during his infatuation.

Apart from all questions of stage, scenery and costume, however, the play was 'the thing' for both theatres; and the art of stimulating or rousing the emotions by means of dramatic representations was the main object of both. Declamation, bombastic speeches and exaggerated metaphorical devices were not unknown to either, while both indulged in disguises, separations, reunions and providential aids and hindrances.[27]

26. *The Elizabethan Stage*, Vol. II, pp. 518–557.
27. Zucker (in his *Chinese Theatre*) draws many interesting parallels, too, between the Elizabethan and the modern Chinese stage. (Last chapter.)

CHAPTER III

THE THEATRE OF THE PEOPLE

R. W. FRAZER[1] finds it "impossible to trace any connection"
between the ancient theatre of India and its medieval
popular theatre. Judging superficially, no doubt there
cannot be a greater contrast than that existing between
the organic construction, consistent characterization, idealistic representation, exquisite lyricism, unity of impression
and lofty moral tone, artistically conveyed, of the classical
drama acted in an organized Royal Court theatre on the
one hand, and haphazard incidents, situations and events,
loose spectacular sing-song representations of the life and
work of Rāma, Kṛṣṇa, etc., with often a curious intermixture
of crude farcical devices, coarse jokes and vulgar expressions
of the medieval folk-plays acted on the village green before
thousands of merchants, artisans and labourers for the
whole night, on the other. This, however, is not the whole
truth; and Mr. Frazer has missed some important links
between these two types of drama.

If one takes the trouble to examine more profoundly
the evolution of several types of Sanskrit drama, one can
easily conjecture where some of the varieties of drama
practised by the ancients were bound to lead. Apart from
the standard drama, *bhāṇa* and *prahasana* (two of the eight
main classes) flourished side by side. A glance at their
salient characteristics will convince one that the medieval
degraded forms of folk amusement are the lineal descendants
of the most ancient types.

In a *bhāṇa* the performer narrates dramatically a variety
of occurrences. Love, war, fraud, intrigue and imposition
are appropriate topics. He may indulge in a supposititious
dialogue with an imaginary interlocutor. Music and singing

1. *A Literary History of India*, London, 1898, p. 270.

precede and close the performance. The *prahasana* is a farcical satire levelled at the sanctified and privileged orders of the community, such as ascetics, Brahmins, men of wealth and rank, and princes. Such plays are marked by extreme indelicacy and sensuality, in spite of a certain satirical aim. Their main object is to incite laughter, as in *Hāsyacuḍāmaṇi* of Vatsarāja.[2]

Now it is obvious that with the ruin of the classical drama proper,[3] after the rise of the Mohammedan power, the lower species came more into prominence and then contributed largely to the village drama. Of course, artistic subtlety disappeared. The old rules of decorum were violated in order to satisfy the desire of the masses to see the death of demons like Rāvaṇa and Kaṁsa. Despite all this, certain elements of the old school lingered in the medieval dramatic performances. The *sūtradhāra* (manager) figured, in one form or another, with a sort of uncouth prologue, and at the end the benediction (*bharatavākyam*) was often pronounced. Singing and dancing, carried to a farcical plane, in and out of season, were the marked features of the rural drama. Again, the main sources of inspiration for both were the great Epics and *Purāṇas* of India, the only difference being the art of concentration on a special episode in the one case and a clumsy reproduction of all the principal incidents of *Rāmāyaṇa* in the other.

In order to draw conclusions regarding the theatre of the people with a view to tracing its connection with the modern Indian stage, and to sifting the material for judging the exact nature of the influence of British drama, it is necessary, in the first place to examine, in some detail, the exact nature of the varied types of popular entertainment prevailing in the several parts of India.

2. Baroda, 1918.
3. The standard old drama is even now occasionally composed according to traditional rules, but it is only of academic interest for a few scholars, as it is seldom produced except by University students, who never perform it in its entirety.

Naturally, it is best to start with the Bengal *Yātrās* first, then to study the *Rāsadhārīs* and *Rāma-līlā* of Upper India and finally to survey the field of the popular theatre with reference to western and southern India, remembering all the time that all these representations have many elements in common and that the bands of strolling players easily carry the traditions of one province to another, since reverence for the Epics is universal and their interest perennial.

A. EASTERN INDIA: *YĀTRĀS*

From times immemorial, the personality of Śrī Kṛṣṇa has fascinated India as no other being has ever done. A halo of complete perfection crowns his head as the eighth incarnation of the god Viṣṇu. In love, war, political shrewdness and philosophy he is claimed to be unique. Compared with him, Rāma looks simple, straightforward and less romantic. Śiva is too rigid and secluded, practising penance on the Himalayas. Consequently, the cult of Viṣṇu-Kṛṣṇa has achieved greatest popularity. Whether the Bengali *yātrās* are a direct continuation of the ancient Vedic drama[4] and whether the opera of *Gītagovinda* of Jayadeva in the twelfth century A.D. forms a link directly with the classical drama, are problems which need not be considered here. In any event, the *yātrās* are like "sacred operas frequently produced in connection with the religious processions of the Kṛṣṇaites".

Yātrā literally means a 'procession', and also a 'pilgrimage'. During the celebration of a particular festival of a deity, huge crowds move in a procession, sing the glory of the deity to the accompaniment of crude musical instruments and indulge in sympathetic dancing in the temple, courtyard or street. Similarly, when people went on a holy pilgrimage on foot or in bullock-carts they used to amuse themselves

4. Dr. P. Guhathakurta: *Bengali Drama*, London, 1930, p. 4.

in a devotional manner with the aid of crude performances representing the glory of a particular deity. No doubt, at an early stage, the *yātrāvālās* used to extemporize the music and words of the plays to suit particular festivals, literary composition or publication being out of the question. Certain conventional methods were, however, taken for granted. Thus, in the case of Kṛṣṇa *yātrā*, Jayadeva fixed the mode of presenting the Kṛṣṇa love-romance. Kṛṣṇa and Rādhā are the eternal lovers. Lalitā is an ideal go-between. Lovers quarrel, part, wander through a series of romantic vicissitudes, singing their passion in some of the most musical Indian lyrics ever composed, and finally unite. As the devotional element decreased the amorous element became exaggerated and degraded, till Kṛṣṇakamal Gosvāmin raised the level of *yātrā* in the later part of the nineteenth century.

Dr. S. K. De[5] writes: "The earlier *yātrā* was some kind of operatic and melodramatic performance, a *volkspiel*, with some dialogue and semi-dramatic presentation, in which improvisation played a considerable part. It had a probable connection with (ancient) religious festivities of a popular character. Generally, the business alone was sketched by the author, the dialogues were supplied by the actors, and the narrative details explained by the *yātrāvālā* or his chorus. Unlike the *sūtradhāra*, the *yātrāvālā* not only controlled and directed the performance but was always in appearance supplying the links of the story by means of the descriptive and narrative passages.

"It is also important to add that there was in the old *yātrā* an exclusive preponderance of songs or recitative poetry, in which even the dialogues were carried on and the whole action worked out. In comparatively modern

5. *The Indian Historical Quarterly*, Vol. VII, No. 3, September 1931, p. 559 f. For a fuller account of the Bengali *yātrā* and its early history, see S. K. De, *Bengali Literature*, 1800–1825, Calcutta, 1919, pp. 442–454.

yātrās, no doubt, secular themes are admitted; the details of the story are more minutely and faithfully followed; there are less music and poetry and more dialogue and dramatic interest, and even lively interludes of a farcical nature are introduced to relieve their seriousness and monotony. (At the present day, the Bengali *yātrā* is being entirely moulded by the Anglicized Bengali drama and theatre, and is therefore departing completely from the older type.) But even these improvements made of late years could not altogether lift the *yātrā* out of its religious envelopment and its essentially poetic or musical structure."

Other *yātrā* troupes specialized in the life-story of Rāma, while some selected popular medieval tales or even imaginary situations and characters. Of the latter type, the most enchanting *yātrā*, even acted to-day in some of the villages, is the *Vidyāsundar* romance. It is, as usual, almost an opera. The story is a slight one. The prince Sundar, enamoured of a princess from a description of her beauty, sends her a love-token in the shape of a small flower-arrow of Cupid skilfully strung in a garland through the agency of a flower-girl Hirā. She in return pines for him. He comes incognito and talks to her through the medium of a female friend and they then accept each other. The king, not knowing the antecedents of Sundar and humiliated by this scandal, orders his execution. However, all ends happily as he turns out to be the real intended bridegroom and the play concludes with the lovers' marriage and the forgiveness of the flower-girl. The principal attraction is the music of Hirā and the interpolated dances. Many plays[6] were composed on the basis of the popular *yātrā* version of Bharatacandra.

If Kṛṣṇa is said to possess a general fascination, the god Śiva is considered to be the most easily propitiated. Consequently, to secure human bliss in all respects, the *Gambhīrā* (the consort of Śiva) festival assumed a great importance. During this festival many devotees put on different masks

6. E.g. by Īśvaracandra Sarkār, Calcutta, 1869.

and played various parts to please Śiva. Mr. B. K. Sarkar, in an interesting volume,[7] discusses many aspects of these *Gambhīrā* or *Gājan* festivals, celebrated in every district of Bengal, "with dance, music, songs, feasts, processions and social gatherings". The several *Gambhīrā* parties keenly compete with each other in decorating their 'pandals' (temporary erections) where an image of the goddess is actually or symbolically present. This festival of five days reaches its most spectacular stage on the third day of *Baḍā Tamāśā*, i.e. 'the great show'. In the evening a sort of mask-play, *Hanumān-mukha*, is held. One votary puts on the mask of the monkey-chief "and makes for himself a long tail with unripe banana leaves". The tail is set on fire and he leaps over a piece of cloth (representing the sea) and returns after thus (symbolically) burning Ceylon. "There are also mask-dances (with crude music) of ghosts and goblins, of Rāma and Lakṣmaṇa, of Śiva and Durgā, of an old man and wife, of a horse, of fairies", etc.

In contrast with these rural mask-dances, the *yātrā* proper has many excellent qualities. Only male performers took part in the acting of this musical drama;[8] the performances took place on the bare ground without any scenic representation. Only a long piece of cloth at the back helped to reserve some space for a green-room. All the performers usually sang in chorus with the leader lingering behind and occasionally pulling the ear of an erring youth in the sight of the audience. An actor often took the liberty of smoking a *hookah* even in the midst of his acting. Naturally, with this type of play, there were many absurdities. Not only did a weeping mother join in with the chorus, but even the slain hero revived in order to take part in it! All this defective, incongruous performance was, however, redeemed by rich poetry set to music, suggesting romantic situations.

7. *The Folk Element in Hindu Culture*, London, 1917.
8. Dinesh Chandra Sen: *History of Bengali Language and Literature*, Calcutta, 1911, p. 724.

This gave life to the piece, and for its sake all the other absurdities were forgotten; by its means passions were aroused and sympathetic appreciation secured. Thus, as Mr. Sen says, even without any modern theatrical aids, these *yātrās* can "rouse emotions which are rare in semi-European performances on the Calcutta stage".

B. UPPER INDIA: *RĀSADHĀRĪS*

Closely associated with the Bengali *yātrā* is the picturesque ancient institution of the Kṛṣṇa *Rāsadhārīs* of Mathurā (Muttra) and its surroundings.[9] The *Rāsadhārī* is by no means yet extinct, and even to-day Sanadhya Brahmins will form small troupes which endeavour to eke out a living by presenting dramatic performances on the theme of Kṛṣṇa's exploits. In these, two boys play Kṛṣṇa and Rādhā and others assume the rôles of cowherds and milkmaids. The performance culminates in a merry-go-round when the fascinating cowherd with a peacock-crown and a perfumed garland dances and sings with the chorus. The devout spectators are so credulous that for the time they often worship the boy as the actual deity. These companies travel far into the south, even to Hyderabad, and to the west in Gujarat, find a hearty reception in Vaiṣṇavite temples of the Vallabha creed, give a series of performances and get rich gifts. They inspire local talent and their performances are imitated by groups belonging to the districts they visit. Thus links are established between several parts of India. During the season sacred to Śrī Kṛṣṇa in *Śrāvaṇa* (tenth month of the Hindu Calendar) these companies are very busy in such sacred spots as Vṛndā Vana with which the life story of the deity is associated. Consequently they can afford to travel during the rest of the year, generally selecting the full moon night for their final performance in an important centre.

9. Sir William Ridgeway: *The Dramas and Dramatic Dances of Non-European Races*, Cambridge, 1915, pp. 172 f.

RĀMA-LĪLĀ

James Prinsep[10] reproduces three excellent plates pertaining
to the Benares festivals and adds important descriptive
notes. The *Rāma-Līlā* occupies, in Upper India, the place
and the season (in *Āśvina*, the last month of the Hindu
Calendar) of the *Durgā Pūjā* (identical with the *Gambhīrā*
Festival) in Bengal. Both are marked by exceptional splendour. The festival of Rāma, in its present form, at any rate,
is said to have originated in the famous version of *Rāmāyaṇa*
by Tulsīdāsa in 1574. The Raja of Benares organizes the
performance in a very thorough manner. "Nearly the whole
of the *Rāmāyaṇa* is read through in the course of twenty or
thirty days, and whatever incidents are capable of being
acted or displayed are simultaneously exhibited. The whole
of the acting is, necessarily, in dumb show; and the *dramatis
personæ* are numerous. The scenery is, as far as it can be,
real: for instance, wherever the Ganges or the sea is required,
the scene is shifted to the bank of some *tulas* (pond or lake);
such incidents as are adapted to the night are performed
by torchlight; separate gardens receive the designation of
the principal localities of the poem."

Dresses and masks are "very appropriate". The dignity,
gravity and patience of the richly decorated children,
impersonating Rāma, Lakṣmaṇa and Sītā, are remarkable.
"Rocks, birds and other paraphernalia are managed nearly
as well as in our pantomimes." Where Rāma restores to life
a saint's wife, the device of the trap-door is used. The
marriage ceremony of Rāma and Sītā is the most pleasing
sight. "The grand assembly of chiefs and princely suitors in
Janaka's palace is worthy of the pen of the author of
Ivanhoe."

"Anybody may join the masked procession (of the demons),
and this year (1825) there were seen a number of jacketted

10. *Benares Illustrated* (series of drawings), Calcutta, 1830, 3rd
Series.

'Sahibs' in white-faced masks, whether intended as appropriate allies of Rāvaṇa's host of demons, or merely as a specimen of masquerade, I will not presume to determine." Finally, the interest culminates on the tenth day when Rāvaṇa is killed in the last battle, when the masses go into hysterics over the victory.

By way of an epilogue, on the next day, Rāma makes his triumphal entry into his capital, Ayodhyā. "Altogether, the immense crowd, the variety and brightness of the costume, the valuable ornaments and beauty of the children, contrasted with the plain white dress of the *mahājans*, the cheerfulness and unmoblike appearance and demeanour of the people, as they shower down flowers and chaplets upon the sacred group (from stone terraces and parapets, canopied with rich pavilions), with the picturesque enchantment of a clear even sky and the intermixture of garden foliage—complete a picture to which no description can do justice, and which will be best rendered intelligible to an English imagination under the title of a genuine Oriental pageant." On another occasion, one of the loveliest spectacles is presented on the river Ganges, when an ancient water fête, devoid of any religious significance, is celebrated.

The devotional medieval romances of Gopichand, Puran and Hakikat are extremely popular with the Punjab masses. Plays based on them are frequently staged in villages, with, of course, the conventional music and dancing. The ideal of renunciation of the world, heroic self-sacrifice and martyrdom are the qualities which endear them to so many hearts. In some cases, "the *kheuras* (singers) divide into two parties, each sitting on the top of a different house and then singing songs in turn by way of dialogue at *Daśerāh* or *Holī*". Such representations are particularly popular among the women.

C. SOUTHERN INDIA

'Strolling players, jugglers, and acrobats tour periodically through the country."[11] Festivals are legion, *Āyudha Pūjā* (worship of sacred implements) on the day of *Daśerah* and *Pangal* (rice-boiling for feeding cows) in January, being the principal ones. Many popular stories capture the imagination, as usual. Lewis Rice[12] comments: "The 'yakṣagāna' stories are generally based on episodes in the *Mahābhārata* or Pauranic works, and dramatic in form, written for recitation on the native stage and suited for performances to rustic audiences. I have sometimes witnessed excellent acting in such performances, primitive as the accessories are."

The *Bhāgavatam* is one of the most ancient folk-plays of southern India. Of course the appeal of the amours and exploits of the boy-hero Śrī Kṛṣṇa have almost the same fascination for the South as for the North. Its mode of representation is pithily described by an authority,[13] G. Shrinivasacharya. Moreover, the dramatic stories of saints like Rāmadās, the pariah saint, always attract crowds from all classes. Many popular ballads, possessing historic interest (such as that of Desinga Raja, i.e. Tej Singh) are seen represented on the stage in Telegu districts. The 'Kathākāli' of the Malabar district, noted in the district *Gazetteer*,[14] fairly gives an idea of what a country drama is like. "The unrefined villagers enjoy the street drama enacted on open stages, on festive occasions, as fervently as the townsfolk do in their (modern) well-equipped theatres."

In Tamil, one of the most ancient and fascinating stories acted on the stage for centuries is that of *Nalataṅgī*. It has a haunting tragic appeal to millions of people. A chaste lady falls into the hands of a tyrant and she has to throw into

11. "Madras," *Gazetteer of India*, Calcutta, 1908.
12. *Mysore*, London, 1907, Vol. I, p. 495.
13. *The Indian Stage*, a periodical of Madras, 1911, p. 33.
14. Vol. I, p. 146.

a dark well all her seven children. She weeps and sings her complaints. The villagers shed tears of sympathy. Ultimately, however, by the divine grace a miracle happens, for her children are all restored to the arms of the desolate mother. Other medieval stories with a pathetic appeal are also popular in Madras villages. The Dravidian race still preserves its original cultural element, despite the fact that the dominant Aryan race has almost completely absorbed it, the stories from *Rāmāyaṇa* and *Mahābhārata* being almost as popular there as in the North. It is here interesting to notice that in the eleventh century a Chola king (Rajareja I) "built a beautiful Śiva temple in his own name and instituted in it a dramatic troupe who had to enact regularly every year the *Rājarājāhnāṭaka* (heroic deeds of the patron)".[15]

D. WESTERN INDIA

In Maharashtra, the most popular type of medieval play is *Laḷita*, generally associated with a dramatic representation of *Daśāvatāram* (ten incarnations of the god Viṣṇu). It is said that the Tanjori drama influenced this species of religious drama,[16] often acted in *Navarātrī* and culminating in *Rāvaṇavadha* on the *Daśerāh*. The play is given in temple halls or inns with the aid of a curtain or two, the manager (*sūtradhāra*) serving as a Greek chorus and the clown (*vidūṣaka*) being the privileged ready-witted man coming in and going out whenever he pleases. The play starts with a prayer (*nāndī*); then Gaṇapati, the auspicious deity, comes with his large belly and elephant's trunk and the manager sings his praises and receives blessings. The goddess of learning comes riding on her peacock carrier. Some questions are asked and answered; but, apart from the clown's jokes and the songs of the manager, the performances generally

15. "One may also consult a very informative article by Mr. K. R. Pisharoti on 'The Kerala Stage' in the *Annamalai University Journal*, Vol. I, pp. 91–113 (Madras, 1932)." Dr. De.

16. *Marathi Encyclopædia*, Poona, 1925, Vol. 16, N—146.

dispense with dialogue. The whole story is told in action, and since the Marathas are a warlike people, they take keen interest in skilful fighting on the stage.

Besides this standard production, several episodes of a romantic nature like that of *Kaca-Devayānī* or *Dāmājipanta* are dramatized for village performances. The most note-worthy feature, however, is the gradual decay of religious inspiration and the growth of a secular element based on realistic farce and contemporary satire. An interesting collection[17] of village plays presents the most diverse kinds of playlets. Foolish astrologers, greedy priests, ignorant story-tellers are all severely satirized in other short productions. Romantic stories of love-adventure in a kingdom of women, the ideal of renunciation and the model relations of preceptor and disciple (e.g. the story of Matsyendranātha) have the same fascination here as in other parts of India.

While in Maharashtra, the Brahmin community generally led in the representation of *Lalita*, in Gujarat the Taragālā Bhojak community was remarkable for centuries of tradition in their particular style of acting. "The *Bhavāi* or popular low drama of Gujarat seems to be the lineal descendant of an ancient primitive drama. It is coarse and obscene. It is performed in open spaces in streets and such other public places as courtyards of temples and the like. No stage is required, no scenery, only a poor curtain, occasionally held by two men at each end; a few torches, and a chorus of two or three men helped by crude musical instruments. The clown (*rangalo*) has his usual licence. The actors put on whatever they can get for the occasion; paint their faces and kindle *rāla* (resin) to create supernatural effects. The companies tour from village to village and even street to street and are patronized by particular castes. The simple surroundings and paraphernalia of the *Bhavāi* will remind one of the similar circumstances of the Burmese drama."[18]

17. *Lalita Sangraha* or *Drama*, I and II, Bombay, 1875.
18. Sir William Ridgeway: *The Dramas . . .*, p. 199.

The performance does not represent any connected plot or story, but consists of a series of unconnected individual personations of one or two or three characters in each scene, presenting thus some popular episode; for example, a quarrel between an ill-matched couple, a highway robbery, or a corrupt friar (*sādhu*) in the company of a seduced widow and a credulous wife. Such characters are introduced as tailors, goldsmiths, moneylenders, profligate Moslem youths and so on. The famous medieval story of the passion of Siddharāja, the king of Gujarat, for the chaste, but ill-starred Rāṇakadevī has been always popular on the stage; but such performances "consist of monologues or dialogues supported by the chorus reciting songs referring to the incidents represented, in singing which the actors also join". The late Mahipataram Nilakanth tried his best to raise the level of these performances and also published a valuable collection[19] of plays.

These performances are essentially secular in character, although at the start the Gaṇapati appears on the stage. Of course, the origin is essentially religious. Even now some Nāgars (highest Brahmins) enact, for the whole night of the vigil, before the sacred image, some of the glorious deeds of the goddess Aṁbā. On the same principle, for the nine nights sacred to the deity, a series of performances are given in many villages in the course of which there lingers only a nominal religious setting, as most of the time is occupied in grossly realistic farces and satires.

Several other folk amusements are worthy of notice as having interesting theatrical elements, which are sometimes exploited in modern drama. Perhaps inspired by the touring *Rāsadhārī* companies from the North, singing parties are formed in Gujarat of men, of women or of both, hymning the glories of the goddess Aṁbā or the amours of Kṛṣṇa and Rādhā; these now often sing of modern themes and national movements. The principal singers lead the chorus

19. *Bhavāi Saṅgraha*, Ahmedabad, 1879.

and the rest repeat after them. The lyrics of Mīrā and Dayārām have been most popular among the ladies[20] of Gujarat. The element of musical dialogue introduced in them gives the institution a theatrical air. Then, there is the *Harikathā* where the story-teller moves in the centre of the audience and narrates a story in a theatrical manner with gestures, studied expressions, etc. Finally, in the midst of *Rāma-Līlā* or *Mahābhārata* performances, many acrobatic feats are performed and the whole story of the great epics is represented with extempore words, in several incidents, in the course of a month's stay of a company in a village. Rope-dancing and many athletic feats are also to be seen performed, like the 'shooting star' when from the top of a tall tree a player slides down on a thin rope.

E. 'MYSTERIES AND MORALITIES'

An attempt to sum up the above evidence regarding the varied modes of the popular theatre may lead one to suggest a partial but real comparison with the medieval 'Mysteries or Miracles' and 'Moralities' of Europe. Dr. Nishikant Chattopadhyay[21] and B. K. Sarkar both try to relate the medieval plays of the East and the West with regard to the part played by them in the evolution of the respective dramas. Dr. Guha-Thakurta, on the other hand, professes to see only the differences between them. Of course, the religious basis and the mode of Church government of the two races being entirely different, striking points of contrast are bound to be felt. Thus, for instance, there could be no question in India of the rulers of the Church trying to stem the tide by forbidding the clergy to act in the churches, while the austere passion of Christ is altogether different from the romantic amours of Kṛṣṇa.

20. K. M. Zaveri: *Milestones of Gujarati Literature*, Bombay, 1924, p. 247.
21. *The Yātrās*, Thesis, London, 1882, p. 45 f.

Once, however, the genius and the environments of the two peoples are allowed for, the two kinds of play appear to have much in common. As in the medieval European drama so also in India "there is no possibility of discovering a homogeneous entity, for a score of diverse elements went to the building up of the great 'Mystery' cycles". At the start there is a pure religious fervour; then a certain realism, even of a gross or farcical nature, is introduced as well as popular bombastic elements (cf. Herod and Rāvaṇa). A certain form of secular drama of social life develops out of both; and much of this entertainment is of an improvised character. The 'Interludium' is farcical, and often vulgar in both cases. The use of verse is, too, a common feature; the introduction of passages of Sanskrit in the one may be paralleled by the passages of Latin in the other. The dramatized stories of Indian devotees may readily be likened to the Saints' plays of Western Europe, while the method of presentation by groups of amateurs provides still another bond between the two.

It must not be forgotten, moreover, that the Roman Catholic ceremonies from which the Western medieval drama developed have a counterpart in the orthodox Hindu temple worship. The Catholic church at Christmas resembles in many respects the Hindu Vaiṣṇava temple at the birth of Kṛṣṇa.

F. RELATION TO THE MODERN STAGE

The typical Indian stage to-day takes its rise from a combination of various elements, the medieval traditional influence being by no means negligible. In these earlier rural performances lay the seeds that were later to blossom out into plays of the present day. "There is freshness of fancy here, a free treatment of material, a rich fund of humour, and at times a true sense of the profound and the tragic."[22] One has merely

22. These words of Professor A. Nicoll (*British Drama*, p. 29) are equally true of Indian medieval performances.

to remember the banishment of Sītā in Rāma-Līlā, the suffering of Draupadī in *Mahābhārata* plays, the heroic self-sacrifice of *Hariścandra* for the sake of righteousness to realize the truth of the statement. As Mantzius puts it, "it would be absurd to measure the medieval drama by the standard of modern or classical principles". After all, these things possessed vitality. Although lacking in refinement or in artistic production, these plays appealed profoundly to the emotion of the masses. This, along with its classical drama, was the rich heritage of the Indian stage when the British influence began to be felt.

In most of the court scenes of emperors, the love of spectacle, music and dance—in keeping with traditional associations—even now plays an important part. A few acrobatic feats are appreciated by the audience even to-day in mythological scenes. Scenes of wrestling and fighting on the stage leading to the death of the antagonist have their traditional aspect when viewed in relation to *Rāvaṇa-vadha* and *Kaṁsa-vadha* which were so immensely popular. The institution of *rāsa* (singing in a circle, especially by ladies) is still loved by Gujarati and Urdu audiences. Moreover, farcical interludes in serious plays, often unrelated to the main plot, especially in Western India, are sometimes borrowed directly from the medieval performances. It may also be noticed that certain classes of professional actors like the *Taragāḷās* have now joined the modern companies, thus bringing with them centuries of histrionic tradition and experience.

Despite the fact that the entire setting is now totally different with its regular theatres, electric lighting and painted scenery, three vital medieval forces still dominate the modern stage. First, the passion for the representation of *Satī*, a chaste wife passing successfully through the ordeal of manifold trials, dates from Sītā and Sāvitrī and forms an important link with numerous medieval romances. Secondly, the devotional attitude of the audience seeks

satisfaction in witnessing times without number the picturesque vicissitudes of devotees who suffer untold miseries
and triumph over sorrow at last. The life stories of almost
all the principal devotees of India have been ransacked and
provide the material for popular plays in most provinces.
Love of this type of play is a direct continuation of the
medieval practice, the only difference being the more rapid
acceptance of a Southern saint by the North and *vice
versa*. And thirdly, romantic love episodes with a pathetic
ring like *Vidyāsundar* or *Rāṇakadevī* are even now eagerly
applauded by thousands of spectators.

The last traditional influence is closely related to the
glorification of historical figures: *Pruthuraj, Shivaji, Pratap*
have been staged as the finest examples of chivalry throughout India. Two principal elements in the medieval performances also were, as has been seen, heroism and love. The
most powerful force, however, even on the modern stage is
the veneration and love for the characters, episodes and
incidents drawn directly from the great epics of *Rāmāyaṇa*
and *Mahābhārata*. What the medieval companies presented
in a confused manner on a series of nights is now more
artistically arranged with a dramatic concentration on
particular episodes and persons; but the impulse for the Epics
dramatized is practically the same. One cannot conceive of
the Indian stage without the inexhaustible resources of the
epics of Rāma, Kṛṣṇa and Arjuna as well as a host of medieval
romances.

CHAPTER IV

THE COMPLETE BACKGROUND

BEFORE discussing, in Part II, the rise of the modern theatres in India, their productions and characteristics for the purpose of assessing the exact nature of the influence of the British Drama, it may be interesting to sum up the argument advanced in the preceding chapters regarding the points of contact between the Indian and the European drama. Such a survey has the advantage of convincing one that a complete background for the epoch-making European influence did exist and that only on a strong indigenous foundation could an imposing superstructure be built.

According to a curious Chinese legend,[1] the Herdman and the Spinning Damsel are ancient lovers inhabiting two stars separated by the Silver River (the Milky Way). Only on one night of bliss this Leander is able to cross to his Hero. The story is not without significance. For centuries the stars of the East and the West dwelt apart. And even when Indian civilization came to be known in the West, years passed before there appeared anything like a just appreciation of the Oriental spirit. The literatures of the two hemispheres looked so alien that it seemed as if the twain could never meet. Obviously the Hindu caste system, its idol worship, complicated mythology and belief in rebirth based on the theory of *Karma* (Deeds) opened the widest possible gulf between the two.[2] The whole attitude to life seemed so different; and indeed it is a far cry from the passive meditation on the One and Invisible in a forest grove to the muscular Christianity warring against Evil within and Wrong without at every step.

1. A. E. Zucker: *The Chinese Theatre*, London, 1925, p. 6.
2. C. F. Andrews: *The Renaissance in India*, London, 1912, p. 269.

Nevertheless, in the modern age an attempt is being made to understand and at the same time to draw attention to the points of similarity rather than of difference. It is being now recognized that it is as great a reward of scholarship —if not a greater—to appreciate the deep unity in apparent diversity, as it is to enjoy the subtle distinctions between the arts and literatures of diverse nationalities at various stages of their evolution. It may, therefore, not be inopportune to stress here some points of similarity between the ancient Indian and the Elizabethan drama. As there is not even the remotest chance that the latter imitated the former, the question is one of striking accidental similarity between the two. Any student of the great Sanskrit dramatists must be struck by a number of passages, incidents, devices and suggestions which recall corresponding ones in Shakespeare. Several inherent points of affinity may lead him to ask: did not the classical masters, as it were, anticipate, in some respects, the greatest world dramatist, born a thousand years after their time, six thousand miles distant from them? Where such remarkable resemblances exist, it is no wonder that Shakespeare should be whole-heartedly welcomed on his introduction to the Indian stage.[3]

In the course of a comparison between the ancient Indian and Elizabethan stages, several important parallels regarding the theatre-building and the mode of presenting plays have been discussed above. Moreover, as regards both types of drama, striking points of affinity have also been suggested while discussing (in Chapter I) the violation of the so-called 'three unities' and the partial observation of 'poetic justice'. It is proposed here to discuss in further detail some other aspects of the close relationship between the two. Some basic differences, of course, are not to be forgotten. Thus,

3. This view differs radically from the one suggested by Professor C. R. Shah's review of a treatise, "Shakespeare Through Eastern Eyes," by Dr. R. G. Shahani, *Bombay University Journal*, January 1933.

for instance, ancient Indian writers did not recognize Tragedy as a distinct art by itself; the Sanskrit drama contains more of poetic description and there is in it a lack of action and movement. Once, however, some discount is made for the distinct national temperaments, it is rather the unity than the difference which surprises the student.

Much has been written on the origins of drama among several nations. Religious worship, as is generally agreed, with all its paraphernalia of dance, gesture, music, songs— and later the assumption of rôles by two and later more characters—is recognized as the prime origin of drama throughout the world. The occasion for its rise in Japan may be a great earthquake, or in Germany—Oberammergau —the devouring scourge of plague; but in any case, it starts consciously with a view to propitiating the gods and in order to ward off war, famine or disease or else to celebrate the festival of deliverance from these evils. In India, Greece and China these origins fade into dim distant prehistoric times. So far as India is concerned, Sir William Ridgeway's theory[4] is not in the least convincing. It is not the cult of ancestral worship, but the idea of divinity and consecration behind those semi-legendary heroes of *Rāmāyaṇa* and *Mahābhārata*, that is responsible for Indian drama. In Greece it was the worship of Bacchus; in the medieval period it was the liturgy of the Christian Church; so it was in India the temple worship of *Rāma* and Kṛṣṇa—more or less, the same story.

Apart from this broad general consideration, one may observe that the Indian classical masterpieces are not mere literary curiosities, but are as pulsating with life in their own way as are Shakespeare's plays. There is a rich feast provided for the eye as well as for the ear. They aim at satisfying the intellect and ennobling the soul. Like the Greek masterpieces they are designed for the theatre as

4. *The Dramas . . . of Non-European Races*, p. 211.

well as for the library. Since theatrical technique has radically changed, the effect originally produced is clearly bound to be entirely different from that which they produce to-day; but this is true of the Greek plays and of Shakespeare's as well. The important thing is that there is in them a constant sense of the theatre everywhere present.

These classical plays, moreover, were not mere ephemeral things. They exercise as powerful a hold on the present-day generation as do the plays of Shakespeare, and for the same reason—their pre-eminent literary appeal. The enchanting Sanskrit poetry is responsible for Goethe's famous eulogy of Kālidāsa. He danced for joy, he said, as he felt 'the flowers of spring and fruits of autumn . . . heaven and earth —all expressed in one *Sakuntalā*'! As all critics have admitted, the infinite musical charms of Sanskrit poetry can never be adequately translated into any language. Apt ornaments of speech not only enhance the significance of the meaning but also add to the poetic enjoyment. In Sanskrit the metaphors are analytical as in the early plays of Shakespeare. They are allowed to develop gradually as in those plays, and often we may remark striking similarities in choice of imagery and style of expression. It is, of course, obvious that the distinct flora and fauna of the two countries should modify the kind of metaphorical expression used in each. The tropics thus, in the moon, the stars, the lotus, the sandal tree, the elephant, the lion, the swan, etc., have a wealth of significance which is lacking in the West, while some of the Warwickshire sports and enjoyments have no counterpart in India. Still, the literary methods employed often appear to be the same in spite of the different forms of expression.

Character and situation are manifestly the principal elements in any form of drama. As regards both of these, the two types of drama strike a very clear note of romance. Moreover, the treatment of the basic human passion, love, is to a great extent the same. The halo of romance round

Śakuntalā, Mālatī and Ratnāvalī is much the same as that surrounding Juliet, Viola, Miranda and others. The dominant passion of love, styled the 'Primary Sentiment' by the Hindus, is a marked characteristic of the English romantic drama; and all of Shakespeare's comedies, like so many of the Indian classics, deal with the vicissitudes of love culminating in marriage or reunion.

What is really striking is the number of parallel situations, in spite of the different cultures of the two races. Śakuntalā and Sītā are both rejected by their royal consorts; so are Hermione and Imogen. These two heroines have the salient qualities of an ideal wife, according to Hindu tradition. All are 'as pure as ice'. They suffer grievous wrong and feel the agony of loneliness and unmerited treatment. Still, they do not complain loudly. At the most there is a murmur of righteous indignation. They turn rather inward and find fault with their lot or fate, for they love their husbands too dearly even to hint at hating them for gross injustice. They forgive gracefully and sink willingly into the loving arms. Desdemona has similar qualities. She dies with the words: "Commend me to my kind lord: O, farewell!" This is not 'deliberate deception'. She could not be otherwise; she remains the emblem of deep love which never spoke out on the stage. While their lords talk, these heroines are comparatively silent.

Their character assumes a peculiar beauty and grace at great moments on the stage. Thus, Śakuntalā, in advanced pregnancy, when rejected by her lord, mutters: "It is not becoming in thee, having awhile since in the hermitage so seduced, after a formal agreement, this person (myself), naturally open-hearted, to repudiate her with such words." In this play the indignant Gautamī displays some of the fine qualities of Paulina, ably pleading for the innocent Queen. When Śakuntalā realizes the loss of the signet ring, she exclaims: "This is the triumph of Fate." Then, in the moment of humiliation, she wishes to be interred in the womb

of Mother Earth. Sītā, also big with child, rises from evil
dreams and mutters:

> "Left me alone! asleep! well, well;
> I will be angry with thee, Rāma.
> I will henceforth be mistress of myself;
> Suppress my foolish fondness, and will learn
> Henceforth to chide thee."[5]

Othello calls his Venetian wife 'Devil'! and even strikes her.
She only mutters: "I have not deserved this" and weeps
like her Indian sisters.

Mālatī is almost as passionately in love with Mādhava
as Juliet is with her Romeo. Her situation is much like that
of the Italian heroine. Nandana, the foolish lover, reminds
one of Cloten. Kāmandakī and Friar Lawrence are persons
who have retired from the world and who try to put things
right. The Indian beloved passes through a most severe
ordeal in a temple of dark sacrifices in a crematorium and
just manages to rush to her lover's arms as he runs to her
rescue, while her less fortunate European sister awakes just
a moment too late in the Churchyard of the Capulets. (A
'fault' which some stage-managers have tried to correct!)
Mālavikā and Ratnāvalī both find themselves in a foreign
kingdom, like Viola; but both are secretly in love with the
several princes, by their reputation; and one may well recall
the words of the last:

> "Orsino! I have heard my father name him.
> He was a bachelor then."

Of course, in the ancient Hindu society, on account of the
custom of polygamy, the condition of being a 'bachelor' was
not of vital importance, yet the passion of love, often felt
at first sight, is similarly expressed in both theatres.

Sometimes, by a most remarkable coincidence, in the
treatment of situations of a like nature, almost exactly
parallel expressions proceed from great poets like Bhavabhūti

5. Wilson, Vol. I, p. 311.

and from Shakespeare. To illustrate, when Rāma is over-
whelmed with sorrow at the loss of Sītā, Tamasā says:

> " 'Tis better thus
> To give our sorrows way. Sufferers should speak
> Their griefs. The bursting heart that overflows
> In words obtains relief; the swelling lake
> Is not imperilled, when its rising waters
> Find ready passage through their wonted channel."

Similarly, when Macduff is struck dumb by intense personal
sorrow, Malcolm advises:

> "Give sorrow words; the grief that does not speak
> Whispers the o'erfraught heart, and makes it break."

Wilson adds another parallel from *Richard III*:

Elizabeth:
Why should calamity be full of words?

Duchess of York:
Let them have scope, though what they do impart
Help nothing else, yet do they ease the heart.

Many of the farcical situations, too, in early English drama
—and also in the plays of Molière—are found anticipated
here on the classical Indian stage. Often is the 'Comedy
of Errors' due to mistaken identity exploited. Thus, in
Mālatīmādhava, Nandana finds himself married to a man
(Makaranda) dressed as Mālatī and is kicked till his limbs
ache and his eyes water! In the *Toy Cart*, Vasantasenā,
through a mistake, mounts the chariot of the foolish and
dissolute doter, Saṁsthānaka (again compare Cloten in
many respects, for both have the same stupidity and cruelty)
instead of that of her lover Cārudatta. This leads to very
serious complications indeed. In *Ratnāvalī*, the heroine dons
the clothes and ornaments of the queen, but Vāsavadattā
herself appears in person at the 'rendezvous'; the king makes
love to the wrong lady and is befooled and humiliated.
Another comedy of errors is graphically described by

6. Wilson, Vol. I, p. 333.

Professor Horrwitz.7 This is by one Rāmabhadra, a contemporary of Molière. Śūrpaṇakhā disguised as Sītā and Rāvaṇa's
butler as Rāma are caught in their own trap. These counter-
feits become enamoured of each other and so forget their
original purpose of murder and abduction. Here one is
reminded too of Caliban, Stephano and Trinculo.

In the handling of tragic situations also, the Sanskrit
drama affords some very interesting parallels. After preferring
the general good of his subjects to his own personal happiness,
and deciding to abandon Sītā in a forest, Rāma finds his
heart torn by internal conflict. He feels tragically alone and
expresses his intense solitariness in the midst of a vast
empire:

> "What now is life?—a barren load; the world?
> A dreary, arid, solitary wild.
> Where can I hope for comfort? Sense was given me
> Only to make me conscious of affliction,
> And firmly bound in an unyielding frame."8

This tragic intensity is not unlike that of Othello. When
innocent Cārudatta is on the point of being executed, he is
troubled solely about his fair name after death. In the same
manner, Hamlet finally entreats Horatio to 'absent' him
'from felicity' and to live to 'tell his story'. What ails Othello,
at the moment of his death, is the mode of relating the
'unlucky deeds' after him.

The noting of affinities in the handling of comic and tragic
situations may readily lead to a consideration of the use of
Dramatic Irony and of several other devices in both types
of drama. In the Sanskrit drama there is no question of
Sophoclean irony as in _Œdipus_, for God is believed to be
always good and just; but ordinary dramatic irony arising
out of comical or tragical situation is certainly present.
There is, for instance, sparkling comic irony in the king's
embracing his queen, believing her to be Ratnāvalī. The
farcical irony of Nandana marrying Makaranda has been

7. _The Indian Theatre_, p. 142.　　　8. Wilson, Vol. I, p. 310.

suggested above. The tragic irony[9] becomes poignant when Sītā reposes on the lap of her lord at a time when he feels compelled to abandon her. The prophetic irony (like 'Thou shalt get kings, though thou be none', cf. *Macbeth*) is suggested when the audience hears of the curse of the sage to Śakuntalā and of the ring atonement.

The most subtle type of irony, perhaps, is present when 'the coming events cast their shadows before'; and people feel or dream of the approaching joy or sorrow. This irony derives its strength from certain omens and prognostications. Just before her rejection, Śakuntalā's left limb begins to throb and she feels uneasy. Sītā screams in her dream: "Where art thou, dearest Rāma?" By a mysterious touch the following banishment is anticipated. Shakespeare's plays present some interesting parallels. As Romeo descends after the only night of bliss, Juliet pathetically asks: "O, thinkest thou we shall ever meet again?" Calpurnia, in her dream, cries: "Help ho! They murder Cæsar!" And what is the significance of the 'Willow' song which curiously haunts Desdemona's mind on that fatal night?

The device of dramatic irony of all types gains in intensity because the Sanskrit dramatists, like Shakespeare, prefer expectation to surprise. This is the first distinctive characteristic of Shakespearean art noted by Coleridge:[10] "As the feeling with which we startle at a shooting star, compared with that of watching the sunrise at the pre-established moment, such and so low is surprise compared with expectation." Of course, one cannot look in Sanskrit dramatists for the most suggestive keynote of the whole piece at the start, as in a Shakespearean play (cf. 'In sooth I know not why I am so sad'; and 'When shall we three meet again, In thunder, lightning, or in rain?'). Both, however, not only at the start, but throughout the several stages of

9. "The best examples of dramatic irony in Sanskrit drama are to be found in Bhavabhūti, who excels in this device" (S. K. De).
10. *Literary Criticism*, London, 1921, p. 195.

the play, take the audience into their confidence, so that it does not remain dumb with confused surprise. The last scenes of the *Toy Cart* and *Cymbeline* are indeed replete with thrilling interest, but the audience knows that Vasantasenā and Imogen are living, this gradually preparing it for a refined enjoyment of the happy catastrophe.

In another striking dramatic device, 'Pathetic Fallacy', there is a great deal of affinity between the two. Both on the Sanskrit and on the Elizabethan stage external nature is supposed in both to take deep sympathetic interest in human affairs. The whole penance grove is touched when Śakuntalā is bidding farewell to all its inmates, animate and inanimate: "The deer let fall the mouthfuls of durbha-grass, the peacocks cease their dancing, the creepers casting their pale leaves appear to shed tears".[11] Similarly, 'even rocks shed tears and the heart of an adamant begins to melt' in divine sympathy with Rāma's profound sorrow. It is here interesting to recollect that at the death of Cæsar and Duncan the whole world is described as in commotion. One hears of thunder and lightning, lions roaring, men walking in fire and night-birds croaking.

Fatalism is noted as an important characteristic of the Elizabethan tragedy, which is, in turn, traced back by Dr. J. W. Cunliffe[12] mainly to the influence of Seneca. But, in the Sanskrit drama, even before Seneca, the mysterious relation of the temporal with the eternal is emphasized. Ultimately, it is divinity which shapes all human ends. No doubt, the element of Fate is modified by the force of Hindu religious faith, with the result that absolute hopeless fatalism of the Stoic school is not expressed. In moments of utter dejection, however, the Sanskrit characters do blame their destiny, in much the same terms as Elizabethan characters. In Shakespeare, of course, these complaints gain in tragic intensity from the gloomy catastrophe. When

11. IV, 92—Williams.
12. *The Influence of Seneca on Elizabethan Tragedy*, London, 1893.

Mercutio is dead, Romeo exclaims: "This day's black fate on more days doth depend." Hamlet's agony grows unbearable as he realizes his peculiar situation: "Oh, cursed spite that ever I was born to set it right." *King Lear* is full of suggestions of some mysterious wire-puller controlling whimsically the helpless puppets on the grim stage of life.

Finally, two fundamental characteristics shared by the Sanskrit masters and the great English dramatist may be noted. First, the essentially human appeal of their plays proceeding not from various 'humours', idiosyncrasies and exaggerated sentiments or caricatures, but from a profound study of types who are individuals as well. The mastery of mundane realities and the power to discriminate between the essential and the accidental are remarkable in both cases.

Secondly, exquisite realism is tinged in all these masters with beautiful idealism. The quality of high nobility in all fine art is thus strikingly maintained. There is neither the study of incest or diabolical crime like parricide as in the Greek tragedy, nor the stereotyped low farcical devices of Latin comedy, in Sanskrit drama. In Shakespeare also high seriousness is never absent from his great plays. The most charming Sanskrit heroines noted above purify the atmosphere they breathe and adorn whatever they touch. The human soul is chastened and ennobled after witnessing the tragic conflict. To observe Duṣyanta repentant on the stage, Vikrama, semi-lunatic, questioning every object of Nature about his beloved, Rāma performing the Horse-sacrifice with the golden image of his Sītā by his side, and Cāṇakya, the king-maker, living deliberately a life of poverty and meditation, is to love and admire the good, the beautiful and the noble in man. Similarly, the audience is struck with awe and admiration for high character at the conclusion of Shakespearean tragedies. One feels proud to belong to the human stock after being exalted by the sight of a few fine souls like Candanadāsa and Maitreya on the one hand and Kent and Lear's Fool on the other.

PART II

THE MODERN INDIAN STAGE
AND THE INFLUENCE OF EUROPEAN THEATRES

CHAPTER V

THE RISE OF THE MODERN THEATRES

I. CALCUTTA

BEFORE the battle of Plassey in 1757, an English theatre was in existence in Calcutta.[1] "The ex-subedar (captain) and his army converted it into a battery to attack the old Fort. But it was rebuilt in 1775–76 by public subscription." Warren Hastings is mentioned among the subscribers. Although only amateur performances were given there at a time when the rich tradition of the ancient Hindu theatre had fallen into decay for centuries and when the theatre of the people had been degraded in villages, we must look upon this theatre as inspiring the reformation of the Indian stage. It is, of course, true that this old playhouse in Tal Bazar was meant solely for the recreation of a handful of Europeans, merchants, missionaries and officials. But a fundamental link with the Indian population was established by occasional invitations extended to rich Bengali landlords.

At this 'Calcutta Theatre', after 1770, sparkling comedies like *The Beaux Stratagem* and *The School for Scandal* and Shakespearean tragedies like *Richard III* and *Hamlet* were staged by one Mr. Massinck or Massing, who had been sent out by David Garrick.[2] "At first the female rôles were taken by men, but later, following the example of the 'Chowringhee (or Mrs. Bistow's) Theatre',[3] women were introduced." Musical comedies or farces were apparently the favourite

1. Raja Binoy Krishna Deb: *The Early History and Growth of Calcutta*, 1905, p. 267.
2. *The Bengali Drama*, by Dr. P. Guha-Thakurta, London, 1930, p. 41.
3. Mrs. Bistow was the wife of a Calcutta business man, and she ran this venture for many years, herself appearing in the rôle of heroine. She met a tragic end on the stage, for her costume caught fire while acting.

fare at the latter theatre. Amateur acting, musical comedies, classical English plays and the presence of actresses were all bound to exert an immense impression on the minds of the rich and cultured Indian aristocracy privileged to be present at these performances.

The second important stage was due to "the efforts of a Russian adventurer, Herasim Lebedeff, who, in 1795, built . . . an Indian theatre in 'Dom Tollah' (the present Ezra Street), for which two English plays—*The Disguise* and *Love is the Best Doctor*—were translated by him into Bengali and performed in November 1795 and March 1796 with the help of 'native actors of both sexes' ".[4] Both plays received 'very liberal support'.[5]

The third stage was reached when eminent Sanskrit scholars such as Dr. H. H. Wilson, educationists like Captain Richardson of the Hindu College, and journalists like J. H. Stocqueler appeared as amateur actors at the "Private Subscription Theatre", where Mrs. Leach won universal praise from 1825 to 1858. Plays such as *Henry IV*, *She Stoops to Conquer* and the *Merry Wives of Windsor* were staged there. Distinguished amateurs continued to appear at the 'Sans Souci' Theatre, established in 1841. All this time "the rich Bengalees who patronized these playhouses were charmed by the novelty of foreign representation, especially by the beautiful scenes and magical transformations, and they felt a keen desire to improve and embellish their own amusements after the model of the European stage".[6]

It is interesting to notice the general nature of popular

4. Syama Prasad Mookerjee, in *The Calcutta Review*, January 1924, p. 110.
5. The plays were advertised in English newspapers. "A synopsis of the play was distributed to the audience. English and Indian instruments were used for the musical accompaniment and some Hindustani music was played. There were also some recitals at intervals of Bharat Chandra's poetry" (*The Bengali Drama*, p. 44).
6. See *Calcutta Review*, January 1924, p. 110.

performances about 1843, which influenced the first Indian efforts in palatial private theatres. When *Aladdin* was announced it was stated to be a "Melodramatic Pantomimic performance, interspersed with combats, choruses, dances, processions, etc.". Again, it was noted that "the difficulty of working new machinery will be entirely remedied".[7] One should remember the type of productions which were popular then in England, for the English conditions were likely to be reflected in Calcutta: "The public does not care a fig for the 'legitimate drama'."[8] To amuse the audience in Calcutta, even after the performance of *Henry IV*, Part I, a popular farce was included in a double bill. Sometimes, on benefit nights for actresses, three farces were given in succession for five long hours. 'Inexplicable dumb-shows and noise' also invaded India. Several species of entertainment were confused. Thus, one reads the announcement of the 'Sans Souci' Theatre, "a much-admired melodrama with new scenery, music and properties, of *The Tale of Mystery* or *The Unnatural Brother*, to conclude with the farce *Three Weeks after Marriage*".[9] More than the 'legitimate drama', musical farces and sensational pieces with all possible theatrical attractions dominated the Bengal stage at this crucial moment.

These English theatres, which were fast becoming commercial, filled the minds of rich landlords with great ideas. At the heavy cost of two lakhs of rupees (£13,000) the popular medieval drama *Vidyāsundar* was acted by men and women in 1835, in the house of Nabinchandra Basu in

7. *The Englishman*, January 2 and 3, 1843.
8. *Britannia*, October 15, 1872, quoted by *Englishman*.
   The writer adds: "Notwithstanding the admiration of the whole world for 'the one great bard', playgoers are the same race now in thought and feeling as that which preferred Dryden and Tate to Shakespeare, and *Pizarro* and *The Castle Spectre* to the finest creation of poetic genius. Novelty and exciting novelty, either in actors or performances, is essential to success; there is nothing to be done without it."
9. *The Englishman*, February 15, 1873.

Shambazar. Although "not a true copy of the scenic representation of the English theatre, it displayed a clear attempt
at innovation. . . . The play was not performed at one and
the same place in the house, but different scenes were put
up and enacted in different parts of the building, when the
audience had to shift with change of scenes".[10] The scenic
representation made the play immensely popular with the
guests.

The next important stage, the fifth, was marked by the
enthusiasm of youths in the educational institutions of that
time. With the students it was a time of renaissance.
Fascinated by the English performances and inspired by
the example and deep interest in theatrical productions of
their professors, in the absence of regular Bengali plays, the
students tried to express their ambition in a double manner.
Dr. Wilson's English version of the Sanskrit classic, *Uttara-
rāma-carita*, was staged in 1831, at the garden house of
Prasannakumar Tagore, with Wilson himself in the cast.
Secondly, since performances after the English mode became
fashionable, and Captain Richardson (of the Hindu College)
and H. Jeffrey (of the Oriental Seminary) were veteran
theatre-lovers, *The Merchant of Venice*, *Julius Cæsar*,
Othello and *Henry IV* were staged in English in a proper
European style, the most notable English actors in Calcutta
being occasionally invited for training and advice in production. The young Indian enthusiasts started a tradition
which was greatly enriched by the second generation.

All the above five stages culminated in the year 1857,
which is generally recognized as one of the most memorable
in the history of the theatre of Bengal. In the coming of
the printing-press to India, in the cultivation of ordinary
vernacular prose by pioneer missionaries like Carey, in the
momentous minute of Lord Macaulay in 1833, and in the
foundation of the three principal universities of India by
the Act of 1857, British civilization had given a tremendous

10. *The Calcutta Review*, January 1924, p. 111.

impetus to the native genius of India. This was the dawn of the Indian renaissance. In the field of the theatre, with the European model before them and the experience of a few odd experiments, young Bengal produced the first original play, a social tragedy, *Kulīnakulasarvasva*, in March 1857, at the house of Babu Jayaram Bysack of Churruck-danga Street, Calcutta; in that year it was published and "was mounted with all the novelty that latest designs of the stage could produce". It marks the beginning of the mode of scenic representation that is now in vogue in Bengal. In this play Beharilal Chatterjee acted a female rôle.

The revival of Hindu drama led at the outset to the fullest exploration of ancient Indian treasures. *Sākuntala* was performed for the first time on January 30, 1857, at the house of Babu Ashutosh Deb, at Simla. Then followed in quick succession Bengali versions of the classical master-pieces. Three outstanding personalities, viz. (1) Raja Jatindra Mohan Tagore, (2) Raja Pratap Chandra Singh, and (3) Babu Kaliprasanna Singh, gave a lead in private theatrical per-formances on the grand scale. Generally, these performances were given "not in an open space, but in theatres neatly and beautifully erected at the lower end of the drawing-room, with scenic embellishment of considerable preten-sions. The opening scene consists in the appearance not of the manager, but of a *naṭa* (an actor) and a *naṭī* (an actress), who entertain the audience with dancing and introduce the actors, stating in brief the chief incidents of the play and describing the parts to be acted by them".[11]

The modern theatre advanced a step further when the first permanent stage was constructed in the gorgeous villa of Raja Pratap Chandra Singh and Raja Issur Chunder Singh of Paikpara, at Belgachia, on July 31, 1858, when *Ratnāvalī* was staged in Bengali. "It was the first Bengali drama that was played to the accompaniment of the

11. 'The Modern Hindu Drama', in *The Calcutta Review*, 1873, pp. 245–273, by Kissory Chand Mittra.

(national) orchestra, after the manner of the English theatres." These Rajas financed the theatre, invited distinguished European and Indian guests, and provided for the former an English version of the play. Along with these classical plays, original productions based on episodes of the Indian Epics continued to be produced.

Rival private theatres were erected, for invited friends only, by other Rajas. A 'Pathuriaghatta Theatre' was started in 1865 by Babu Jatindra Mohan Tagore, at his own residence. It was not very spacious, but was "very beautifully got-up", and "the scenes were singularly well painted, especially the drop-scene, which was ablaze with aloes and water-lilies and was entirely Oriental". Sometimes the scenes were painted by distinguished English artists and the songs and orchestra were entrusted to various experts.

Social farces, like *Eki-i-ki-bale-sabhyatā* (*Is this Civilization?*), by Michael Madhusudan Datta, on the English model, began to be produced by the Shobha-Bazar Private Theatrical Society and other amateur companies, including the Jorasanko Tagore troupe, about 1865, either as independent pieces or as laughter-provoking afterpieces. The merriment was often heightened by "the perfection of the whole spectacle, in song, scenery, dress, acting, orchestral performance and general management". Many plays created a sensation in the town and elicited prompt applause from Indian and European guests on Saturday nights for years. The rush became so great (there being no fee charged for these performances) that, in order to regulate the free admission, tickets had to be issued in many cases, and hundreds of enthusiasts sought these free tickets with 'certificates' for the qualification of playgoers.[12]

Being disappointed by such private theatres meant only for privileged classes, Girishchandra Ghosh, 'the father of the Bengali theatre', boldly launched the idea of a public

12. *Abhinetṛ Kāhinī* (*Story of Actors and Actresses*), by Amarendranath Datta, Calcutta, 1914, p. 21.

theatre for the middle class run by amateurs. This genius, a book-keeper at Messrs. Atkinson Tiltan & Co., secured the co-operation of another gifted actor, Ardhendushekhar Mustafi; and after struggling for several years by acting with but few theatrical accessories, in the manner of the *yātrā*-players, and winning laurels in difficult rôles, they succeeded in establishing the 'National Theatre' in 1872. This was the first regular theatre in which actors received salary and tickets were sold to the public. With admirable insight and energy they attempted all kinds of stagecraft, and experimented in tragedy, musical comedy, farce and pantomime.

Their productions partook of all the salient characteristics of the English stage. The services of "a poor English sailor named McLean who came for alms at Baghbazar" were utilized for painting by the able scenic artist Dharamdas Sur. At a rival theatre, 'the Bengal Theatre', actresses were introduced, for the first time on the Indian stage, in 1873. In the same year 'the Great National Theatre' was constructed on the model of the European 'Lewis Theatre' at Calcutta.

So far as the public Bengali playhouses are concerned, therefore, 'the National Theatre' of Girish was the ancestor of all those now existing, such as 'The Star', 'The Minerva', 'The Manmohan', and 'The Arts' of to-day.

Girish, himself an eminent dramatist, also directed the course of the several types of plays which were produced on the stage. Pauranic plays like *Hariścandra,* based on incidents and characters of the ancient Indian epics, mythology and legend, became immensely popular, after the classical translations had lost their hold on the popular mind. Along with these, Shakespearean adaptations were tried with considerable success, Girish himself excelling as Macbeth. Later on, with the development of the national sentiment, historical plays like *Pratap* and *Shivaji* fascinated crowded audiences, the English chronicle plays serving in some respects as models. Social tragedies were also boldly staged and much admired, while the interest in musical and satirical farces of contemporary manners and customs remained unabated. Finally, there evolved a most skilful realistic type of play by Dvijendralal Ray which was pro- duced with great success, on the one hand, and the highly poetic and symbolic type of play by Dr. Tagore which could seldom succeed on the stage, on the other. The works of these two dramatists are among the finest flowers of the literary renaissance, for they have assimilated the best of the Western ideas.[13]

2. BOMBAY

The conditions in Bombay present a noteworthy contrast to those prevailing in Calcutta. In the first place, Bombay is the most cosmopolitan city of India, without the homo- geneous culture of the Bengal Hindus. From this it follows that in the former case one hears a babel of tongues, while in the latter there is the standard language of a race. Thus while the medium of dramatic expression is fixed in Calcutta, the commercial theatre of Bombay makes all sorts of experi- ments in Urdu, pure Gujarati, Parsi Gujarati, with an occasional element of Marathi. Secondly, Parsis, the most intelligent minority in India, have made their headquarters in Bombay. They bring with them ancient Persian traditions profoundly modified by Hindu culture. Again, they have a genius for completely adapting themselves to Western standards. In a sense, they are the pioneers of the modern theatre in Bombay, both in the amateur and in the pro- fessional field. As a community, they are responsible for bold experiments in stagecraft, but at the same time they made this too commercial for higher development. Thirdly, Bombay had not the same time to evolve slowly through

13. For a few interesting extracts drawn from certain periodical articles on 'The Early History of Bengali Theatre' by Mr. Brajendra Nath Banerji, see Appendix A.

the several stages noted in Calcutta, on account of the former's later development and the absence of very rich landlords there. Fourthly, in her peculiar situation, Bombay has not been able to produce theatrical successes which are at the same time literary masterpieces, in the manner of Girish, D. Ray and Dr. Tagore, except on the Marathi stage. It must not be forgotten, however, that Bombay had other great advantages. The position of woman, for instance, is decidedly superior in the west, where there is a considerable freedom which does not exist in the east, with the majority of the Mohammedan population. This accounts for the greater freedom of representation in drama. Finally, the Marathi, Parsi and Gujarati companies, on account of their business instinct and their free use of Hindustani, can travel from province to province and create a love of the theatre in the remotest places in India, and this the Bengali theatre cannot do. How far such an influence has been an unmixed good is another question.

With these reservations, the stages in the establishment of the professional theatre were very similar in Bombay. "The original Bombay Theatre, which stood on the old Bombay Green (Elphinstone Circle) was built by subscription in 1770 (on a site granted by Government), and for a few years only managed to pay its way."[14] European amateurs used to perform here, generally providing fare consisting of musical comedies, farces, pantomimes, with occasional productions of Shakespeare and of serious plays. Some of the distinguished Parsis and Hindus were bound to be impressed by these novel performances. An original advertisement gives characteristic information: The price of a seat in the pit was Rs. 8 (12s.); and no gentleman was allowed behind the scenes. "On Tuesday evening, the 12th instant, will be performed the Favourite Farce of the *Apprentice*, after which the Interlude of the *Manager's Ante-Room* to conclude with the *Village Lawyer*. A moiety

14. *The Gazetteer of Bombay City*, Vol. III, p. 364, Bombay, 1910.

of the net receipts to go to charity."[15] Similarly, from an extract quoted in *Life in Bombay* (1838), one gathers that there was an improvised 'Artillery Theatre' at Matunga, where "in November 1820, all Bombay society, including the Governor, witnessed a performance of *Miss in Her Teens* and the *Padlock*".

In 1842 a private theatre was built by Jagannath Shankerseth, and became available for European and Indian productions at a fixed daily rent.   K. N. Kabraji described it, in 1850, as standing alone ('The Bombay Theatre' being destroyed) "like an oasis in the desert".[16] This year is again memorable in the annals of the western Indian stage, for the chief of Sangli was profoundly impressed by performances of native plays by the Kanarese Players, who eventually came under his patronage. The chief asked one of his gifted clerks, Vishnupanth Bhave, to follow in the footsteps of the visiting players, to collect a troupe, and to produce plays in Marathi with music on a Karnataki basis. Bhave himself composed some pieces, achieving particular success with amorous and pathetic themes. This experiment was a purification of medieval performances on indigenous lines. After the demise of the patron, these Bhave players turned professional and toured many cities and provinces, influencing the modes of production there, and themselves also incorporating several devices and stage-tricks of Parsi companies who were imitating the English model.

A phase of the age of patronage is also noteworthy in connection with the Kathiawad Rajas, who liberally endowed at the start local players, as in Morbi, Vankaner,

15. *Bombay Courier*, September 2, 1820.
16. The physical conditions of Old Bombay then are worth noting for a proper perspective. J. Douglas, in his *Glimpses from Old Bombay* (London, 1900), notes: "Fifty years ago (1850) Bombay was a very different place from what we see to-day. With some exceptions, it was a city unpaved, unlighted, undrained, unventilated. There was no gas, no tramways, no hotels worthy of the name. Hospitality then did duty for hotels."

Palitana, etc., derived some pleasure from command performances, and then released these companies from all
obligations, permitting them to turn professional and to
tour in many districts. But these chiefs were at no time so
profoundly interested as were the Bengal landowners, who
themselves acted and invited to their shows such persons as
the Governor-General, high officials and prominent public
men.

As Mr. A. V. Kulkarni has noted,[17] after 1851 the Bhave
Players went to Bombay, witnessed a European performance,
and on the same stage, later on, produced their typical play,
which was "much admired by the Governor's Secretary".
Religious spirit, 'scientific' singing by a sort of 'chorus' in
the midst of dialogue by other characters, crude dances and
quaint costumes and make-up and certain skilful sword-play
were their outstanding qualities. With all their defects,
Bhave's Pauranic productions had a fixed system, some
dignity, and intense musical charm. One has to remember
that the audience was very devotional in character.

Rival troupes, of course, sprang up and began to compete
on professional lines, as may be gathered from the history
of the 'Sanglikar' (of Bhave), 'Altekar', and other companies. The types of productions ran on parallel lines with
those noted in relation to the Bengali theatre. In the first
instance, most of the incidents and situations of the ancient
epics and legends were exploited to the fullest. In these
performances more curtains were added in the Parsi style
and some English farcical devices were gradually incorporated.

Inspired by witnessing European performances, the
'Kālidāsa Elphinstone Society' of Bombay staged the
English version of *Śākuntala*, as Dr. Wilson and others did
Bhavabhūti's masterpiece in Calcutta. Similarly, at Poona
in 1872, *Julius Cæsar* was staged by university students.
Occasional help of European actors like Player Cloe and

17. *Marāṭhī Raṅgabhūmi (The Marathi Stage)*, Poona, 1903, p. 19.

actresses such as Miss Eltia May was sought by colleges at heavy expense. Following the example of English productions, Sanskrit classics were also staged by college amateurs. These efforts led to 'bookish plays', i.e. plays from English and Sanskrit adapted to the Marathi stage. In this type of performance the 'Aryoddharaka Company' of Poona particularly excelled. Professionals followed suit with the special accessory of music and songs. Only one, 'The Maharashtra Company', made a heroic effort to produce only prose plays, keeping its eye fixed on 'legitimate drama'. Otherwise, the passion for music is an outstanding quality throughout. Before this company, some of the finest plays seen on the Marathi stage were produced by 'The Shahunagaravasi Company' in prose. This troupe produced some of the best adaptations of *Hamlet* and *The Taming of the Shrew*. It had a brilliant galaxy of actors, including Ganapatrao Joshi and Balavantrao Jog.

After several able performances of these adaptations of classics, the third type of historical plays began to be staged from about 1890. One has to recollect that the Maratha power was a dominant feature of Indian political life till the early nineteenth century. In the case of Maharashtra, therefore, the patriotic note gains a peculiar intensity. Quasi-historical plays with a deep national appeal were sure to be censored by the Government. Therefore the subtle Marathi genius used to couch the patriotic appeal in an allegorical form or in a legendary setting. The heroic sentiment was the marked feature of several plays popular on the stage, like *Bajirao*, *Shivaji*, *Pratap*, etc. Some excellent English historical research by chroniclers such as Colonel Todd, Grant Duff and others, often provided suitable material for these historical productions.

Finally, social plays exposing flagrant evils, like *Huṇḍā*, or farcical skits ridiculing contemporary follies in marriages and the like became popular. *Śāradā* was the first social play, written for a prize competition, as in the case of the

Bengali social drama. Ibsen and Shaw then began to exercise a marked influence in plays like those of Mr. Varerkar after 1910. Social tragedies were also boldly launched on the stage, deeply affecting the audience. It is this last influence which proved to be lasting in its effects.

From the rapid survey of the Marathi theatre, one may gather that on account of a fixed medium of literary expression and of the power of assimilating foreign influences, a high standard is usually maintained in many Marathi productions, especially by the 'Bala Gandharva' (musical) and the 'Maharashtra' (prose) companies. The Marathi theatre ranks next to the Bengali to-day. Again, as in Bengal, the English and Sanskrit adaptations have been staged side by side with conspicuous success. There has not been any conflict between the two; only, as in the English Renaissance theatre, many experiments based on foreign models were freely made, and ultimately the national genius of Bengal and Maharashtra assimilated some of the best features of Western models. They both retained the passion for indigenous music by a frequent infusion of songs, partly on the Shakespearean model. Both welcomed tragedies and social satires and farcical skits in the English manner.

Despite the glory of this remarkable achievement, the sad fact remains that there is not now a single permanent Marathi theatre in Bombay. Many companies visit the city and give excellent performances, but cannot afford to continue throughout the year, as some Parsi, Urdu and Gujarati companies do. The fault lies with the Bombay audience and the types of inferior productions given by some other troupes.

The Parsis, with the gift of imitating Western models, were the true pioneers in Bombay theatrical productions, although they were originally inspired after seeing the (Bhave) Marathi players in that city. They started as amateurs about 1851, giving performances only on Saturday nights. As some organizing syndicates began to derive huge profits from these experiments, rival Parsi and Gujarati companies hired or built their theatres and began to run on a commercial basis, trying to vie with each other in all possible melodramatic and farcical devices—thus expending enormous sums on all kinds of stage machinery, disregarding all canons of art, often indulging in gross anachronisms.

It should not, however, be forgotten that the Parsis had no proper medium of expression[18] and that their audience of Gujarati and Urdu or Hindi-speaking people made it immensely difficult for them to reach a high literary level in their plays. Again, the Parsi community have the talent for histrionics and are very resourceful in stagecraft. They do not grudge spending generously for rich settings. Moreover, by ransacking all possible sources they can think of—Persian and Sanskrit mythology and epics, English novels, farces and plays, medieval legends and historical events from diverse races, and modern social problems—they opened a wide vista of vast possibilities for dramatic themes. Finally, by their very powerful acting, tragic and farcical, and their habit of touring throughout India, they emphasized the great need of varied action and rapid movement along with marvellous scenic effects on the Indian stage.

Without going into details, one may mention that Dadabhai Thoothi, Dadabhai Patel, Kuvarji Nazir, Khori, K. Khatau, K. Kabraji and K. Balliwala were among the most outstanding pioneers in the Bombay theatre. Most of them were well educated in English, and some of the actors had visited England to study theatrical conditions. Generally, their plays were adaptations of English comedies to suit Parsi life and manners. They continued the English practice of giving small farces in Gujarati, Urdu or English at the end of the principal play. With a view to commercial success, they ordered stage machinery from England, adver-

18. They generally use Parsi-Gujarati with many Urdu words. Again, as they do not know Sanskrit, their pronunciations of words are also different.

tised boldly the novel attractions of 'Transformation Scenes'
or 'Dissolving Views', and even went to the length of showing
with the aid of a bioscope pictures of the Franco-Prussian
War, or of the Zulu and Abyssinian Wars. They had an
English girl acting as a pianist and an English expert as an
interpreter of scenes. Pantomimes like *Aladdin*, and even
pure operas, were given closely on English lines, Dadi
Ratanji Dalal being the greatest scenic artist of Bombay at
that time. Mostly, they made a point of publishing their
plays, in contrast to pure Gujarati dramatists.[19] To the Parsi
community also belongs the credit of introducing women
on the Bombay stage, for it was Khatau who brought the
accomplished actress Gohar to the notice of western India.
The Urdu stage was the creation of the Parsis. Native
Christians and some Moslems have sometimes co-operated
and started joint ventures. Moslem poets and scholars like
Aga Hashr Kashmiri have composed powerful plays based
on English or Persian or Sanskrit plots which have been
staged with conspicuous success in many parts of India.
Some Hindu actors are also to be found in such cosmopolitan
troupes. The principal Urdu theatre of Calcutta, owned by
Madan Ltd. (a Parsi firm), has the unique advantage of a
modern revolving stage and Anglo-Indian actresses for
spectacular scenes.

The Gujarati theatre proper arose out of discontent with
Parsi high-handedness in the management of the new
theatre. Ranachodbhai Udayaram, the pioneer dramatist,
gives a graphic description of its origin.[20] He was disgusted
with the low farcical and vulgar devices of the Gujarati
Bhavāi. Consequently, he translated for the stage some
Sanskrit classics, wrote the most popular Pauranic play of
Hariścandra, and also produced the first social tragedy,
Lalitāduhkhadarśaka Nāṭaka. Some Gujarati teachers like

19. Cf. a series of articles on the "Parsi Stage" in *Kaisare Hind* of
    Bombay from November 25, 1928, by Mr. Dhanjibhai Patel.
20. See *Rangabhūmi* (*The Stage*), Vol. I—4, p. 400.

G

Narottam started the venture as amateurs, then three partners founded 'the Gujarati' company as a business concern in 1878, after which 'The Bombay Gujarati' of Dayashanker, 'The Morbi' of Vaghaji Oza, and 'The Deshi Company' of Dahyabhai Dholsha established the modern Gujarati theatre. Gujarat, like Bengal and Maharastra, has the advantage of a standard vernacular; unfortunately, she has not yet won the reputation of the other two. The Gujarati is essentially a commercial community. Following the example of the Parsis, all sorts of experiments in sensational themes and marvellous stage effects were made in Bombay to attract large audiences. After the usual but very rapid stages of evolution from Pauranic plays and lives of the saints to English adaptations, plays with ultra-romantic themes, historical and social productions are the order of to-day. The former indirectly preach patriotism, Hindu-Moslem unity; and the latter generally satirize contemporary evils. Perhaps the most deplorable features of modern practice are the incorporation of low social farces, often unrelated to the main plot, generally as alternate scenes (instead of giving a separate skit at the end), and the rarity of the publication of acted plays.

C. MADRAS

With the exception of high-class amateur productions Madras is several decades behind the western Indian stage and at least half a century behind the Bengali theatre. Of course, the Madras Theatre includes the Tamil, Telegu and Kanarese theatres, of which the first is the most backward. As compared with Bombay's eighteen or twenty well-equipped theatres, Madras has scarcely four or five, most of the new theatres being designed for cinema exhibitions. Tamil plays by professional companies still deal mostly with mythological themes like *Daśavatāram* in gorgeous spectacular settings. The general level of actors from the stand-

point of education and culture is so poor that they cannot
stage good English adaptations. By way of compensation,
it may be noted that they excel in the indigenous arts of
Dravidian dances and songs. The Telegu companies of the
Andhra district and Kanarese theatres of Mysore are certainly, in all respects, much more advanced.

In 1875 the 'Madras Dramatic Society' was founded,
under whose auspices amateur Europeans gave performances
in English. As in Calcutta and Bombay, some of the high-
class families had the opportunity of witnessing English
productions. About 1880, when medieval 'paddy-field' or
open-air plays were still the principal source of dramatic
amusement, the Poona Sangli Troupe visited Madras. Inspired by their novel performances, one Govind Swamirao, a
Marathi resident, started to act Tamil mythological plays with
the aid of crude scenery and native music. About 1882 the
'Fort Bijour Theatre' was built and the Oriental Dramatic
Club was founded, wherein about 1885 the European
harmonium, Hindustani 'Gazals', and English farcical songs
were introduced. In 1890, Krishnamacharya of Bellary
started the first amateur dramatic society of Southern
India, the 'Sarasa Vinodini Sabha'. Inspired by some of
their productions in Madras, and on the model of the European 'Madras Dramatic Society', Mr. P. Sambanda and
other college students founded the premier amateur dramatic
institution of India, 'The Sugun Vilas Sabha'.[21] This was an
epoch-making event in the annals of the Indian theatre.
Several reforms of vital importance were introduced, as one
may gather from a few articles in that society's periodical,
The Indian Stage, in 1911. The ancient and medieval system
of prayers at the commencement of a play was replaced by
the novel practice of giving a song from behind the drop-
curtain. The story of the plot was not to be narrated in
advance. The buffoon, if he figured at all, was not to be
present on the stage all the time. Everyone was not to sing

21. See its *Illustrated Souvenir*, 1929.

and dance. Instead of constant singing and fighting on the stage with only some links in prose, plays on a Shakespearean model with only occasional songs were to be produced, and on many occasions only prose plays were staged. All these points were indeed distinct improvements.

Most members of this excellent institution are 'university wits' and high officials, including several High Court judges. They have staged Shakespearean comedies and tragedies in English, Tamil and Telegu, side by side with adaptations of the Sanskrit classics; in the true spirit of the renaissance they accept joyfully whatever is best in international art. Historical plays with a national fervour and social farces and tragedies are also produced by them. These plays are given in the Victoria Memorial Hall, where the society has its headquarters. Now it is on the eve of building an up-to-date theatre of its own, £8,000 having been laid aside for that purpose.

The influence of this society is not confined to Madras, for select actors travel to all important places in the south, including Ceylon, with the noteworthy result that they establish a healthy amateur dramatic tradition, giving birth to numerous local companies to follow in their footsteps. Not only the amateurs, but the very professionals are often tempted to imitate them in their plays, their style of acting, their scenic arrangements, and their make-up.

In their turn, the pioneer Madras amateurs were greatly influenced by a visit of the Bombay Parsi Theatre Company to Madras in 1897, when, in an improvised theatre, it thrilled the audience by means of novel and brilliant scenery, costume and stage technique on European lines. This venture was a huge success, and other Bombay companies visited Madras, including 'Balliwala' with his repertory of Shakespearean adaptations. In 1898 the 'Museum Theatre' was built and 'Kanaiya and Company' was started. Respectable people began to visit theatres for the first time. Later on, other professional and amateur Tamil and Telegu societies were formed, including a Boys' company ('Bāla Vinoda Nāṭakasabhā') and a Women's troupe ('Bālāmaṇī Company'), wherein all rôles are played by women. Unfortunately, the former have not as yet a suitable repertory for players of their age and the latter have no status in Hindu society.

Whereas the Tamil professional theatre is patronized by a low-class audience, the Telegu stage is able to maintain a comparatively high level on account of its middle-class playgoers. Consequently, there is not a marked difference between the amateur and professional performances on the Telegu stage. Since 1890 it has been developing rapidly, while passing through the mythological, 'bookish', historical and social types of productions. The modern tendency is to expose mercilessly through the medium of a tragedy or a burlesque the most glaring social evils, such as the sale of a bridegroom (*varavikrayam*), or of excessive drinking (*madhusevā*), or of prostitution (*cintāmaṇīyam*). Some amateur companies also act Shakespearean drama in English, while *The Merchant of Venice* and *Hamlet* have been popular on the professional stage as in Calcutta and Bombay. Of all the historical plays, *The Fall of Vijayānagar* has a naturally poignant appeal to the people of southern India, for this part of India maintained its independence from the Moslems till 1565.

The Kanarese theatre is the youngest in southern India. After the visit of the Marathi Players, its medieval entertainment, *Yakṣagāna*, underwent a rapid change. The Raja of Mysore himself was deeply interested in the new dramatic movement and encouraged it. Translations of Sanskrit classics and Shakespearean adaptations were staged with success. At present there are three noteworthy companies in Mysore, apart from a Boys' troupe. One may note that so far only one tragedy, a translation from the Marathi, has been staged, the popularity of Pauranic themes, of musical elements, and of social farces being predominant. On occasions episodes from the *Arabian Nights* and sensational pieces based on novels of Reynolds (*Nirupamā*) attract audiences. This stage, however, shows considerable activity of late and is likely to advance rapidly, as the educated people there are now taking a keen interest.

Thus, in southern India, the professional theatre has neither the earlier useful history of private theatres patronized by rich landowners of Bengal, nor the peculiar advantage of support by an intelligent mercantile community in Bombay. The effect of this disadvantage is aggravated by the fact that the original Dravidian culture has been a great deal effaced, and by a deep-rooted lethargy in the race, due to centuries of servitude. Consequently, its theatre has not the very intelligent type of playgoer who may insist on a more modern and less mythological type of dramatic fare. Above all, the Madras theatre is most unfortunate in the fact that English-educated people were not the pioneers of the professional stage, as in the case of the Bengali, Parsi and Marathi theatres.

Space need not be devoted to the rest of India here, for the Hindi theatre is a later development due to the influence of touring Urdu companies, and it is passing through the same stages of development in the United Provinces after the appearance of the dramatist Harischandra. In Sind there are occasional performances in colleges of Shakespeare in English and Sindhi, but the professional stage is mostly in the hands of touring commercial companies using Urdu as the medium of expression. Similarly in Punjab, the dramatic activity is gradually spreading from schools and colleges to performances in Gurumukhi, the chief difficulty being the want of properly cultivated dialects, although here, too, the new spirit is apparent.

The following considerations, based partly on the above scattered remarks regarding the rise of the modern theatres in India and partly on their subsequent development, may prove useful:—

(1) The English merchants and officials brought the con-temporary European theatre with them, and held it as a model before the high-class and educated Indian audiences. It fired the imagination of a people who had the rich heritage of the past, which had, however, grown faint during the Moslem rule. The fascination of the novel spectacle and admiration for the rulers led to imitation.

(2) The new theatre came full-fledged. There was no question of the model to be followed. India simply adopted the mid-Victorian stage with all its accessories of painted scenery, costume and make-up.

(3) The greatest service which the British theatre did was to create a genuine love of amateur acting as an art. This was a new idea and came with a magical effect when high officials and eminent professors were seen in several rôles on the stage. Consequently, the new theatre acquired a dignity and a status which could not have been achieved otherwise.

(4) Not only this, but the presence of distinguished women on the stage and in the auditorium opened a great vista before India, which had the *Purdah* system of the Moslems. This made possible the appearance of several good actresses on the one hand, and of advanced ladies in the auditorium on the other.

(5) Along with the marvellous theatrical appeal came the deep and abiding influence of the richest dramatic literature to the young and eager minds of the college students, in the true spirit of the renaissance. Shakespeare, with his universal appeal and his many features in complete harmony with the spirit of the ancient Hindu drama, was loved and admired, passionately studied, and enthusiastically produced on the college stage first in English and, later on, in the vernacular.[22]

(6) In such productions the aid of several English actors and actresses was sought, and a spirit of co-operation

22. To verify the truth of these remarks one has only to look up the records of the rise of the modern Bengali theatre.

resulted. On many occasions the Anglo-Indian Press also paid a glowing tribute to vernacular productions, playwrights and actors, one of the latest being a chorus of encomiums on the death of Amritlal Bose in 1929. Distinguished Europeans were often entertained at Indian theatres with English translations or synopses of vernacular plays.

(7) European scenic artists have also been invited to help, and Anglo-Indian girls have figured on the Indian stage.

(8) For the evolution of the new theatre, some of the educated actors visited England and other countries and brought back novel ideas and stage technique.

(9) So far as the professionals are concerned, spectacular shows have played the most important part.

(10) Light operas and loose farcical productions were eagerly seized from European example in order to attract the crowd. Such pieces stimulated the performance of several medieval skits with a few changes.

(11) But the English theatre also handed the legacy of shrewd comedies of manners which pointedly drew attention to glaring evils.

(12) The greatest service to the Indian stage was the gift of Romantic Tragedy. This idea came from Shakespeare, as the widespread production of *Hamlet* in India proves.[23]

(13) Once tragedy was accepted, exaggeration of certain elements was bound to creep in, as one may notice especially on the Urdu stage.

(14) The English tragi-comedy intensified the love of this type of play ingrained in the Indian mind, and led to its full cultivation.

(15) The types of plays produced on the stage have generally followed the order of development from mythological and saint plays to historical and social tragedies and farcical and satirical sketches of contemporary manners and customs, passing through the middle stages of Sanskrit translations and English adaptations and patriotic historical

23. Cf. Appendix C.

plays (praising heroism, self-sacrifice, chastity, and love of the motherland).

(16) In the spirit of the Renaissance, not only Sanskrit and English, but Persian, Arabic, Spanish, and French materials were exploited for stage purposes, the distant time and place lending peculiar charm.

(17) There was never a real conflict between the Sanskrit classical model and the English dramatic model, for translations of ancient masterpieces were frequently produced along with clever Shakespearean adaptations on the Indian stage with remarkable success, due to the many links of inner harmony existing between the two (as discussed in Part I).[24] This seems clearly to prove that Dr. Gupta was mistaken in his view when he argued for the conflict of models with the ultimate triumph of the one over the other. His discussion is merely academic, as he overlooks the stage history of Sanskrit and English productions in all parts of India.[25]

(18) Lastly, the Indian theatre could not grow naturally on its own lines, as was the case with some other countries. The full-fledged foreign theatre came to a subject nation and overawed it completely, with the obvious result that many efforts were made simultaneously for a commercial success, and the several types had not the necessary period and free atmosphere to grow in due course to fulness, beauty and strength.

24. For instance, compare the productions of Girish in Bengal or the 'Shahunagarwasi's' repertory in Maharashtra on the professional stage and the 'Sugunvilas Sabha's' record in Madras.
25. Unpublished thesis: *Shakespeare in India*, London, 1924, p. 191.

CHAPTER VI

THE INDIAN STAGE TO-DAY

IT is indeed true that the Indian stage as it has developed in the course of the last eighty years reveals a great variety of culture, from the primitive Tamil theatre to the most artistic productions in Bengal. One has to remember, however, that a fundamental unity is secured in the midst of this utmost diversity by means of the Hindu ideals and the general attitude towards life. The Indian mythological heroes have commanded the same uniform reverence through-out the length and breadth of the country. Plays based on *Rāmāyaṇa* and *Mahābhārata* have aroused unbounded universal enthusiasm and the phenomenal success of *Hariścandra* in all the provinces of India was largely due to Parsi effort in Urdu.[1] The Hindu culture has thoroughly permeated even southern India where the population is largely Dravidian. Thus, the same peculiar note is heard everywhere in one form or another.

It is a curious fact that there is no indigenous Moslem stage in India. As Dr. Abdul Latif[2] has pointed out, stage representation is against the Islamic doctrine. The Mohammedan religion looks down upon all idols, images, or pictures of God, saints, etc., and the very essence of theatrical art demands impersonation which is so repugnant to Islam. From early days, therefore, the theatre proper does not seem to have flourished in Moslem countries. One should not forget, however, that in the course of chanting dirges for the Prophet, there is almost a passion-play enacted, though unconsciously. This latent talent for acting was given a suitable opportunity with the rise of the modern Indian

1. This is a fact. In order to cater for miscellaneous audiences throughout India, mixed Hindi-Urdu is generally employed.
2. *The Urdu Literature*, section on Drama.

theatre. Certain Moslem actors, such as Ashraf Khan have distinguished themselves on the Urdu stage; and certain playwrights, such as Aga Hashr Kashmiri have written powerful plays.

In the course of the following study of the vernacular versions of Shakespearean and non-Shakespearean plays on the Indian stage, a distinction must accordingly be made between the cultured productions on the Bengali and Marathi stage on the one hand, and the popular Urdu stage versions on the other, with several intermediate types in the Gujarati and Telegu theatres, yet at the same time one cannot fail to notice that the same national love of the emotional, the imaginative and the idealistic rather than of the intellectual and the purely realistic is evinced by the entire nation.

THE URDU STAGE

After realizing this common spirit, one may turn to examine the stage conditions prevailing in the several theatres of India, for it may, perhaps, be well to make a brief preliminary survey of such conditions, both primitive and advanced, before proceeding to the question of the place English plays occupy on the various stages. The highly popular Gujarati-Urdu[3] stage of Bombay may be taken first.

The *kavi*.—There the manager, who is also either sole or joint proprietor of his company, engages a *kavi* (a poet) to write plays to order. Such *kavis* get a fixed salary and are in duty bound to write one play every six months or so and to transfer all its rights to the manager. If the play happens to score a huge success, the proceeds of one or two 'benefit nights', or sometimes a fixed bonus, is handed over to the *kavi*. Moreover, this poet has to do many odd jobs, such as adding to or altering or cutting scenes and providing songs, i.e. the words fitting a situation, sometimes

3. Bombay companies generally produce plays in both vernaculars.

suggested by the manager, and on the musical notation decided by the expert of the company.

Both the manager and the *kavi* keep a constant eye on the changing fashions and tastes of contemporary life. They may note a successful historical play prepared by a rival company and within a month a similar play with even more melodramatic situations is hastily staged. Favourite tricks, songs and devices are so skilfully imitated that the clutches of the law are escaped. The patriotic vein is found to be particularly profitable and, as a result, topical sentiments are thrust into the plays in order to elicit applause.

The manager is usually unscrupulous. He does not necessarily confine himself to one *kavi*. He holds out great inducements to public favourites, offering immense prices for plays he imagines may prove successful. The poor *kavi* may be asked to fill up gaps here and there, or to supply a few songs with popular airs or to dash off a number of farcical scenes (often unrelated to the main plot); if he fails in any way, he may be dismissed with scant courtesy. On the other hand, the *kavi* is equally unscrupulous, for, disregarding his contract, he is constantly seeking better terms from other more prosperous commercial managers. His principal traffic lies in the composition of 'catching' scenes. He may borrow ideas, themes, incidents from any native or foreign sources; only he must succeed in giving them the right Indian stamp and create a startling impression of novelty on the audience. He must, of course, build on the firm foundation of the national tradition and conventions.

When the manager dominates and boldly interferes in the composition and production of plays, the system of collaboration has for him a great attraction. He often thinks of a vague plot and then distributes the writing of the usual three acts of a tragi-comedy to three 'poets' noted for their several gifts of serious, comic and musical composition. Artistic unity naturally often suffers if there is no competent mind to fuse all the elements together.

Actresses.—Although on the ancient Hindu stage female rôles were generally played by women, the tradition was discontinued after the Moslem conquest on account of the inferior status of women and the 'purdah' system. Thus the native histrionic talent was confined to the salon of the dancing girls and to certain types of village performances. The new contact with the West, however, brought about a change, although orthodox opinion, afraid of all criticism, was very slow to introduce reforms. When the gifted Parsi actor-manager Balliwala returned from his European tour, he made the bold experiment of introducing a few women on the popular stage of Bombay. Gohar, Mary Fenton and Munnibai are among the best actresses seen on the Urdu stage.

The story of the English actress, Mary Fenton, daughter of an officer in the Indian army, falling in love with the acting of the celebrated K. P. Khatau is graphically told by one Gangakanta.[4] She excelled in the rôles of Parsi heroines in light social comedies and was universally admired. Gohar played several Shakespearean rôles with success, whereas Munnibai recently won laurels in a Hindu domestic tragedy. Despite about a dozen good actresses on the Gujarati-Urdu stage during the last half century, however, the popular prejudice, based on social considerations, has made it extremely difficult for women to act in professional theatres.

Boy Actors.—In a manner not unlike the practice of the Elizabethan 'Boy companies', boys in India are generally selected in professional companies for their gift of singing, though, unquestionably, handsome features and charm of personality are additional qualifications. On account of the prejudice against actresses, the young boys selected play as chorus girls and later on rise to be understudies and finally to the rank of 'stars'. With only the rudiments of education, the gifted 'Sundarī' (named after Desdemona) and 'Bāla Gāndharva' made their début on the Bombay stage.

4. *The Gujarati* periodical, Bombay, October 15, 1916.

As young heroines, they have fascinated thousands of play-goers. Their peculiar talents have secured for them considerable 'shares' in the profits, until they themselves became partners or proprietors of their own companies.

Although a few independent 'Boy companies' exist in the Deccan and in Madras, most of the boy actors have to cast in their lot from childhood with adults in several companies. These boys have to undergo severe tests for dancing and for singing and for expressing every idea by means of appropriate gestures. Unfortunately, in many cases, more attention is paid to artificial and strained gesticulation than to the study of phonetics or to the cultivation of pronunciation.

There being no compulsory primary education in India, children of any age from eight or nine may be seen on the Urdu-Gujarati stage. These poor creatures are overworked and not properly treated by the managers. They seldom know much of outside life and thought, and in some cases die prematurely. It is true that precocious boys draw a high salary; and there are instances of princes falling in love with boy heroines and paying immense sums to company-managers by way of compensation, with rich gifts for the actor who thenceforth resides in the palace for command recitals.

Adult Actors.—Apart from the numerous ordinary adult actors, three stock types may be distinguished: (*a*) The Harlequin or the Tarlton of a company usually draws the highest salary (cf. 'Mulchand Mama' and 'Master Mohan' with the maximum £100 a month). He enjoys extraordinary liberty, for his sole object is to create unbounded merriment in the theatre by playing little practical jokes or by improvisa-tion. He constantly offends against Hamlet's dramatic canon. (*b*) Next in importance stands the pair of romantic lovers who figure for years together in changing rôles (cf. 'Saubhāgya' and 'Sundari'). When they grow middle-aged and cannot do justice to their parts they have to train a younger pair. (*c*) The third type is the thundering hero who can play the tragedian and is good at fencing. The rant and bombast of the protagonist and his antagonist and their power of stressed rhythmic repartee are lustily applauded by the pit and gallery.

Production.—The principal actor of a permanent company is usually the producer, though the financial manager may interfere if he chooses. Tragedy, high opera, musical comedy, pantomime, etc., being not developed yet as recognized distinct types, the producer usually prefers a musical tragicomedy with full scope for scenic spectacle. For his cast, he has his band of about fifty actors, of all ages and experience, to choose from. The *kavi* and the expert musician are at his service. He generally entrusts the dancing discipline to a chief actor who plays the heroine. He spends over a month in rehearsals.

Every company follows the repertory system; and new plays are being constantly added to the old stock. The novelty of a play captures the imagination of the masses. The new favourite, if it is a success, continues to be produced every Saturday night and Sunday afternoon for a year or two. Old favourites are revived on Monday and Wednesday nights. When a new play loses its hold on the popular mind, it is transferred to a weekday and another 'new' play produced on 'the gala night'. Very seldom are two plays given on the same day. Only on important communal holidays one play is given in the afternoon and another play at night, the overworked actors earning an off day and a feast from the manager on the following day. Thus in the course of a week, actors are rehearsing on three evenings and appearing in plays on the other four. As the plays usually last from 9.30 p.m. to 2 a.m., the poor actors live an unnatural life and seldom get complete rest.

There is no regular theatrical season as in the West. Plays continue to be produced throughout the year; and if some leading actor must take a holiday for reasons of health or private business, his salary depends on his contract or on the manager's good will. If the understudy does not come up to a sufficiently high level another play has to be substituted. Sometimes it is not considered desirable by the managers to stage old favourites again, for the original actors who made them famous have either died, retired or migrated to other companies.

In the mode of production, again, there is a noteworthy contrast to the European standard of to-day. In the midst of the noise and bustle of the Urdu theatre, opened an hour before the performance, one hears three bells at short intervals and with the third bell a thundering gun shot is heard as the drop-curtain, gorgeously painted with mythological legends, goes up. The chorus girls sing a prayer or a 'welcome' to the accompaniment of the harmonium and rhythmic drum beats. This song ends with an offering of flowers to the distinguished patrons and with garlanding the portraits of the pioneers of the respective company or of deities. Then the action commences. It must be noted here that electric lights are burning in full brilliance in the auditorium throughout, continued darkness, as in cinema shows, being strongly disliked. One may see admirers singing to themselves favourite songs from the 'opera book', i.e. the programme (4d.). In it the cast of characters is given with explanatory notes as to who is who, but seldom the names of the actors. Also, a detailed synopsis of scenes, even as many as twenty, is printed for explaining situations and background. Generally the producer and often the dramatist are also not mentioned. Only the managing proprietor figures in bold type. Things are, however, on a better level in advanced theatres which are trying to copy the practice of European productions in Indian cities.

Once the drop-curtain goes up, the change of scenes takes place in the full view of the audience till the end of each act. There is no fixed standard of scenic design established so far. In most theatres, painted curtains are hung up to suggest the locality of the setting. Apart from these pictorial hangings indicating streets, houses, gardens, palaces, there is often the use of a 'flat', run in two pieces on grooves from opposite wings and clamped together when they meet midway on the stage. 'Box sets' and 'transformation scenes' are often admirably contrived. The startling changes of scenery are accompanied by the unnecessary thundering noise of gun shots.

How far the love of spectacle is deep-rooted on the Urdu stage may be well judged from the following English extract from the play-bill of the favourite mythological play of *Nala and Damayantī*, by 'the greatest of Urdu playwrights', Pandit Shaida (on page 114).

It is interesting to compare this play-bill with the nineteenth-century English mode of advertisement, where a similar indication of the stage sets was provided. The remarkable point here is that the Urdu stage still clings to century-old devices directly borrowed from the English practice.

Similarly, the system of alternate scenes noticeable at the Old Vic or Sadler's Wells performances of Shakespeare to-day still prevails in most Indian productions, with the convention that farcical scenes are usually acted before the proscenium and important scenes on the full stage where scenery is arranged during the interval. Characters mostly enter and leave the stage by the side openings which serve as doors. Like the Elizabethans, they walk out 'on the stage'— hardly 'into a habitat prepared'. Notwithstanding the scenic devices of the nineteenth century, with the wonderful stage effects of storms, seas or rivers in commotion, castles, sieges, steamers, aerial movements and the like, it often strikes a shrewd observer that the illusion is by no means complete, for the picture scenery is not an environment in which actors move and have their being.

Love of sheer dazzling Oriental costume is gradually giving place to more appropriate dresses on the stage. The Parsis of Bombay made an excellent beginning in studying the proper models from original authorities and engaging

H

NEW PLAY!   NEW PLAY!
AT THE
CORINTHIAN THEATRE
ETC.

THE LOVE STORY OF THE AGES

NALA AND DAMAYANTI

A Spectacle of Super-Extravagant Splendour
in Three Acts
etc.

With an All-Star Cast Featuring India's
Popular Stage-Star

MASTER MOHAN

in the principal rôle of 'Bidushak'

The Play is replete with gorgeous dresses, wonderful trans-
formation scenes and weird and enchanting effects. . . .
The entire gorgeous scenery designed and painted by
India's Greatest Living Artist

Mr. K. HUSSAIN BUKSH, of Lahore

See?   See?   See?

The Sleepy Lotuses transform themselves into Fairy visions.
The Vision of Princess Damayanti.
The bursting of a lotus and the appearance of Goddess
        'Saraswati' therefrom.
The flight of the Swan.
The 'Swayambara' of Damayanti.
Narad's descent from the clouds.
The miraculous appearance of Kali with the Flaming Sword.
The transformation of five Nalas.
The transformation of 'Karkota' in a forest fire.
The Durbar-Hall of King Nala.
The transformation of seven Fairies, etc.

a set of expert tailors. In make-up, also, greater care is now taken to avoid anachronisms and absurdities. No doubt it is true that the Urdu stage spends more lavishly on elaborate scenery, costume and make-up than any other theatre of India. Perhaps the glaring defect lies in want of proper lighting effects. Brilliant light in the auditorium throughout the performance, along with often unconcealed, powerful electric lights of most diverse colours on the stage, can seldom create any genuine illusion of a particular season or time of day or night. A proper study of appropriate colour-schemes is a crying need of the stage. A great number of songs are generally introduced in all possible contexts (even fighting heroes and dying heroines sing on the Urdu stage), and the beauty of native music is marred by slipshod Parsi and semi-European tunes to the accompaniment of the monotonous, noisy harmonium and *tabalā* (drum beats).

Management.—When such faults are pointed out a pro-ducer generally blames either the false taste of the commercial manager or the vicious demands of the cosmopolitan Bombay audience. Most of the managers, who are either sole proprietors or partners of a company (rarely a limited concern), conduct their theatres entirely on a commercial basis. They seldom care to spend much on the comforts of the theatre, so long as they succeed in attracting large crowds to their latest venture. Most of the theatres are poorly ventilated and sanitary conditions are far from satisfactory. The defective acoustic properties and the restlessness of the audiences are also partly responsible for the rant and bustle on the stage. Police authorities often connive at the discomfort and unhealthy conditions of the Grant Road theatres situated in unclean localities. They interfere only on

5. It may be noted that in the absence of many reserved seats and of the 'queue' system, there is a regular scramble for seats an hour before the play, when the gates of the theatre open. The spectators can get a cup of tea and cigars and *pān-sopārī* in the theatre from the hawkers, and thus a good deal of dis-turbance is caused.

political grounds, obscene jokes or vulgar scenes being seldom banned. The municipal supervision is also, often, far from satisfactory.

Advertising is confined to a few vernacular papers, the names of only two or three leading actors being announced even in recent years. One reads posters in the principal streets, regarding a 'new' production; but there is nothing comparable to the pictorial mode of advertisement of the West to-day. Outside the theatre, in a fixed wooden frame, dates and names of plays are inserted every day. Otherwise the old Elizabethan practice still persists on the Urdu stage, for between acts the producer appears before the drop-curtain, in the costume of his part, thanks the audience and invites them to witness a subsequent play. In the provinces, two or three musicians carry the advertisement in a horse-cart through important places in a town and distribute play bills.

The commercial rivalry between theatre-managers in Bombay leads them not only to spend all their resources on the most startling scenic displays and brilliant costumes, but also to win over well-known actors by all possible inducements and to use the Elizabethan device of a 'claque'. Not only a "prepared company of gallants to applaud his jests and grace out his play"[6] is hired by a manager, but sometimes, a similar body is engaged to hiss off a rival show on the first night, in order to proclaim it as a 'failure' or a 'fiasco'. To drown all criticism, however, the managers spend lavishly rather than sensibly in mounting a piece, £4,000 to £5,000 being reported to be spent on a single production both for dazzling scenic effects and for elaborate costumes of many different nationalities.

Managers seldom profit by press criticism, since this is still in its infancy, especially so far as the Gujarati-Urdu stage is concerned. Their sole concern is the box-office returns. In the sale of tickets also, on first nights and for many days

6. E. K. Chambers: *The Elizabethan Stage*, Vol. II, p. 550.

in the case of favourites, a few contractors are previously given on loan the best tickets to be sold on a commission basis. They sell them at the door sometimes for five or even eight times the original price; and thus the managers often quietly pocket the lion's share of the profits. Of course, many officials and several creditors (for the managers often borrow large sums) and their families have to be given free accommodation when they choose to visit the theatre even if that entails the providing of an extra line of chairs very close to the footlights.

An ordinary manager of a Gujarati-Urdu company generally spends about £1,000 per month for running expenses. Most of the young actors have to be lodged and fed by him. Consequently he hires a building and runs a kitchen. Even many married actors prefer to stay with the company (a full staff comprising about a hundred persons), their families living in distant villages. The standard of living is indeed poor, for the manager always complains that he cannot make both ends meet.

Audience.—When the managers are accused of being blind to the dictates of art, they inevitably transfer the entire blame to the shoulders of the unthinking playgoers. The typical Bombay audience is more like the Elizabethan than like the twentieth century European audience. Here one may notice the new monied classes, along with a sprinkling of the riff-raff of society who win their livelihood by pleasure and gambling. Apart from the small educated class, men and women of all classes flock to the theatre; and so there is a resultant catholicity of appeal.

Thus, as Dr. C. J. Sisson[7] neatly sums up: "The Bombay popular stage offers in many respects a parallel to the Tudor stage of England. . . . The theatres are commercial ventures which aim at profit from the delectation of the people, and which are not, and do not pretend to be, concerned with the

7. Lecture on *Shakespeare in India*, London, 1925, p. 25 and pp. 15–17.

drama as literature. They are not patronized by the cultured classes or by respectable women. . . . The audiences demand action, spectacle, and variety entertainment all in one, and they delight in rhetoric and declamation. . . . The general attitude of the 'respectable' classes towards the community of actors is precisely that which is familiar to the student of the Elizabethan age. There are no actresses, for women's parts are acted by boys and men. . . . All actors go through a severe apprenticeship, and the singers, dancers and fencers are experts, even as they needed to be on the Elizabethan stage.

"The companies are generally co-operative concerns, with 'fellowship in a cry of players'. . . . Such companies are financed by business men of the stamp of Henslowe, who control them very much after his fashion. . . . Plays are written to order often, and are invariably bought outright, so that the author has no further rights in his play. The best companies maintain a paid *kavi* or playwright, whose duties are to write new plays, to redramatize old and well-tried subjects, to refurbish old plays or alter or add scenes or topical matter where required. Collaboration in the writing of plays is frequent, the comic part being entrusted to one *kavi*, the serious part to another, the 'romantic' love scenes to a third, and the songs to a fourth. . . . The intricate history of Elizabethan companies and theatres is reflected in the history of Bombay companies. They too are formed, suffer defections, fuse into one another or unite for a time, move from theatre to theatre, or build theatres for themselves, and travel in the provinces."

While these remarks are fundamentally true, it is to be remembered that though Dr. Sisson's remarks justly apply to the Urdu and Gujarati popular stage, they cannot be applied equally to the Bengali and Marathi stages, which present much further advanced theatrical conditions. Therefore it is necessary to review briefly the present position of the Marathi theatre of Poona, of the Bengali theatre of

Calcutta and of the Tamil, Telegu and Kanarese theatres of Madras. Such an analysis will greatly help to explain the nature and scope of the varied influence of British drama on them.

THE MARATHI STAGE

In strong contrast with the *kavi* system, both in Maharashtra and Bengal the playwrights enjoy a much more dignified position. In the first place, there are great dramatists who rise from the lowest rung of the ladder from actors to become 'sharers', start by writing a few necessary passages in plays to be produced, or adding a few songs, then proceed to pen full plays, in collaboration, or alone, exclusively for their companies. Later on they publish these dramas and sue for literary fame. To this class belong Girish Ghosh and Amritlal Bose, Ghadkari and others. And secondly, there are gifted playwrights such as Dvijendralal Ray, Kolhatkar and Khadilkar who do not belong to theatrical companies, but have some experience of stage-craft, possess a keen eye for effects and have mastered stage technique. They publish their plays and permit competent companies to perform them on payment of a suitable royalty. Some of these bear in mind particular actors for different rôles and even coach the players during rehearsals out of sheer love of the theatre

Here a fundamental distinction may be drawn between the Gujarati-Urdu companies on the one hand and Marathi-Bengali troupes on the other, for the former scrupulously guard the MS. and seldom publish, the latter treat the authors with respect and realize the dignity of plays as literature. All the rights usually belong to the playwrights. Again, the entire attitude being different, the producers treat the published play as of supreme authority and do not take any liberty with the original except by permission. No extra comical stuff or farcical songs are thrust in, in the manner of the Urdu companies. Therefore, it is not to be wondered at that the Marathi and Bengali plays present artistic wholes. The secret of the status of competent play-wrights lies in the fact that in these districts a number of educated and cultured managers aimed deliberately at the improvement of theatrical conditions. Even here, on the other hand, the dramatists are not over well remunerated owing to the lack of long 'runs'. Nor does the sale of printed copies bring in any considerable profit, for the level of general education is still poor.

Actresses.—The Marathi theatre has seldom displayed the courage to try the experiment of introducing actresses on their stage in a way comparable to that of the Urdu stage. Extremely orthodox opinion still prevails in that district. Many people connected with the theatre there strongly hold the view that gifted boys can do full justice to female parts, can act without unnecessary shyness, can speak more distinctly and can win a higher glory by overcoming the handicap of nature.[8]

There is, however, one fact worth recording. Certain women, belonging to the dancing class, now and then form their own troupes and play Marathi pieces remarkably well. They do not admit any men to their company, male rôles being all played by women. Thus they tend to the other extreme. No doubt their courage and resourcefulness deserve high praise.[9]

Boy Companies.—Another distinguishing feature of the Marathi stage is its very rare employment of boys in adult companies. Pantomimic representation by boys dressed as girls in plays has never been popular on the Marathi stage, as it has been in the Urdu theatre. Only on occasions pre-

8. Cf. the Report of 'The Marathi Dramatic Conference', Poona, 1929.
9. "Mrs. Hirabai Barodekar and her two sisters have made a great mark on the modern Marathi stage. She, a well-known singer, is the director and the proprietor of the 'Nutana Saṅgīta Maṇḍalī.' Their plays fetch very good houses at present in Bombay" (Professor Shah's Notes).

cocious boys figure on the stage if they are required. This youthful talent, however, finds another channel of self-expression, for several boy companies, with all the members under sixteen or eighteen, are formed and play light comedies with great success. These professional troupes are under the control of their financial managers. The great difficulty in their way is the want of a suitable repertory, as they have to play dramas intended for adults.

Adults.—The Marathi and the Bengali theatres reveal a more healthy tone and a greater artistic endeavour on account of the presence in them of fairly well educated young men. Even some graduates and undergraduates now consider it a legitimate profession to follow. Most of them are genuinely inspired by the passion to lift the stage to a higher level. The supreme instance of a selfless unbounded devotion to the histrionic art is furnished by Professor Shishir Bahaduri of Calcutta, who resigned his post and gave an exemplary lead in founding a national theatre for Bengal. To the Marathi stage belongs the good fortune of producing two of the greatest Shakespearean actors in India—Ganapatrao Joshi and Bala Jog. It is no doubt true that many of the ordinary actors are insufficiently educated; but on account of medieval stage traditions in the villages, they have in them a latent talent which constant practice often brings to light.

Production.—The same repertory system is followed on the Marathi and Bengali stages as in the Urdu theatre, the only noteworthy distinction being that in Calcutta, instead of giving a long continuous performance, managers prefer to give a double bill of shorter pieces in Bengali. The entire spirit of production, on the other hand, is different on the Marathi stage from the one noted above in connection with the Urdu productions. The Marathi theatre being comparatively poor does not attempt to rival the splendour of scenery and costume of the other stage. Thus it concentrates its effort on natural acting and scientific music (unspoiled by spurious European imitations). It follows the same system of alternate scenes but is guilty of fewer anachronisms than the Urdu productions. As the plays are mostly published beforehand, and the stage directions given, they are followed as far as the financial resources of the company permit. Although things are far from satisfactory, the intelligent managers are fairly conscious of their limitations.

The greatest blemish of the Marathi productions is their excessive love of songs and constant repetitions.[10] In the midst of a serious play, therefore, the action stops, and the other characters lose all interest in the performance while the favourites are charming the audiences as in a music hall. To counteract this folly, an excellent effort, the only one of its type in India, is made by one company to produce only prose plays, with no songs at all. This troupe is doing very valuable work but finds itself occasionally in financial difficulty.

Management.—Both the producer and the manager often evince a genuine desire to profit by criticism in the Press, which is more assiduously cultivated in relation to the Bengali and Marathi stages than in the Gujarati-Urdu theatres. The treatment given to Marathi actors is much better and on a higher plane than that accorded to their Urdu brothers. Most of the actors in good companies are educated Brahmins.

THE BENGALI STAGE

Apart from the several common points noted above in relation to the Marathi theatre, there are certain aspects of the Bengali stage which deserve especial emphasis:

(1) *Actresses.*—Notable actresses have figured on the Bengali stage for over fifty years and have fascinated audi-

10. It is interesting to notice that favourite songs have to be thrice or even five times repeated when the jubilant audience continue to applaud, whistle and cry 'Once more!'

ences, as one can judge from the biographical sketches of Sukumari Datta, Tarasundari and others.[11] Although most of them belong to the class of concubines and dancing girls, they have displayed remarkable talent in various kinds of acting. The distinguishing feature of the Bengali theatre is that all female rôles are now played by women. Some caste Hindus may find it awkward to act with them; but on the stage, the dignity and high standards of Hindu ideals are uniformly maintained by them.

(2) *Girl Actresses.*—Another noteworthy aspect of the Bengali theatre is the employment of young girls in the parts of boys. They perform them exquisitely. These girls are generally selected for their musical gifts and grace of movement. This leads us to the third peculiarity of the Calcutta stage, the novel use of song and dance. Unlike the practice on the Urdu and Marathi stages, most of the actors or actresses are not supposed to sing in diverse contexts, but only a few lyrics are artfully introduced, generally at the beginning or end of acts.

Finally, the Bengali theatre has the greatest claim to be considered genuinely national for the simple reason that while it welcomes the best influence from foreign sources it tries to preserve some of the finest traditional traits and to assimilate other elements intelligently.

THE MADRAS THEATRES

It is not possible to devote much space to the Madras theatres, for they are decades behind all the rest in India. Unfortunately, the Tamil professional theatre is still indulging in medieval practices and is trying to arouse enthusiasm by the introduction of plaintive songs and of many acrobatic feats on the stage. Hindu mythological plays are still being staged with the worst features of dazzling scenery and costumes borrowed from the Urdu stage (cf. the recent

11. *The Story of Actors and Actresses*, in Bengali.

productions of Kanaiya and Co.). The Telegu stage is, on the other hand, developing more rapidly, while the Kanarese theatre is taking remarkable strides in Bangalore under the patronage of the Mysore Maharaja.

From the above remarks it would appear that each important theatre in India has its own characteristic charm. Generally, every good actor wishes to excel in arousing the three main sentiments of love, heroism and pathos, though it must be admitted that physical valour on the stage is at great discount in Bengal. Whereas proper recitation and restrained acting are much appreciated by eastern India, magnificent scenery, quick movement and thrilling situations have greatly fascinated Bombay audiences. Despite so many handicaps of education and training, the stage-business of several Parsi actors, the musical appeal of the Marathi stage and the cultural presentation of characters by the Bengali artists would commend themselves even to foreign visitors.

CHAPTER VII

STAGE-VERSIONS OF SHAKESPEAREAN COMEDIES

INDICATING the possible danger in all free adaptations of foreign plays, from his knowledge of a German travesty of *The Beggar's Opera*, St. John Ervine[1] expresses his wish to see, in his own language, any foreign drama in a translated form as close as possible to its original. Principal G. G. Agarkar[2] in the course of a masterly preface to the Marathi stage version of *Hamlet* strongly expresses the same view. He holds that the mind of the audience should be broadened by bringing it in contact with a distinct civilization and different conventions: "Does not the mere mention of 'a free adaptation' serve as a cloak for all possible licence and abuse of the original?"

Theoretically speaking, these arguments are quite sound as they stand. For a select audience, a close translation exerts fascination, on account of their qualities of high intelligence, sympathy and understanding. The question of professional production, however, raises extraordinary problems, for it must be remembered that the few great successes of very close versions, in India at all events, have been exceptions to the general rule. An average playgoer, so long as he gets value for his money, does not trouble himself about the accuracy of the translation. Moreover, even where a common international standard of life exists, as in Europe, it is often impossible adequately to transfer the conditions of one dramatic literature to the conditions of another, without making various alterations. Nay, even in England itself Shakespearean plays had to be 'improved' drastically for the Restoration stage within fifty years of the poet's death. Consequently, one has only to consider the immense

1. *The Observer*, December 28, 1930.
2. *Vikāra-Vilasita* (*Tragedy of Thought*), Poona, 1883.

gulf which separates the West and the East in religion, politics, social and economic existence—in the entire attitude to life, in order to realize the problem of the Indian theatre, especially when it is in a chaotic situation in the midst of many bewildering influences. To illustrate this fundamental diversity, from the other point of view, it must not be forgotten that even excellent adaptations of Oriental plays, keeping as closely as possible to the spirit and expression of the original often fail in a strange land, as is exemplified by the recent failure of the Sanskrit classic, *The Toy Cart*, at the Lyric Theatre (Hammersmith) in London.

Under the circumstances, the Marathi scholar, V. M. Mahajani, whose several excellent adaptations of Shakespeare succeeded admirably in India, was indeed justified when he dwelt on the necessity of making considerable modifications in the original before an acceptable stage version could be produced. Even Mr. Agarkar confesses the need of rendering the Shakespearean verse into Marathi prose, of changing English names to significant Indian ones, of omitting the verbal quibbles of the original and of substituting the corresponding references from Hindu mythology for Greek and Roman ones. Such a procedure is bound to lead to confusion of manners and customs, as the translation otherwise follows its source line by line. This is neither pure literary translation for the library nor proper adaptation for the stage. Therefore, Mahajani's contention[3] for a full adaptation with as much fidelity as possible to the spirit of the original is certainly justified.

In such a necessary modification, the national genius of a race is sure to assert itself completely. The use of songs may here be used as an example of this. Professor E. J. Dent[4] neatly sums up the characteristic English attitude to music while discussing Shakespeare's songs: "The Shakespearean drama, though it never employed music in the most

3. Preface to the adaptation of *All's Well That Ends Well.*
4. *Foundations of English Opera*, Cambridge, 1928, p. 7.

essentially operatic way, was none the less addressed to an audience highly susceptible to the art. . . . A large number of songs are scattered through the plays for no other purpose than to give an excuse for the appearance of a singer. Such songs as those of the Clown (in *The Twelfth Night*) are part of the singer's personality. . . . Old Merrythought is drunk, the Clown is mad and Ariel is a supernatural being. English poets can never accept the idea of a normal man expressing himself in song." The typical Indian attitude to music is precisely the opposite of this. Contrary to the English belief, the Indian audience justifies "the principle of heightening the effect of a dramatic moment by making the actor break speech into song." To the Indian, as to the Italian—with whom he has many points in common—"music is a means of self-expression or rather of self-intensification"; not "a thing apart, a message from another world", as to the Englishman.

It is, after all, a matter of national tradition. "The fact was that in England, the spoken drama was already far too highly developed and far too deeply rooted in the heart of the people for its musical counterpart to be accepted as an equivalent, much less as a transfiguration of its most powerful emotional workings."[5] Exactly the reverse is true of the ancient Hindu drama where the usual emotional expression is through the medium of music. The predilection for music was maintained even on the medieval popular stage and at the Moghul Royal Court. Naturally enough, therefore, considerable modifications have to be made in this direction in order to render the Shakespearean plays popular on the Indian stage.

On the other hand it must be remembered that the Indian dramatic tradition and the characteristic Hindu temperament made the work of adaptation quite easy. No Voltaire in India called Shakespeare a "drunken savage". No dust was raised before admitting the great English dramatist. The

5. *Foundations of English Opera*, Cambridge, 1928, p. 3.

Indian literary world, instead of being torn asunder by controversies as in France, Germany and Italy, at the start,[6] was profoundly impressed by one whom they at once recognized as 'belonging to all countries'. The reason is not far to seek. Many inherent points of harmony between the ancient Hindu drama and the Elizabethan drama have been noticed above. The so called 'Three unities', for instance, never stirred the Indian mind. Tragi-comedy was the characteristic contribution of the Hindu drama; prose and verse were there used for expression on the stage. In fact, it was the privilege of the Sanskrit dramatist to inspire the most diverse sentiments (rasas) in the mind of the audience through the performance of one play.

Moreover, it is essential to understand the modern education of an average Indian boy. In his secondary course, not only is English a compulsory subject but also the chief medium of education. Thus, he is better prepared for the appreciation of English literature than an average schoolboy on the Continent. In particular he has often the opportunity of acting or of reciting Shakespearean passages. Thus Shakespeare is studied in schools and colleges; and the conditions for his favourable reception on the stage exist.

While summing up the argument for Shakespearean adaptations, one may recall Dryden's observations on poetic translation.[7] He carefully distinguished between 'metaphrase', 'paraphrase' and 'imitation'. A mere verbal copier "dances on ropes with fettered legs". In order to avoid obscurity in literal translation and to secure perspicuity and gracefulness, he recommends the gifted "later poet to write like one, who has written before him, on the same subject; that is, not to translate his words, or to be confined to his sense, but only to set him as a pattern, and to write, as he supposes that the author would have done, had he

6. Cf. *Cambridge History of English Literature*, Vol. V, Chap. XII.
7. Preface to Ovid's *Epistles*.

lived in our age, and in our country". These remarks especially fit in with stage-versions of foreign plays. Even "customs and ceremonies" of another age and place will have to be modified so that the play may be fully enjoyed by the audience.

It is now time to come to the main business of this dissertation—a general consideration of the adaptations of English plays in western India. A start may suitably be made with Shakespeare's comedies, some of which are among the most popular pieces of the Indian stage.[8] These are dealt with here in the order of the generally accepted canon of Shakespeare's works.[9]

(1) Both the Marathi and the Urdu versions of *The Comedy of Errors*[10] seem to have been successful on the western Indian stage. In a short preface to the first edition of 1877, it is mentioned that "the adaptation was undertaken for production"; and that "the play was extremely well received". Instead of Ephesus, the scene is laid at Sarangapur, a town in Deccan. Necessary changes in names, manners and customs were effected to suit the new environment. Otherwise this prose rendering follows the original very

8. All stage-versions are dealt with here, but literal translations and academic exercises are of course omitted.

9. *Love's Labour's Lost* was translated into Urdu, but is not known to have been staged in any part of India.
   The Two Gentlemen of Verona was not only adapted into Marathi as *Kāntipuracā Don Gŗhastha (Two Gentlemen of Kantipur)*, but was also certainly staged by the Shahu company as early as 1880 (cf. *The Marathi Actors* (in Marathi), Poona, 1919, p. 16), but, unfortunately, the version has not yet seen the light.

10. M. *Bhrāntikŗta Camatkāra (A Miracle of Confusion)*. By R. B. Jathar and B. R. Pradhan, Icchalkaranjikar Company, Akola, 1877.
    U. *Gorakhadhandā (A Labyrinth)*. By Narayana Betab, The Parsi Alfred Company, Quetta and Bombay, 1912.
    G. **Rāmā-Ratana* (Names of Characters). By N. K. Vaidya, Subodha Gujarati Company, Bombay, 1903.
    B. **Bhrāntivilāsa Nāṭaka (Comedy of Errors)*? Based on Vidyāsāgar's story with dialogue. Staged in Calcutta on August 25, 1888.

I

faithfully, almost sentence by sentence. The concluding
couplet is happily rendered in verse. The presence in the
company of two sets of youths with like features must have
aided the success of the performance.

The Urdu version, as may be judged from the theatrical
conditions of Bombay Parsi companies, outlined in the last
chapter, has not the same reverence for the original. The
publisher, the company's manager, K. P. Khatau, claims
that: "An imaginary ornament is cleverly tacked on to the
original to add a pathetic interest; and at the same time a
record has been established by Playwright Betab, Painter
Husain Baksh and Musician Jandekar in producing the
play within two months."

The original situation does not suffice for the Urdu stage;
catering for a less cultured audience, the adapter introduces
a new and thrilling plot of murder and intrigue. The play
opens with a spectacular scene in a coal mine; there are
many songs thrust in, some farcical and others pathetic;
and the final additional scene is devoted to the celebration
of the marriage of Antipholus of Syracuse (Antonio Rumī)
with Luciana (Lucy). Moreover, in the relation of the Courtesan, styled 'The Bar Maid of the Green Hotel', Shakespeare's
reticence is sacrificed in order to excite peals of cheap
laughter. In this connection, singing and dancing are freely
indulged in (cf. I. vii). An extra scene of raillery between
Adriana (Adā) and the Courtesan indicates the method of
exploiting every possible situation hinted at by the original.
The only inter-relation with the additional plot (which involves the intrigue of Sir James to murder his uncle Emperor
Louis of Shama) is secured by a unity of place in the Green
Hotel and by the character of Antipholus of Ephesus.

(2) Another early Shakespearean comedy, *A Midsummer
Night's Dream*,[11] was staged on both the Marathi and the

11. M. *Saṅgīta Premamakaranda* (Musical, *Honey of Love*). By
A. N. Ukadive, Nāṭyakalā Company, Poona, 1904.
B. *Jahānārā* (*Hermia*). By Satishachandra Chattopadhyaya,
Unique Theatre, Calcutta, 1904.

Bengali stages, about 1904. An Urdu version of Lahore is mentioned by Dr. Abdul Latif, but is not known to have been acted. There are three other Marathi translations; but Ukadive's adaptation was the only one tried on the Poona stage. It did not achieve much success. The spirit of the adaptation, however, is remarkable. The small preface starts with a Sanskrit quotation which extols the enjoyment of pure poetry as a blessing of God; pays a glowing tribute to the English poet's genius; and refers to numerous translations of his works in many languages. "A true adapter is one who holds a spotless mirror in front of Shakespeare for revealing his great personality in the work."

A Midsummer Night's Dream presents special difficulties to an Indian adapter. First, for achieving success, he must build on certain traditional beliefs of a nation. Therefore, a parallel is sought in a Himalayan semi-mythical race of the Yaksas, celebrated by Kālidāsa in his famous *Cloud Messenger*. Even a more difficult problem is the rustic under-plot of Bottom and company. The idea of celebrating a royal marriage by performing a play and securing pensions has no counterpart in medieval Hindu tradition. Thus, the beauty of the Pyramus and his Thisbe performance was sacrificed for a hackneyed device of a love intrigue between a big-bellied man and a slender girl. To this buffoon Titania makes love. Apart from these main changes, the play closely follows, in prose, the original. It may be noted, here, that the situation of Helena (Radanikā), the emblem of cc 'stancy, appeals easily to the Hindu mind; and her songs have a peculiarly pathetic ring. The concluding scene of the customary three acts is a grand court scene, celebrating the fourfold union, with (boys dressed as) courtesans dancing and singing.

In the Bengali version, which is artistically more beautiful, a Mohammedan setting is given to the adaptation to suit the Bengal conditions. Here the Persian notion of fairies (*parīz*) naturally fits in. Again, a rustic, pining for the sight of a wonderful fairy, at midnight, in a flower garden, is easily duped by Puck (Mariyama), who puts a donkey's head on him and befools him. The rustic play is altogether omitted. A few melodious songs are introduced at striking moments. Usually, at the end of scenes, an actress starts a song and a chorus of young girls joins from the two wings.

The same attitude of reverence for Shakespeare is revealed in the preface. The piece opens in a suggestive manner, for it does not contain the customary traditional Prologue as in the Marathi version, but a flower garden, a flower swing with fairies seated on it, singing as they swing. In the final tableau, there is the display of an aerial vision with Oberon and Titania embracing in the centre of the stage, the pairs of lovers on both sides and Puck below his master, for he also finds a bride, the Fairy Marinā![12]

(3) *The Merchant of Venice* has always proved the most popular Shakespearean comedy on the Indian amateur stage, for it has been acted in English, either in parts or in its entirety, from the beginning of English education in India. Even to-day the fourth act is the greatest favourite with the students of the secondary schools. Accordingly it is not surprising that a good number of vernacular adaptations of that play exist in India. Nevertheless, the number of acted versions is indeed small.[13] Dr. Gupta ably discusses the

12. An interesting feature of this publication is the printing of the full cast of the first performance, rather a rare imitation of the European practice. Thus, the reader is informed that Hermia (Jahānārā) was acted by Tarasundari, Helena (Ajinārā) by Bhuvanamohini, Lysander (Jāfarkhān) by Kunjalal Chakravarti, Demetrius (Majafarkhān) by Tarakanath Palita, and Puck by Ranubabu.

13. M. *Saṅgīta Praṇaya-Mudrā* (Musical, *The Ring of Love*). By V. S. Gurjar, Mahalakshmiprasada Company, Bombay, 1904.

   U. *Dil-farôsh* (*The Heart-seller*). By Hashr, The New Alfred Company, Bombay, 1900.

   G. *(1) *Jagata Siṁha* (or *A Pound of Flesh*), partly based on a Bengali novel. Vankaner Company, Gujarat, 1904.

   *(2) *Vibudha Vijaya* (*Triumph of Intellect*), a free version. Morbi Company.

   B. (1) *The Merchant of Venice*, with English names, an exact literary merits of two Bengali versions (Chapter III, Part II), one, *Bhānumatī Cittavilāsa*, being the first Indian adaptation of any foreign play in 1853; but he does not mention the acted adaptations at all.

The Mohammedan setting of the Urdu adaptation is justified by the age-long religious differences existing between the Moslem population of Bagdad and the Jewish traders. The Bond story, the Casket story and the Ring episode are in the main the same; but there are no scrolls inside the caskets and Portia indulges in a good deal of amatory singing. As regards Jessica's elopement (a Masquerade being out of the question), a characteristic Oriental device is adopted; the credulous Jew is befooled by Gratiano, in the guise of a soothsayer who prevails on the former to try the divine cure for the amorous Jessica in a temple at midnight, whence, of course, she runs away with her Lorenzo. There is no talk about her squandering money on 'a wilderness of monkeys'; but an effective curtain is secured at the end of Act II when the runaway couple have just set sail on a high sea and the Jew frets and fumes in despair.

Gratiano is made into a negro slave and his amours with the white Nerissa (Salimā) are fully exploited. Instead of Shakespeare's most suggestive opening, a hint is taken from *As You Like It*, and after the conventional song the audience sees Bassanio (Kāsim) in the position of Orlando praying to God to protect him from the wiles of his usurping elder brother. Another hint is taken in I. iv from *Romeo and Juliet*, by the Munshi, when the impatient Jessica is exasperated by the circumlocutions of her elderly nurse. Moreover, on the model of the scenes of revelry in Restoration comedy, Mahamud, the elder brother of Bassanio and his unsuccessful rival for Portia (he chooses the golden casket),

translation. By Manmohana Ray, Minerva Theatre, Calcutta. (2) *Saudāgara* (*The Merchant*). By Bhupendra Bandopadhyaya, Star Theatre, Calcutta. First night, December 4, 1915.

is seen indulging in wine and women and coarse songs to
the glory of 'English brandy' with his boon companions.
Again, in the manner of an English opera, the moment the
lovers meet they start singing amatory songs with the
addition of exaggerated gesticulations.In such an atmosphere,
one need not say, the incomparable poetry of the fifth act is
altogether absent. The success of the piece may have been
due largely to the distinguished acting of Sorabji Oghra as
Shylock.

The Marathi version, which remains very faithful to the
original, with the exception of many songs introduced in all
possible contexts, had not even half the success of the
Urdu free adaptation. Here the religious antagonism between
Brahaminism and Buddhism is substituted for the Christian
and Jewish antipathy; but the effort seems rather strained
and artificial, for such strained relations have vanished for
centuries.

An excellent cast was secured for a performance of the
play on the Calcutta stage in 1915. From a complete list
printed in the first edition of *Saudāgara* (*The Merchant*), it
appears that the 'Managing-Proprietor' (Amarendra Datta),
'Rehearsal Master', 'Dancing Teacher', 'Music Teacher' and
'Stage Manager' were men of reputation. Shylock was acted
by A. Datta himself and Portia (Pratibhā) by "Miss Kusumak-
umari" (this system of the naming of actresses being borrowed
from English practice). This version does not make use of
the Bengali blank verse, but is rendered all in prose with
songs, not quite so numerous as those in Urdu, in Marathi
or in Gujurati.

One delightful innovation, of an otherwise fairly faithful
rendering, is the creation of Page Joy (Āhlāde), a son of
Launcelot Gobbo, in the service of Portia. He has many
innocent quarrels with Nerissa, who gets jealous of him.
Such a rôle assumed by a young girl has a peculiar charm
for the Bengal audience. In accordance with the orthodox
Hindu practice, Portia keeps aloof from the suitors and only

occasionally appears in a balcony above. The chorus of young girls sings a commentary on each choice.

(4) Both the farcical comedies of Shakespeare have been produced on the Marathi stage; but, perhaps no other genuine version of a comedy of the poet has succeeded in India in achieving the glory of *The Taming of the Shrew*,[14] as acted by the Shahunagaravasi Company at Poona and Bombay. Possibly on account of the absence of blood and murder and sentimental pathos, this comedy was not adapted for the Urdu stage; at best, in an altered form, it would serve on it, as an unrelated underplot, in a drama of horror and intrigue. Curiously enough, Bengal also did not care to adapt it.

Anyhow, the most popular Marathi version was done by a gifted scholar with a keen sense of humour, with an intimate personal knowledge of actors and of the theatre and with reverence for the English dramatist. It is acclaimed to be such a perfect stage version that even if Shakespeare were a Hindu, he could not have improved on it. Principal Bhate said, in one of his lectures, that for once the original was surpassed in dramatic beauty. Of course the task of the adapter was facilitated by the fact that interest, here, is centred in plot and action, and not so much in subtle characterization. Its rollicking success was, unquestionably, due to three of the finest actors western India has produced, Ganapatrao Joshi (Petruchio), Bala Jog (Katharina) and G. Supekar (Grumio). A dramatic critic[15] has paid a glowing tribute to the Grumio who was so admirably fitted for the task that the audience went into raptures over his acting. The success of the play may be measured by the fact that

14. M. (1) *Trāṭikā* (*The Shrew*). By Professor V. B. Kelkar, Shahunagar Company, Poona, 1891. (Prose.)
(2) *Sangīta Caudāve Ratna* (*Efficacy of a Sound Thrashing*), the same with songs added. Balvant Company.
(3) *Karkaśādamana* (*Taming of the Shrew*), with songs. By Patankar Company, Bombay.
15. A. V. Kulkarni: *Marathi Stage* (M.), p. 59.

long standing debts of the company were easily cleared, in 1893, by a long and prosperous run of this play[16] and of a version of *Pizarro* at Poona. The play has gone into many editions (5th edition in 1924), and even to-day its revival ensures a crowded house in Bombay or Maharashtra.

The Induction is, of course, omitted; for, as it is, Shakespeare himself seems to have quite forgotten all about it at the end of the play. Otherwise, consistent with the requirements of Hindu life, Professor Kelkar has followed the original, act by act, almost scene by scene. Most of the English situations, ideas and passages are ably preserved. Nothing is sacrificed. Instead of the ironical "Sweet Kate!" the address *Ānandī*! (the Cheerful!) admirably fits in. Some of the sly insinuations in the original scene of courtship are eliminated. On the whole, every liberty taken wtih the original is in harmony with the purpose of Shakespeare himself, any vulgar additions in the manner of *Sauny the Scot* being out of the question.

Later on, for a musical company, songs were added in various contexts; but the Balvant Company never attained the level of the earlier first-rate acting of their rivals. Another musical version of this favourite comedy was staged by the Patankar Company, notorious for cheap imitations and many vulgar innovations in order to pander to the taste of the labouring classes of Bombay. Observing the huge success of the Shahu Company's version, the manager, an intelligent man with some knowledge of English, developed Professor Kelkar's adaptation, as a pure business proposition, for his inferior audience. This production, in 1901, also attracted large crowds; but could not attain any dignity or recognition among the cultured Marathi classes.

In the Prologue, which is on orthodox lines, a musical tribute is paid to the great English poet. The names of the characters are significant. The Marathi heroine's name means 'The Shrew'; Petruchio is 'the bold one' (Himmat-

16. L. N. Joshi: *Life of Ganapatarao* (M.), Poona, 1923, p. 113.

arāva); and Bianca is 'the fascinating one' (Mohanā). As may be expected, most is made of the love scenes between the last and her lovers, amorous songs being frequently thrust in; and the bedchamber scene in the house of Petruchio is made more appetizing by additional coarse touches not warranted by the original

(5) The other Shakespearean farcical comedy, *The Merry Wives of Windsor*[17] was also mounted by the Marathi stage. While *Richard III* and *Henry V* have been translated into Marathi and have exerted a subtle influence, the English chronicle plays have never been produced there, for the obvious reason that foreign history as such seldom proves attractive to an average playgoer. The elementary passions and the universal appeal are, no doubt, present in Shakespeare; but the whole spirit of those plays is quite alien to India. Accordingly Falstaff could figure in an Indian garb only in his amorous adventures. The production, however, did not prove popular, for Ganapatrao Joshi had not the same gift for humour and love as he had for pathos and heroism.

This scholarly prose adaptation, styled 'A Farce in five acts', is, on the whole, well done. Only a few necessary changes have been effected, the principal one being the love relations of Anne Page and Fenton, before marriage, in accordance with the Hindu custom. The English dowry system is parallel to the Marathi *huṁḍā* practice. The mock duel between the rival lovers being out of the question, a fight with cudgels in the streets gives a true Oriental colour to that episode. Utilizing the usual stage device, the fat 'Rao sahib' (Sir John) makes several comic remarks from behind the screen in Mathurābāi's (Mrs. Page's) drawing-room. He is forced into a basin of refuse and then carried to be thrown on a dunghill. For the constant demand of sack, 'a bumper of strong tea' is ordered by the dissolute knight, as drinking

17. M. *Caturagaḍhacā Vinodī Strīyāṁ* (*Merry Wives of Chaturagadha*). By P. G. Limaye, B.A., Shahunagar Company, Bombay, 1905.

by a high-class Hindu gentleman would not be tolerated. Instead of Windsor Forest, the vast temple of Pingaleśvara near the crematorium, is selected as the rendezvous. The final touch given to the play by an ingenious addition is noteworthy. The corpulent and coarse knight is wonderfully resourceful when he boldly asserts that the whole episode was his own contrivance for he meant to act as Kṛṣṇa to facilitate the nuptials of 'Arjuna' (Fenton) and 'Subhadrā' (Anne)!

(6) Of the sunny, refined and exquisite comedies of the middle period of Shakespeare, *Much Ado About Nothing* was translated, but not acted, while *As You Like It* and *Twelfth Night* were both adapted for the Indian stage. The former[18] was acted at Poona in Marathi, at Madras in Tamil and possibly at Bellary in Telegu. Neither the Bengali nor the Urdu stage produced this pastoral comedy, although the former had an adaptation and the latter made full use of several theatrical situations from it.

The popular Marathi version opens, in the orthodox style, w th an actress singing of the difficulty of satisfying the varied tastes of the audience. This Gordian knot is easily cut by girls praying in a Chorus. Immediately after this prologue, one hears Orlando (Vīrasena) bewailing his misery to Adam in a song. All the characters and the dialogue have been preserved, only slight modifications being effected for the frequent introduction of songs. As usual, the romantic atmosphere of the Middle Ages and of Indian chivalry is utilized. Charles the Wrestler easily fits in, since even to-day some Indian princes patronize *mallas* for royal sports. Again, 'The Forest of Arden' is even more in accordance with the Hindu ideals of retirement from the world and quiet contemplation than with the Western notions of life.

18. M. *Premagumphā* (*The Arbour of Love*), a musical play. By
   V. S. Patvardhan, Nāṭyakalā Company, Poona, 1908.
   Ta. *Vidame* (*As You Like It*). By P. Sambanda, 'Sugun Vilas
   Sabha' (Amateurs), Madras.

Also, it may be noted that the incident of the melancholy Jaques moralizing on the wounded deer has a deep appeal to most of the vegetarian Indian audience. Similarly, a verse rendering in Marathi of "All the world's a stage" is in tune with the Indian mind. Finally, the boy actor, now dressed as Rosalind, now as Ganymede, has the same fascination for the Indian as for the Elizabethan audience, and the aged Duke joining the hands of pairs of happy lovers at the end, is in harmony with the Indian stage tradition.

As the famous Madras amateur actor and playwright, Mr. P. Sambanda, informed the present writer, the Tamil production of this play was a conspicuous success in Colombo, when the Club was touring in Ceylon. The forest scenes aroused great enthusiasm. Hymen was omitted in this version also; and the names aptly selected, as may be judged from 'Rājivalī' (Rosalind). 'Suśīlā' (Celia) and the like.

(7) The other romantic comedy, *Twelfth Night*,[19] was also fairly successful in western India, both on the Marathi and the Urdu stages. In a preface to the Marathi version, the adapter attributes the success of this light comedy to the *rasa* of *Hāsya* (laughter) from start to finish. For the setting of the scene, a romantic mythological land 'Indrabhuvana' is imagined. The names of the characters are, again, chosen with the usual skill, Orsino becoming 'A love-dreamer' (Premānanda), Sir Andrew 'A jolly good fellow' (Sadānanda), Malvolio 'Passion's Slave' (Madanasena), and so forth.

The play opens with an original theatrical scene in which

19. M. *Bhramavilāsa Nāṭaka* (*A Comedy of Confusion*). By B. H. Pandit, B.A., LL.B., The Old Sangit Nataka Company and Icchalakaranjikara Company, Poona, 1910.

U. *Bhūla-bhūlaiyān* (*A Comedy of Errors*). By Munshi Mehadi Hasan, The New Alfred Dramatic Company, Bombay, 1905. (This comedy is mentioned by Dr. Gupta as an adaptation of the *Comedy of Errors*. The same mistake is made by Dr. Abdul Latif. Both seem to have overlooked the comedy of errors arising from the presence of Viola-Cesario and Sebastian.)

the audience sees a boat in which Viola (Vijiyā) and Sebastian (Satyavṛta) are discussing their present position. Before long, however, the clouds gather and the sea is seen in commotion as the curtain is lowered. After this, the Shakespearean arrangement is followed scene by scene. Even the songs of Feste are faithfully rendered with only slight necessary modifications. This is also true of the snatches of Sir Toby. The letter read by Malvolio is rendered entirely in prose. Although the topical allusion to the Puritans is lost, such self-conceited fools really belong to all ages. The standard Marathi prose does credit to the adapter. The only fault is that a too literal mode of rendering makes the meaning only partially clear in the theatre.

The Urdu version of this comedy, as usual, takes many liberties with Shakespeare's text. An entire scene was added at the start for the spectacle of the *Durbar* (Court) of Safadarajaṅga, King of Bokhara, who is in love with Dilerā princess of Bagdad (Viola). This irrelevant scene was, however, dropped in actual production. In the first scene of the Urdu play, Dilerā and Jāfar (Sebastian) are seen escaping in a railway train from the invading army of Safadarajaṅga; but the train is caught in a storm of thunder, rain and lightning; a bridge crashes and the twins are seen struggling in the sea waters below. Viola, in the strange land of Illyria (Tartar), dresses as a young doctor to suit the Moslem convention. She is also named Jāfar by the Duke. The main story is then followed as in the original.

The principal departure is the treatment of the Malvolio episode. An entirely new intrigue is substituted by the Urdu poet. The sensational underplot has as its one advantage that of having a pretence of relation to the main plot. The favourite device of songs sung by most characters is, of course, fully utilized.

(8) Of the later, unpleasant, plays, *Troilus and Cressida* was neither translated nor adapted for the stage in India; but the other two were rendered in Marathi and produced

in western India, while *Measure for Measure* was also staged, in part, by the Urdu and, in its entirety, by the Bengali stage. It is interesting to notice that of the two Marathi faithful adaptations of *All's Well that Ends Well*,[20] the earlier and more literary prose version by V. M. Mahajani was not staged, whilst the later more colloquial rendering with a free use of songs proved popular. In this musical piece, the characters are named according to their qualities, e.g. Lafeu becomes 'the good one' (Sajjanasiṁha) and Parolles 'the wicked one' (Durjanasiṁha). It must be confessed that in no age can one justify Helena's appeal to the King in a song, Bertram's protest in a song and the king's fury also expressed in music!

Only on rare occasions a slight rearrangement of scenes is made for the purpose of introducing a spectacular display. For instance, in Act II, a soldier and an officer are seen talking before the proscenium and then the middle curtain is raised to reveal the full splendour of the Imperial Court where the king is talking to Lafeu. Otherwise, the original arrangement is mechanically followed with alternate scenes. One peculiar Oriental trait may be noticed. Departing from the original in III. iii, Helena, bewailing her lot in a song, dwells on the wicked deeds of her past life. She even holds herself responsible for the premature deaths of her mother and her father. The original note of righteous indignation is indeed faint here. Finally, in the concluding song, after justifying the title, the moral of this unpleasant play is summed up for the benefit of the audience.[21]

20. M. (*Saṅgīta*) *Priyārādhana* (*Propitiation of the Lover*), a musical play. By V. S. Patvardhan, Nāṭyakalā Company, Poona, 1894.
   U. **Husnārā* (*The Ornament of Beauty*), with scenes from *Measure for Measure*. Bombay Parsi Company, 1900.
21. It is not possible to discuss the Urdu version here, for the writer could not secure a copy. Even the usual so-called 'opera-book', i.e. a summary of the plot with the words of the songs, could not be obtained.

(9) *Measure for Measure*[22] was even a greater success both in western and in eastern India. The Marathi version had a fairly good run, partly on account of an all-Brahmin cast of brilliant actors. In a series of songs in the 'prologue', one serves the significant purpose of propitiating the god Cupid, the presiding deity of the comedy, and another is meant to be a tribute to Shakespeare. All possible situations are seized, as may be expected, for the introduction of songs. Otherwise it is a fairly close version.

To the Indian mind, saturated with the hoary traditions of mighty emperors (cf. Vikrama) travelling incognito to study the frame of the popular mind at first hand, the Duke's device of temporary retirement exerts a deep fascination. The consequent dramatic irony, scene after scene, keeps the interest alive to the end. Even more than Vincentio, it is Isabella, 'more pure as tempted more', who casts a magic spell in the Indian Theatre. Her transparent innocence, and her frank and bold appeal to her brother are fully admired. In the two scenes (II. iv and III. i), where her character reaches great heights in the presence of a passionate Angelo and in the conversation with Claudio (he muttering 'Death is a fearful thing'), her every sentence will be cheered by the sympathetic gallery. The final poetic justice of her marriage with the Duke is sure to arouse unbounded enthusiasm.

A few exquisite Hindu touches add to the beauty of the situations. The song, 'Take, O take those lips away', finds a most appropriate echo in a musical expression of the lovelorn goddess Pārvatī pining for her Lord Śiva, with haunting associations of Kālidāsa. Hindu ideals are grafted on Christian ethics in the prison interviews. Again, in

22. M. *Samānaśāsana* (*Equal Punishment*). Anonymous (music by G. G. Deva), Nāṭyakalā Company, Poona, 1909.
    U. *Shaheedē nāz* (*The Martyr to Beauty*). By Aga Hashr, Original Alfred Company, Bombay, 1905.
    B. *Vinimaya* (*Give and Take*). By Virendranath Ray, Vidhura-njana Natya Samaj, Calcutta, 1910.

conformity with the best Hindu practice, the royal priest joins the hands of Vincentio and Isabella as they smile consent. In the finale after the didactic message of upright government, justice and chastity, a wish for 'the uplifting of the Motherland' is expressed.

The Urdu adaptation tries to exploit as many Shakespearean situations and incidents as possible with the addition of thrilling scenes of its own invention. The play characteristically opens in a magnificent garden where girls are singing to the glory of Nature. Immediately the central curtain is raised and a spectacular Court scene dazzles the eye. The bodyguard Kātil is on the point of murdering the king for his 'mercy' (*rahm*) on one who had an illegitimate amour with his sister; but Angelo (Safarjang) just succeeds in saving Vicentio (the king). In the next scene one hears a distinct echo of *The Merchant of Venice* in the long discourse on the diverse attributes of 'mercy'. The king, apparently as a gesture of renunciation, invests his sole authority in Angelo, but really means to study the deputy's character. As a counterpart of Lucio, Mistress Overdone and the Clown, the stock device of a vulgar farce of Fitnar's amours calculated to hoodwink the foolish husband, a constable, is utilized.

Other striking changes may be noted. The chaste and beautiful Isabella is not coy and bashful, but a Moslem virago handling the situation boldly. The Duke assumes even more rôles, including that of a servant to Angelo, in some scenes. The mistaken identity is made convincing in a scene of midnight revelry when Isabella artfully makes the Moslem Angelo drink till his brains are steeped in liquor. At such a critical moment Mariana slips into his arms. In the course of the last theatrical scene, the keynote of the play, 'mercy', is dinned into the ears of the audience; and the curtain rings down on several happy couples, the only exception being in the case of Lucio, who is not compelled to accept the hand of his 'whore'. One need not add that almost every one sings.

The Bengali adaptation is more chaste and artistic. Certain modifications effected to suit medieval Hindu life may be noted. A poor soldier (Claudio) is secretly married to the Minister's daughter, Juliet, and elopes with her but is arrested. The young king has moods of quiet contemplation. When he is pressed to marry a lady of his choice, he entreats his mother and his aged minister to permit him to go on a great pilgrimage for a complete study of life before he enters upon matrimony. The young general Angelo is to be his deputy. Angelo, flushed with power, insults and deserts his honest wife, who in despair makes an attempt to throw herself in a river; the royal ascetic, however, saves Mariana and lodges her in his hermitage. The two scenes where Isabella's character is shown in its beauty and charm and the concluding scene replete with many thrills are well rendered.

The medium of expression is Bengali blank verse with the occasional use of prose as in Shakespeare. The songs are but few and are introduced in an appropriate, suggestive manner. Here, again, the Shakespearean model preserves the dignity and artistic unity of the whole version. Isabella (Mohinī) the virtuous virgin, waits for her dear lovelorn brother in a lonely house at midnight. She admires the beauty of the firmament and sings, as she swings, "How sweetly do the stars smile!" and so on. Her solitary domestic life has a peculiar appeal to the Hindu heart, the nunnery being out of the question at such a tender age; and her songs possess a haunting charm.

Out of the serene romances of Shakespeare's mature period, *The Tempest*[23] was produced on the Marathi stage; but the too literal translation of K. B. Belsare being unsuitable for the theatre it had to be withdrawn; whilst the other versions—two Bengali, the second Marathi and one Telegu—do not seem to have been mounted at all. Two Marathi versions of *Pericles* are extant; but no professional

23. M. *Tuphānu (Tempest)*.

company staged either of them. An Urdu free adaptation, styled *Khudādāda* (*Given by God*, i.e. Natural), was, however, produced by a Bombay Parsi company in 1891; but it was not printed.

(10) On the other hand, *Cymbeline* and *The Winter's Tale* proved two of the most successful comedies on the Indian stage. The former[24] was even a greater favourite in all parts of India, obviously on account of the profound appeal of the chaste Imogen to the audiences. The Marathi version, which ran into several editions, is generally considered to be a standard prose adaptation by a Shakespearean scholar.

In the course of his masterly preface to the first edition of 1879, Mahajani states his definite aim of entertaining the audience by making certain necessary modifications in the original text. Thus, the queen could not be a widow remarried in Hindu society; and Imogen had to be a little younger and unmarried. The custom of open burial and the offering of flowers had also to be modified. Similarly, Posthumus's vision of his parents did not harmonize with Indian notions. Then the adapter, in a spirit of reverence, admits that "if there are faults in this version they are due to the mirror itself and not the original thing of beauty". The prevailing *rasa* of pathos, particularly love in separation, is discussed; and the peculiar Shakespearean charm of ably harmonizing various *rasas* of pathos, heroism, and laughter is praised. Particular emphasis is laid on the excellent

24. M. *Tārā* (*Imogen*). By V. M. Mahajani, M.A., Chittakarshaka Company, Poona, 1879.
   U. *(1) *Zulmē nāravā* (*Unjustified Tyranny*). Staged by Empress Theatrical Company, Bombay, 1899.
   (2) *Mithā Zahr* (*Sweet Poison*). By Munshi Mustafa Saiyadalli, The Parsi Company, Bombay, 1900.
   G. (Part) *Cāṁparāja Hāṁdo* (hero of that name). By Vaghaji Asharam Oza, Morbi Company, Bombay, (c. 1900).
   B. *Kusumakumārī* (*Imogen*). By Chandra-Kali Ghosh, at the Old Jorasanko Theatre, Calcutta, 1874.
   Ta.**Siṁhalamānadha* (*The Ruler of Ceylon*). By P. Sambanda, 'Sugun Vilas Sabha' and University Amateurs, Madras.

'poetic justice' meted out to several characters in the final
scene, and the forgiveness of Iachimo is noted as an act of
magnanimity. "The atmosphere of this romance is not
unlike the Sanskrit classics."

Mithā Zahr (*Sweet Poison*) was the more popular of the
two Urdu versions. It is characteristic of the Urdu publications that, sometimes, the manifest debt to Shakespeare is
not at all acknowledged. Here is an instance to the point.
The title indicates 'the sweet potion' given by the physician
to the queen. Moreover, it suggests the queen's character
for the simple reason that although she smiles and smiles
she breathes venom. The original text has been greatly
tempered by the Urdu poet. Imogen is the niece of the king,
while Cloten is the son. The queen's sole aim is to secure
Imogen's hand for her worthless son, the point of gaining
the crown for him being missed. The foolish Cloten, a member
of 'The Golden Gang', is forced by his mother to make love
to Imogen. There is no mention of 'his meanest garment'
or his visit to Milford Haven. In the battle he dies at the
hands of Iachimo!

An additional underplot is developed in which the fool is
ridiculed by his boon companions who make him drink
heavily and go into the snares of a dissolute blind woman.
Most of the alternate scenes are occupied by this vulgar
farce. Finally, the battle scene is fully exploited; martial
songs are introduced and there is the greatest possible
bustle on the stage. With a full theatrical sense the last
scene with its many sudden revelations is kept much more
faithful to the original.

The Gujarati playwright takes only the dramatic episode
of the wager from *Cymbeline* and develops it on original
lines in his historical play of the time of the great Akbar.
At his magnificent court at Delhi, in the course of a discussion
concerning women, the Rajput chief boasts of his virtuous
queen, Sonarāṇī, at Bundikota; a dissolute Moslem chief
challenges him and a wager is fixed by the Emperor. It

being impossible to visit the Rajput harem, through the intrigue of a flower-woman who poses as the aunt of the hero, the Indian Iachimo gets all the clues mentioned by Shakespeare. Cāṁparāja is on the point of losing his head when the accomplished Sonarāṇī, dressed as a dancing-girl, finds admission to the Moghul Court and ultimately her honour is vindicated. Although this novel treatment is developed independently in harmony with the medieval legend, the debt to Shakespeare is unmistakable.

In the Bengali adaptation, after the prologue in the ortho-dox style, the minister of a State and his brother discuss the disappearance of the princes and the king's doting on his devilish second wife. Since Cloten is absent, the queen's persecution of her stepdaughter does not find a sufficient dramatic motive. Her evil genius is her maid-servant Kuṭilā ('The wicked one'), a new character, based on the analogy of Mantharā in *Rāmāyaṇa*. A clown on the classical model is also introduced to divert the king's mind after he has banished Posthumus (who is secretly married to the princess). The lament of Imogen follows more the Indian traditional vein than the Shakespearean expression. The challenge is an echo of the original; but the admission to Imogen's bed-chamber at midnight is secured through the agency of Helen, who also comes in occasionally and urges Iachimo to exercise haste. The queen's confession saves the whole situation and finally the gods shower flowers from the sky on the happy couple on the stage! In this free prose version, the introduc-tion of only a few songs from behind the screen at suitable moments is indeed a noteworthy device of the Bengali stage.

(11) Three adaptations of *The Winter's Tale*[25] are known

25. M. *Vikalpavimocana* (*Dissolution of Doubt*). By Nevalakar, Nāṭyakalā Company, Poona, 1894. Later, revived with the addition of songs, 1908.
   U. **Mureedē Shak* (*The Disciple of Doubt*). By Munshi Hasan, Alfred Company, Bombay, 1898.
   G. (Part) *Candrahāsa* (name of the hero). By Vaghji A. Oza, Morbi Company, Bombay, 1894.

to have been staged in India. Other two Marathi and two Bengali adaptations do not seem to have been produced at all. The Marathi stage version follows the usual high standard of the Poona Nāṭyakalā Company. Necessary modifications of locality, names, manners and customs are happily introduced. In the later popular revival, Hermione importunes Polixenes to stay and teases him about his 'home-sickness' in a song. Just a hint from Shakespeare is expanded into a graphic delineation of home joys. The adapter, however, fails to correct the initial drawback of supplying a sufficient motive for the jealousy of Leontes. The ideas in the original have been well assimilated, as may be judged from the reference to *swayaṁvara* (choice-marriage) according to the ancient Indian tradition, instead of the reference to 'courtship' in the English poet. "Paddling palms and pinching fingers" being foreign to Hindu society, the only ground of suspicion lies in a supposed amorous address, side-glances and sweet smiles. The philosophical song of the miserable King of Bohemia, at the end of Act I, is an innovation which soothes the mind of the sympathetic Indian audience. The principal departure in Act II is in relation to Paulina. She is not so young here; but an elderly lady who has 'nursed the king himself in his infancy'. She thunders heroically and defies the wrath of the king. Her rhetorical sentences are always sure of success. For the oracle of Delphi, the divine judgment of the royal family preceptor is invoked. A Sanskrit verse serves as a riddle.

The Court scene (III. ii) impresses the whole theatre deeply. Poor Antigonus bleeds profusely on the stage and dies in his conflict with the bear. In Act IV an old shepherd comes forward and informs the audience in his soliloquy that twelve (not sixteen) years have elapsed and that his foster-child is now marriageable. Florizel and Perdita sing a number of amatory songs. The Hindu pedlar also has talent in displaying his wares and his wiles. In the last act, the match between Paulina and Camillo being absurd according to the Hindu ideals, she retires from the world. Finally, at the request of the reformed king, all sing a prayer to God to dispel the darkness of infatuation and suspicion. Another chorus follows for the glory of the Motherland.

The Gujarati version which is curiously mixed up with the Pauranic story of the devotee Candrahāsa does not care to acknowledge any obligations. However, the debt to Shakespeare is obvious; Oza, a teacher in an English school, was at least familiar with the English poet's plots. This play has enjoyed a huge success for years on the Gujarati stage. Considered from a literary point of view it is a poor production and the songs are trivial; but the element of romance and pathetic situations made it popular in those days. To illustrate the measure of the liberty taken with the plot one may refer to a novel farcical match arranged for Leontes by the villain Hirji. The king, when the rogue is exposed, goes almost mad and indulges in hysterical speeches of repentance for past deeds and in wild passionate utterances for Hermione. Perdita is deposited at the palace of Polixenes and she naturally loves Florizel. Finally, everything ends happily. All that is finest in Shakespeare is here utterly lacking.

*   *   *

From the above survey it would appear that out of the seventeen comedies (keeping apart the English Chronicle Plays) of Shakespeare, thirteen were staged on the Marathi stage, eight on the Urdu stage and only five on the Bengali stage in India. Out of those remaining, *Love's Labour's Lost* has been adapted into Urdu and *Much Ado About Nothing* into Marathi. A Marathi version of *Pericles* (*Sudhanvā*) is extant, although only the Urdu rendering was staged. Thus, in the whole range of Shakespearean comedy only *Troilus and Cressida* remains unaccounted for. The palm naturally belongs to the Marathi theatre.

It may be observed that the most enthusiastic and

abiding reception has been accorded to Professor Kelkar's excellent Marathi adaptation of *The Taming of the Shrew*. This farcical comedy is also mentioned as one of the most attractive plays of Shakespeare on the German stage.[26] Of the other two comedies mentioned there, *A Midsummer Night's Dream* and *The Merchant of Venice*, the former succeeded admirably on the Bengali and the latter on the Urdu stage.

Regarding the 'improvements' on the original text, one must remember the different levels of culture of the three principal theatres of India, viz. the Marathi, the Urdu and the Bengali. The fact that scholars and college professors were deeply interested in the theatre and approached the English poet with respect and admiration accounts largely for the high level of the Marathi stage. To add to this, educated actors interpreted the adaptations with sympathy and understanding. This attitude of reverence and affection in playwrights and actors was responsible for the least possible liberty being taken with the original plays. The only glaring defect of the musical comedies in Marathi is the excessive use of songs. Music in the drama should always be regulated to harmonize with the spirit of the production. However, there are many popular prose versions with a few appropriate songs which call for special admiration. Tried by critical canons these adaptations will hold their own anywhere.

For melodramatic extravagances of the type of Lacy's *Sauny the Scot* and for curious combinations of plots as in D'Avenant's *The Law Against Lovers*, one should turn to the Urdu stage. Here the licence taken goes beyond all expectation. It is not possible to discuss most of the vulgar Urdu adaptations in the light of any dramatic theory, for the essential unity and probability are missing. The Urdu poet is hardly able to read any English. He simply hears a story or reads it in his vernacular. Then he seizes upon the

26. Sir Sidney Lee: *William Shakespeare*, p. 619.

most theatrical situations and gives them racy and powerful expression. Lighter shades of character he cannot draw. To play to the gallery he adds an extra farce, even in the adaptation of a comedy. Scenes of blood and fury in rhetorical style he thrusts in. What Hazelton Spencer says of the adaptation of *The Faery Queen*[27] is even more true of the Urdu adaptations. Yet as he rightly concludes: "Ridicule is easy; but let not the modern (European) playgoer cast a stone at either the pedestals of china-work or the monkey ballet."

Moving from the west to the east of India, one notices at once that the Bengali theatre has never taken seriously to the Shakespearean comedy. The Bengali drama is the most original in India and tries to develop on national lines; but when it does adapt for the stage, it remains fairly close to the original with fewer and more artistic modifications than even those of the Marathi stage. For a fuller examination of the problem, however, one must turn here to the Shakespearean tragedy, where the greatest glory resides.

27. *Shakespeare Improved*, Cambridge, 1927, p. 319

CHAPTER VIII

STAGE-VERSIONS OF SHAKESPEAREAN TRAGEDIES

To an Indian student accustomed to the Hindu classical dramatic tradition of musical comedy and farce, with occasional use of tragi-comedy, the Shakespearean tragedy came as a great revelation. As has been observed above, the internal conflict in the soul of Rāma is revealed by Bhavabhūti; but 'this story of exceptional calamity' does not 'lead to the death of a man in high estate'. It is true that the painful decision of the banishment of Sītā proceeds from the character of her lord; still, the fact remains that the tragic conclusion of the Hindu epic is converted into a forced happy ending by the dramatist, presumably to comply with the ancient critical canons. Only subordinate figures meet their death in the classic plays, and, even so, these deaths are merely reported, never shown to the audience.

The sense of 'painful mystery' was not absent from the ancient Indian drama, but it was completely veiled by means of the Hindu philosophy. Such an attitude does not lead to a great tragedy. In Shakespeare, for the first time, the University student came across a profound study of the genuine tragic atmosphere. Shakespeare's mode of approach proved particularly impressive. The impression gained in beauty, vividness, and depth as the English Professor[1] recited and even occasionally acted the scenes. Thus a real taste for Shakespeare was cultivated at some schools and at most of the colleges. The characteristic catholicity of mind of an average Hindu made it possible for him to retain his enjoyment of the flowery beauties of Kālidāsa and at the same time to appreciate the tragic depths of the

---

1. This is the impression of the writer who studied under the late Dr. R. Scott and Dr. E. A. Parker in Wilson College, Bombay.

English dramatist. The model of stage-production was, concurrently, presented by the European theatres in Calcutta, Bombay, and Madras, where Shakespearean tragedy, notably *Hamlet*, was constantly in the repertory. Thus, both the theatre and the University co-operated in providing a sound basis for amateur Indian acting.

Some of these 'University wits', specially in Maharashtra, began to write about 1875 also for the professional stage. They approached Shakespearean tragedy in a spirit of reverence and seldom 'improved' its catastrophe. With the dawn of the new learning, the ancient tradition started to lose its vitality, and, after all, it must be remembered that its continuity had been broken by a gulf of centuries.

For the other set of ignorant professional adapters, the melodramatic elements of song, show, incident, declamation, oratory, and the like in Shakespearean tragedy proved seductive. The Moslem *kavi* seized avidly on sensational themes of murders and diabolical crimes. The elements of lust, the supernatural, and fate were fully exploited. This characteristic attitude will easily explain the Urdu adaptations of Shakespearean tragedies. Thus, while considering the several stage-versions of Shakespearean tragedies, one has constantly to remember the different levels of culture in the Indian theatre.

Taking the English Chronicle dramas first, it may be observed that out of the plays dealing with the seven English kings, adaptations only of *Richard III*—apart from its two Marathi translations with Hindu names—and of *King John* have been staged in India; *Henry V* and *Henry VIII* have been translated into Marathi, but were not acted. *Richard II, Henry IV* and *Henry VI* are not known to have been rendered in any Indian language, though it is surprising that Falstaff did not figure on the Indian stage other than in his farcical amours with the merry wives of Windsor. Possibly, the English historical plays proved too intimately related to their own time and

place to be easily transferred to the Indian stage. It is not
without significance to notice that even in Germany, where
Shakespeare is most popular in the theatre, most of the
English histories are not among the favourites.[2]

(1) As may be expected, the dominant Marlowesque personality of *Richard III*,[3] as a study in sheer external conflict,
proved attractive to the Urdu stage. Curiously enough,
however, after a partial exploitation of the situation in the
original, the well-known Urdu *kavi* turned to the plot of
King John and made the best he could of its last two acts.
Like Richard, the hero Nādirjaṅga is a most powerful
thundering figure swayed by the sole passion of unscrupulous ambition. He is certainly not weak and vacillating
like John.

In the last act (Act III) Arthur advances with an army
of supporters. All the wicked plans of the usurper miscarry
and he is imprisoned. Arthur ascends the throne and marries
Blanche, and at her entreaty confines the tyrant to life-
long imprisonment. Thus the play ends altogether in a
different key, and has not even the pretence of a Shakespearean tragedy, despite its many deaths. It is also interesting to note that instead of the excellent comic relief and the
side-study of the bastard Falconbridge, a very crude and
free version of Molière's *The Mock Doctor* is incorporated.
For the many elements of low farce and lascivious song the
kavi himself is, of course, responsible. Finally, the triumph
of truth (*nekī*) is vindicated and the evil in man (*badī*)
condemned.

(2) *King John*[4] was, however, treated with more dignity
and beauty by the Marathi adapter. In the preface it is
made quite clear that the version was designed to meet the

2. Cf. the list by Sir Sidney Lee: *William Shakespeare*, p. 619.
3. U. *Saide-Havasa* (*Prey of Ambition*). By Aga Hashr, Parsi
   Theatrical Company, Bombay, 1906.
4. M. *Kapidhvaja* (named after the King) or *Kapaṭa-prabhāva*
   (*A Study in Intrigue*). By L. N. Joshi, Shahunagar Company, Poona, 1904.

needs of the particular company and that it is to be taken as an imaginative study with the medieval Maratha setting. Again, the female interest lacking in the last two acts of the original is supplied by granting a longer lease of life to Constance, who is allowed to return to England. This version is ingeniously dedicated to "the unfortunate Queen Constance (Citrasenā), on the occasion of her first incarnation on the Marathi stage".

In Act IV the Prince Arthur and Hubert (Sañjīvana, i.e. the Reviver) scene is also faithfully rendered. It is bound to be generally effective on the Indian stage on account of the presence of clever boy actors in most troupes. The first noteworthy change occurs in IV. ii, when, instead of Peter of Pomfret, Constance in male attire (Piṅgalākṣa) is introduced with the Bastard. In the midst of the conversation John asks her: "Who art thou?" Constance: "An Astrologer!" John: "May your astrology be consumed to ashes!" She: "May your immorality be consumed!" John: "I now know you." She: "I have indeed known you long ago!" and so on, in the style of 'Stichomythia'. The allusion to the foreboding 'five moons' is retained. In IV. iii, she sees her son in prison and believes that he is proceeding in safety to the French camp, but actually he dies as in the original. The most striking original scene is V. v, which is replete with irony and pathos. She, covered in black, at night, on her way to the French camp, utters a soliloquy of gratitude to Hubert, meditates dire revenge on the usurper, and, in the manner of Lady Macbeth, invokes the spirits of darkness to help her. She dreams of Arthur's coronation! The following scene opens at night in a temple in a crematorium, with the ailing John on one side and the dead body of Arthur on the other. She sees only the tyrant and wants to stab him as he sleeps; but he stops her, confesses his crimes, and points to the dead body of her son. Her dagger drops. Broken-hearted, she commits suicide. John expires next. The Bastard dwells on 'Union is strength',

instead of on England's glory. On the whole, it is an excellent
adaptation, as the spirit of the original is beautifully preserved and the few additions are tactfully introduced.

(3) After the English historical tragedies, it is convenient
to approach the other Shakespearean tragedies in the generally accepted chronological order. *Titus Andronicus*[5] may be
dismissed first. It is no wonder that only the Urdu stage
was attracted by this monstrous story of lust, revenge and
torture. Curiously enough, the Shakespearean Theatrical
Company of Bombay started with this play in 1910 and did
not produce any other drama by the great dramatist. The
managing proprietor, V. K. Nayak, spent £1,000 on elaborate
Roman scenery and costumes; and yet this version failed
to attract large audiences, for two reasons: (*a*) the high-
sounding Roman names did not appeal to the people; and
(*b*) scholastic touches given by many Arabic words fell flat
on the ears of the illiterate playgoers. It is noteworthy,
however, that V. K. Nayak[6] as Titus and the gifted actress
Gohar as Lavinia won considerable success.

The "Opera" booklet of this play is a unique publication
of its type, for it contains a masterly essay of twenty-eight
pages on 'dramatic art', ancient and modern. This is followed
by an able preface by the same writer, Nayak. There are
apt quotations in English, and a small biographical sketch
of Shakespeare, with a list of his plays and of the Urdu
versions.

(4) The lyrical tragedy of *Romeo and Juliet*[7] proved

5. U. *Junûnē Vafā* (*Mad Fidelity*). By A. B. Latif Śād, The
   Shakespearean Theatrical Company, Bombay, 1910.
6. "This great actor died in 1913 or so; he was a very ambitious
   man and a gifted actor and producer. He would have done
   something really great had he lived a little longer" (C. R. Shah).
7. M. *(1) Pratāparāvaāṇī Maṁjulā* (named after the Lovers).
   Staged by a Poona Company in 1882.
   (2) Śaśikalā-Ratnapāla (named after the Lovers). By Kanit-
   kar, Native Institution, Poona, 1882.
   (3) *Śālinī Nāṭaka* (play named after Juliet). By K. V.
   Karmarkar, Patankar Company, Bombay, 1900.
   (4) *Mohana-Tārā* (named after the Lovers). By K. R.

immensely successful on both the Marathi and the Urdu
stages in western India and was also well received in the
south, though one cannot explain why none of the three
Bengali adaptations was produced by any professional
company in the eastern provinces. It is interesting to
notice that as many as four versions were tried in the
Marathi theatre, and hints from the original love story were
taken by many playwrights. The first two Marathi adaptations were not as successful as the two later ones. Karmarkar's rendering is very faithful to the original with a very
few changes due to different manners and customs. After
the orthodox prayer, the two *rasas* of the drama—love and
pathos—are emphasized in a song. Instead of 'Queen Mab',
Mercutio (Hirojī) dreams of the goddess Beauty and of his
subsequent disappointment. According to the Hindu practice on festive occasions, Juliet is seen singing in a chorus
in a garden. The lovers get a few minutes to talk. The Hindu
Juliet is metaphorically described as an 'idol' instead of
"a saint," and her lover is the 'devotee' visiting the temple
instead of the "holy palmer." They gently touch but do
not kiss. The famous soliloquy "Gallop apace" is rendered
freely in two songs and prose.

In 1908 the play was turned into a musical tragi-comedy
(*Tārā-Vilāsa*) by D. A. Keskar. This version, however, was
not staged. In the same year a tragical adaptation proved
highly popular in Poona. It is remarkable for one principal
departure from the original. Here Rosaline (only mentioned
by Shakespeare) is brought on the stage as Kamalā. After
her youthful romantic passion, she has to marry Tybalt, but
remains still deeply enamoured of Romeo. She also happens
to be a boon companion of Juliet. The secret passion of
Rosaline serves as an excuse for developing an underplot.

> Chapakhane, B.A., LL.B., The Cittakarshaka Company,
> Poona, 1908.
> U. *Bazmē Fāni* (*The Fatal Banquet*). By Mehar Hasan, The
> Alfred Company, Bombay, 1897.
> Ta.*Ramaṇa-Jvālitā (named after the lovers). By P. S. Durai.

Apart from this novel line of development, the main story runs as in Shakespeare. Considerable scenic adjustment is effected in this version to suit the new requirements. Thus Act I is subdivided into eleven instead of into five scenes as in the original. The marriage ceremonial gains in spectacular beauty when the lovers are married secretly with proper Hindu rites in the presence of the god 'Fire', and blessings in Sanskrit verses are showered on them by the Hindu priest. Shakespeare's IV. i tests the skill of the adapter. Nevertheless, it is made thoroughly effective on the Indian stage. As Friar Lawrence is both a hermit and an apothecary, he declares that Juliet is stung by a poisonous serpent, and therefore she should be confined alone in a temple for medical aid and divine blessings. The plan miscarried on account of Rosaline's intrigue. The adapter introduces an extra realistic comical relief by means of a discussion between two Brahmin priests relating to their share in the prescribed charities after the death of the heroine!

The Urdu version is styled *The Fatal Banquet*, for the pair of star-crossed lovers fall in love at first sight in the course of the festival; but it is turned into a crude tragi-comedy in three acts. It has, no doubt, the singular advantage of the absence both of extra characters and of the customary unrelated farce. The artistic beauty of the piece, however, is ruined by ignorance and folly. At the same time, it must be remembered that the play was a huge success, measured in terms of the box-office; and what does the *munshi* or the manager care for else?

In the usual spectacular fashion, the play opens in the court of the Prince of Verona (Emperor Shahā). The dancing girls entertain the courtiers, who drink and sing Bacchanalian hymns. Family feuds amongst nobles are discussed. The court fool (Jarif) indulges in lewd jokes. In such an atmosphere there is no question of the Shakespearean spirit being retained. In fact, the adaptation aims only at following the main lines of the original plot. By a sort of 'Tateification' everything ends happily after Paris is killed in combat with Romeo. It may be noted that on account of the similarity in the mode of the disposal of the dead, the final scene is laid in a churchyard as in the original.

Romeo loses the finer essence of his tragic idealized love and indulges in a world of voluptuous dialogue and songs. A few subtle wit combats of Mercutio are well turned to advantage; but his genius and his vision of 'Queen Mab' are gone. The Nurse, indeed, plays the same tricks, does not give out Romeo's message at once, and also creates ironical confusion regarding Tybalt's murder; but after this she loses all her importance. On the whole, from the literary point of view, this version has hardly any merit.

(5) Since *Julius Cæsar* was not acted, although it was adapted into Marathi and translated into Bengali, one may now proceed to the examination of the several stage versions of the most popular of Shakespearean tragedies in the whole world, *Hamlet*.[8] It may be recorded that no Shakespearean play, most faithfully rendered, has ever evoked such unbounded enthusiasm and admiration in India as the Marathi *Hamlet*. From 1882–1883 on to his death in 1922, Ganapatrao Joshi, easily the greatest Shakespearean actor of India, interpreted *Hamlet* as a 'tragedy of thought' in such a wonderfully impressive manner that it was the one tragedy which, despite its having been acted by him hundreds of times, was always in demand wherever the company toured. Although he also excelled in the rôles of Othello and Macbeth, it is generally acknowledged that Hamlet was the brightest

8. M. *Vikāravilasita (Tragedy of Thought)*. By Principal G. G. Agarkar, M.A., Shahunagar Company, Poona, 1883.
   U. *Khûnē-nāhaq (Unjust Murder)*. By Munshi Mehdi Hasan, Parsi Alfred Company, Bombay, 1898.
   B. *Harirāja (Hamlet)*. By Amara Datta, Classical Theatre, Calcutta, June 21, 1897.
   Ta. *Amalāditya (Hamlet)*. By P. Sambanda, 'Sugun Vilas Sabha', Madras, 1911.

jewel in the crown of his glory. Undoubtedly, part of his tremendous success he owed to the co-operation of Balvantrao Jog, as Ophelia, and to the rest of an admirable cast.9

This Marathi version by Principal Agarkar is itself a model of genuine scholarship and taste. In a masterly preface the learned adapter discusses the problem of 'Translation and Adaptation'; and then he proceeds to a critical appreciation of the text.

With absolute fidelity Shakespeare is rendered in standard Marathi prose, act by act, scene by scene, almost line by line. Only a few minor changes are made. In II. ii, the Hindu Polonius quotes some apt Sanskrit verses bearing on the youthful lovelorn condition of Hamlet. For Æneas's tale to Dido and Priam's slaughter, striking use is made of the familiar and touching episode from *Mahābhārata* relating to 'the story of Aśvatthāmā's death' in dignified Marathi verses. 'Hecuba' gives place to 'Kṛpī', the old mother of the Hindu hero. In the play within the play, III. i, only a few explanatory touches are added to clear the full meaning of Hamlet's subtle remarks. The satire on contemporary performances gains in point as it exactly fits in with the defects of the medieval Indian stage. Ophelia's sweet but painful songs find a fitting echo in Marathi lyrics.

There are two more Marathi adaptations, but no company had the courage to stage them, for the obvious reason that

9. Mr. E. H. Atkin was "taken by surprise" in 1894, as he could follow Shakespeare scene by scene and as the acting was "good and powerful throughout". To Mr. J. R. Roberts, in 1902, it was a "revelation that the dramatic art had attained to so high a pitch in India as that displayed by the Shahu Company. Ganapatrao's rendering of the great characters of Shakespeare is beyond all praise. He is a finished actor of the highest quality and of marvellous talent. I would say the same of Balabhanu, who does the female parts". Major F. B. Younghusband was "astonished at the ability and talent" of Ganapatrao and Balavantrao in 1902. (See Marathi *Life of Ganapatrao*, pp. 139 and 174.)

all efforts to invite comparisons with the Shahu troupe would lead to inevitable disaster. Even amongst the reading public this tragedy enjoyed an exceptional popularity. For another great stage success in western India it is necessary to turn to the Urdu version. Although described on the title-page as a "Translation in Urdu of *Hamlet*", this is really a free adaptation. It is interesting to notice in connection with this production that the famous manager-actor, Khatau, tried his best to follow Henry Irving's model for dress and scenery.

So far as the plot is concerned, the main argument of the original is preserved; but the events and incidents are curiously altered and mixed up. Except in the case of a few striking sentences here and there, there is no question of a close verbal resemblance. Many beautiful scenes are mangled. Again, instead of an artistic comic relief, a poor vulgar farce is substituted, which definitely destroys the dramatic harmony. Of course, songs are needlessly thrust in on every occasion. The additional farce is thus patched up with the main plot: Marcellus (Sulemān) is in love with Rahanā (friend of Ophelia), who is beloved by Anwar (brother to Horatio). Mansūr (son to Cornelius) is also in love with Ophelia. In two of the seven farcical scenes Hamlet himself figures. The culmination of the love intrigue is reached when he kills his foolish rival Mansūr, who is bent on compelling Ophelia to his wishes at midnight in a churchyard!

The play opens in the favourite Urdu fashion in the midst of the royal Court festivities, celebrating the nuptials of Claudius and Gertrude with dance and music. The Prime Minister Polonius is won over by the wiles of the Queen; and so Claudius is crowned King. In Hamlet's powerful lament, at the end of the scene, ideas are taken from several portions of the original. The catastrophe also strikes a novel note. It starts with the mention of a "double stage" for the play within the play, which is styled *Khûnē Nāhaq* (*The Unjust Murder*) instead of 'the mouse-trap'. The Prince of

Denmark has his misgivings, and delivers his message to Horatio after exacting a solemn oath from him. Then he sits in a corner to watch the effect of the play on the guilty pair. Here the Queen instigates the murder, while the murderer hesitates. Claudius changes colour and wants to run away; but Hamlet prevents him. Laertes offers to fight a duel. They wound each other, the touch of poison circulating rapidly through Hamlet's veins. The Queen rushes to help and asks for a cup of syrup. At this stage, Cornelius, father of Mansūr (killed by Hamlet), passes a poisoned chalice for the purpose of wreaking revenge on the Prince. Hamlet refuses to drink, and she, thoroughly exhausted, drinks and dies. Cornelius runs away. Laertes makes his confession. Hamlet finally shoots his uncle. He, however, expires before Claudius.

The greatest weakness of the version lies in its travesty of Shakespearean characterization. The genius of Hamlet has fled. His Moslem counterpart does not delay on account of any philosophical reasoning. He has simply a vague doubt about the genuine nature of the Ghost. He would certainly not have spared Claudius while praying. His relations to Ophelia and Gertrude are not delicately treated. Indeed there are very few soliloquies. Hamlet is just a melodramatic hero. The atmosphere of the original simply does not exist. Moreover, the Shakespearean problem of the Queen's guilt is solved absolutely. Here she goads her incestuous lover to murder her husband. And poor Ophelia? She is sought by several lovers, but prefers the eccentric one. She goes mad on account of her lover's waywardness and jumps into the sea from a bridge (for the sake of spectacular effect!) Horatio has no personality, and Fortinbras and the Grave-diggers do not figure at all. (This economy was necessary, since *Hamlet* is a fairly long play, and a new farcical element and a number of songs—which were bound to be encored—had to be incorporated for the need of the theatre.) The result is the utter ruin of the great tragedy.

Curiously enough, the free Bengali version, acted in Calcutta in 1897, with Nagendra Chaudhari as Hamlet, does not acknowledge directly any obligation to Shakespeare, but simply quotes on the title-page, "I could a tale unfold", etc., from *Hamlet*, I. v. Writing this play for the smaller cast of the Classic Theatre, A. Datta considerably 'improved' Shakespeare in the Hindu garb. Still, it must be confessed that these alterations are more artistic than those of the Urdu rendering. The first scene opens on a Kashmir battlement. The guards talk and hear of the King's death and of his last message that his son should succeed him. In the second scene, Hamlet and Horatio, lodged in a distant place, have bad dreams. The following scene discovers Ophelia on a lovely morning waiting for her lover. They hold a sweet discourse. Then the Minister Polonius arrives and brings bad tidings. In the course of the fourth scene the Hindu Claudius, the commander-in-chief (he could not be a near relative), hatches his plans. The last scene of Act I reveals Hamlet standing alone at night before the burning body of his father when he sees the ghost rising from the flames. The Queen's adultery and Claudius's treachery are revealed. "Leave her to God, but avenge my foul murder!" it cries. Hamlet takes a vow to appease the manes of his father with the blood of the criminal.

The complication is developed in Act II. A devoted Brahmin clown (Dadhimūla) tries to serve the Prince by acting as a spy on the guilty lovers. The day for the coronation is fixed, but there is a secret plan to instal the Queen and to appoint Claudius as regent. Hamlet dwells constantly on 'adultery', 'ingratitude', 'suicide', and the like in a meditative mood and confides freely to Horatio. Poor motherless Ophelia is disconsolate when Hamlet, with mind partly unhinged, asks her to wait for a year. In the third act there is a love scene between Suramā (Hamlet's sister) and Horatio. In Act IV Fortinbras supplies information about the conspiracy. Claudius has a devoted wife like

Portia waiting for her lord at midnight. Finally, in the last act, Gertrude turns into a complete virago like Lady Macbeth, and decides to sacrifice her son for her own happiness. In the confusion of midnight at a friend's house, on account of mistaken identity, Gertrude strikes her lover at a time when he was already wounded by Hamlet, who utters the words 'My father's murderer!' But before this Claudius had mortally wounded the Prince under the pretence of believing him to be a thief. Ophelia then goes mad and throws herself into a river. Finally, Horatio is declared king and Hamlet's sister becomes Queen of Kashmir.

The faithful Tamil version follows closely the original like the Marathi adaptation. Here Dravidian names befitting southern India have been chosen with great propriety: Hamlet is 'the spotless sun', Ophelia is 'the helpless damsel', Polonius 'the protector'. In one respect it gains in naturalness over the Marathi version, for such ancient Dravidian practices as the mode of burial closely resemble those of Denmark. A stage critic[10] of Madras casts some light on the acting of this piece when it was revived by the 'Sugun Vilas Sabha' amateurs on February 25, 1911: "Mr. P. Sambanda's personation of the hero was faultless. . . . We are not sure if we have not seen Mr. Rangavadivelu do his Ophelia better. . . . We feel it our duty, however, to criticize in the strongest terms the transformation of the pathetic scene of Ophelia's death into an occasion for amusement, by reproducing all the grotesque realism associated with a class of funerals in the streets of Madras. Apart from the question of their incongruity in Gujarat, where the scene is laid, they bring down the tragic dignity of the piece. Ophelia on a simple Indian bier, followed by silent mourners, without the blowing of conches and beating of cymbals, must have drawn tears (instead of the actual chorus of laughter) from the audience. . . ." Then the critic congratulates the actor-

10. *The Indian Stage*, March 1911, p. 67

adapter on his uniform success in his excellent Shakespearean versions.

(6) The most poignant of all tragedies, *Othello*,[11] has been well represented in all parts of India and has been a conspicuous success on all its stages. Perhaps the finest adaptation of a Shakespearean tragedy in India is the Marathi stage version of this drama by the gifted actor, poet and playwright, Dewal. Many producers and actors have found it perfectly suited to the Marathi stage. At the start, the adapter himself played Othello and Patkar Iago. This acting was only surpassed by the "all-star cast" of the Shahu troupe. Later on, the Tipnis brothers played the chief rôles, in which all ambitious actors wish to shine.

In a short but important preface Dewal mentions the early scholarly version by Kolhatkar by which he had profited. This literal adaptation was tried, but failed. Then the adapter's genius rehandled the material. He instinctively felt the need of being faithful to the spirit of the original and, at the same time, of making modifications which the exigencies of the Marathi stage necessitated. He curtailed long speeches and varied the construction of sentences to suit the genius of his vernacular. He made a special effort to create the atmosphere of a particular historical period in

11. M. *Jhuṁjārarāva* (*Othello*). By G. B. Dewal, The Aryodharak Company, Poona, 1880, The Shahu Company, Poona, and Maharashtra Company, Poona.

U. (1) *Shaheedē vafā* (*The Martyr of Fidelity*). By Munshi Mehdi Hasan, The Empress Victoria Company, Bombay, December 14, 1898.

(2) *Shēr-Dil* (*The Tiger-Hearted*). By Najar Dehlvi, Parsi Alfred Company, Bombay, August 1918.

G. (Part) *Saubhāgya-Sundarī* (*Othello and Desdemona*). Bombay Gujarti Company, 1903.

B. (1) *Bhīmasiṁha* (*Othello*). By Taranicharana Pala, at Calcutta on February 21, 1875.

*(2) *Othello*. By Devendranath Basu, Star Theatre, Calcutta, March 8, 1919.

Ta. *Yuddhalolam* (*Brave in Arms*). By P. S. Durai Swami Iyengar, 'The Sasi Vilas Sabha,' Madras.

India for giving verisimilitude to the story. Thus, the hero is a south Indian Maratha adventurer with the dark Dravidian colour; and the heroine is a fair high-class Hindu damsel. The disparity in colour, birth, education and social rank is exquisitely dealt with.

The play opens in 'Veṇipur' (note the phonetic affinity with Venice) and has its evolution at 'Sona beṭa' (an island like Cyprus). With only a few scenic adjustments, the version is faithful; although the dialogue, of course, is not literally translated—a very necessary improvement is made in the coarse and vulgar expressions of Iago (cf. couplets like "If she be fair and wise", etc., rendered in a favourite sing-song fashion)—at the same time enough is tactfully preserved of his insinuations to paint him as 'the demi-devil' that he is. Given a consummate actor, Jādhavarāva is a perfect incarnation of Iago. III. iii, the Temptation scene, becomes fully convincing on the Indian stage. The foolish pratlings of Bianca are appropriately rendered in Hindu *dohras* (rhymed verses). The edge of her coarseness, too, is blunted.

The highest credit belongs to Dewal for not thrusting in a single extra song. It is indeed difficult to rival the beauty and significance of 'the willow song'. Much as he admires the ballad, the present writer, however, must confess that for once Dewal surpasses this both in melody and dramatic appeal. The medieval tragic story of a lovelorn Hindu princess (for Barbara) finds a most melodious expression of its poignant sentiments pertaining to the condition of the banished Sītā. These words have been set to an intensely melancholy strain of music. This perfect lyric has become a household song in Maharashtra. Yet it must not be forgotten that its inspiration is Shakespeare's. The last magnificent speech of Othello is exquisitely rendered in Marathi prose.

The Urdu versions of *Othello* are, no doubt, greatly inferior to the one just discussed. It is true, however, that both adapters have enough sense not to thrust in an additional unrelated farce. They prefer, out of reverence for

Shakespeare, to develop the inherent comical elements in the tragedy. Consequently, in both adaptations, Roderigo is caricatured to an extreme degree. Such a farcical interlude for pleasing the spectators is certainly better than the usual mode of coarse buffoonery witnessed on the Urdu stage.

The earlier production, in which the famous actor Jahangir Khambhata acted Othello with conspicuous success, "was inspired by the tremendous enthusiasm aroused in the playgoers by *Cymbeline* (*Zulmē-nāravā*)", as is stated in the preface to the "opera-book". The manager says that "English and Gujarati reviews have joined in a chorus of praise". After paying a glowing tribute to "the greatest of poets", he states that "the acting of *Othello* is extremely difficult". Then he deplores "the tendency in the audience to demand some extra farcical absurdity"; but he will not encourage such "hybrid taste". Instead, he will only permit the rich fool Roderigo to be exploited to the fullest.

The later Urdu adaptation was also produced with success by the son of the celebrated Kavasji Khatau. In order to preserve the original local colour of Venice and Cyprus, the management spent large sums on painted curtains and costumes, although Moslem names were given to the characters speaking Urdu. The main line of argument is fairly well preserved, with some few striking modifications. The play opens in a garden, where the prime minister of the Venetian state, Brabantio, is entertaining the General Othello (Shēr-Dil). After dance and music, at the request of Desdemona (Zarnigār), the veteran commander narrates his exploits. She directly falls in love with him. They hold a sweet discourse in song. The next scene discovers Roderigo, mad for Desdemona, extorting money from his unwilling parents. In the third scene, Othello helps Desdemona to elope with him by means of a rope-ladder (a hint from *Much Ado About Nothing*). The next scene is Shakespeare's I. i. Here Iago, a lord of Venice, swindles the fool of his money. In the course of Act I, Iago's sole motive of revenge is stated to be Othello's illicit amours with Emilia. The last scene, I. vii, is Shakespeare's I. iii.

Act II opens on a 'river-bank of Cyprus', where Othello arrives with his bride. The General exhibits the head of the arch-enemy. Universal rejoicings follow. Later on, in II. v, Roderigo's 'hotel-keeper' assaults him for his follies and amorous professions. The conviction of Othello is complete at the end of this act. In the last, Act III, with full Moslem pomp and ceremony, Roderigo, completely befooled, goes in a procession to marry his beloved. In the later scuffle he is wounded by Iago and then removed to a lunatic asylum, where the next scene opens. Roderigo's father comes in time to rescue his maltreated profligate son. The final scene, which is on the Shakespearean model, is distinguished by the death of Iago on the stage.

The Bengali adapter of 1875 is perfectly conscious of his difficult task, and, in a profound spirit of reverence, com-pares himself to "a dwarf trying to catch the moon". It is a faithful rendering almost line by line, Othello being a dark Maratha adventurer in Bengal. Instead of the Turkish invasion, the Moghul army's attack is substituted. With only occasional blank verse, the general medium of expression is prose. In the place of 'the willow', a sensitive plant growing on the banks of the Yamunā is mentioned. On the whole the rendering is too close to appeal to a wide class of audience.

The later Bengali version, which ran only for a limited period at the "Star Theatre" in Calcutta, was acted by a good cast, Palita playing as Othello, Apareshbabu as Iago, and Tarasundari as Desdemona. As the title *Othello* indicates, it was a close translation of the original, and consequently failed to catch the imagination of the people. Other Bengali translations and adaptations of this tragedy are not known to have been produced by any professional company.

The partial Gujarati adaptation follows more the Urdu method of production than either the Marathi or the Bengali model. Nevertheless it is a fact that the play named after

Othello and Desdemona was a phenomenal success on the Bombay stage, that the "Gujarati Company" made huge profits, and that the actor who took the part of Desdemona ("Sundarī") continued to call himself by that name. This tragi-comedy in three acts (with songs) develops on original lines in Act I, while Acts II and III show more intimacy with the Shakespearean story in the vernacular than any intimacy with the original. Here Othello is a handsome young prince who does not know his own identity and falls in love with the only princess of another kingdom, Desdemona.

Before the play opens, the situation is like one in *The Winter's Tale*. In the first act there is an echo from *Cymbeline*, for Cloten (Aughaḍabhā) is pining for Desdemona at the in stigation of his stepmother. By the favourite Shakespearean device, Desdemona, dressed as a boy, escapes with Othello, while his friend, dressed as the Princess, makes love to Cloten. The true lovers ultimately find their way to the kingdom of Othello's father. The King, not knowing his son, gives him permission to marry Desdemona, and appoints him the Commander of the army by removing Iago from the post. Thus the motive for revenge is established. Emilia is asked to steal the ring (not the kerchief) of Desdemona by Iago. II. vii is the 'Temptation scene'. Roderigo is turned from a fool into a knave, an accomplice of Iago. A new complication is created by Iago's daughter, married to Othello's friend, who tries to save Cassio. Othello throws his innocent wife into a river after half strangling her. She is rescued in the last act by Othello's mother, who is leading a pious, retired life. Later on a farcical situation is developed by Iago's daughter trying to make love to Desdemona dressed as a boy, which reminds one of *As You Like It* and *Twelfth Night*. In the final scene an effective curtain is secured by the sensational exposure of Iago by Desdemona, by the dramatic recognition of Othello and his mother by the King, by the installation of the hero, and the marriage of Iago's daughter and Othello's friend.

The Tamil version is more on a line with the Marathi and Bengali than with the Urdu and Gujarati adaptations. This close rendering was successfully staged by Madras amateurs. In the course of a review, a critic[12] observes: "The adapter has taken great pains to reproduce the real sense and force of the original; still, we must confess that the rendering in some places is painfully literal. . . . Next to *Hamlet*, perhaps, *Othello* lends itself least for either translation or adaptation in Tamil—a language not over-rich in its vocabulary for descriptions of complex mental conditions and feelings or fine shades of character. . . ."

(7) *King Lear*[13] has been staged both in the Marathi and in the Urdu theatre, and with considerable popularity in the latter. The extant Marathi version was not considered suitable for the professional stage by the Shahu Company. Consequently, L. N. Joshi was asked to adapt that great tragedy for the Marathi stage. It was the last ambition of the great Ganapatrao to act Lear on the high level of his Hamlet, Othello and Macbeth; but before he could achieve that end and then retire from the stage with the crown of Lear, he died suddenly in 1922.

In his long preface to the adaptation, Ranade contrasts *King Lear* with the *Barbarossa* of Brown and mentions the difficulties of adaptation. He boldly calls his three notable changes in the original "real improvements" on Shakespeare himself: (*a*) Lear and Cordelia live; (*b*) the King of France plays a prominent part in the last act; and (*c*) the whole kingdom of Lear is finally handed over to France. Otherwise, this rendering follows the original closely. The Court

12. *The Indian Stage*, January 1911, Madras, p. 19.
13. M. *Atipīḍacarita* ("much sinned against", i.e. named after Lear). By S. M. Ranade, Aryodharak Company, Poona, (*c*.) 1880.
    U. (1) *Hāra-Jīta* (*Defeat and Victory*). By Munshi Murad Alli, Victoria Theatrical Company, Bombay, 1905.
       (2) *Safed Khûn* (*The White Murder*). By Aga Hashra, (?) Parsi Company, Bombay, 1906.

scene of Lear is given a new orientation to suit the Eastern atmosphere. The Fool's speeches, being too subtle for the audience, are expanded and his songs fairly well rendered in Marathi verses.

Both the Urdu stage versions turn the tragedy into a three-act comedy with the usual farcical additions and amorous songs. They do not care to maintain the level of the adaptation of *Othello*, for here they found a great villain in Edmund but no Roderigo. The Fool proved too subtle for them. Accordingly, in the first version the Fool becomes the hero of a vulgar farce in four long scenes, with jealousy for his betrothed, hotel scenes, cross-purposes in the loves of doting gallants and young wives, thefts and confusions due to mistaken identity. A hint being taken from Malvolio, the Fool is declared to be a lunatic and confined in a cell. The other loose adaptation also develops its farce on similar lines, with the favourite device of songs in chorus.

The scene in the first version is laid in Egypt, partly to give an appropriate background for Moslem characters, but mostly for the purposes of a spectacular display of Egyptian scenery and costume. The play opens with the full para-phernalia of a Court scene with Gloster as the Prime Minister. The intrigue of Edmund runs on parallel lines to that in the original. Act II discovers Gloster and Kent in the garden of Regan planning to send Lear under the protection of Cordelia. Edmund overhears this and betrays his father. In the famous storm scene, "wild forest and hills covered with snow", Lear's ravings are impressive. Edgar is also there; but not the Fool. In the prison scene of Act III, Lear and Cordelia are saved in the nick of time. After the murders and suicides, Lear gives the crown to Cordelia! The audience goes into raptures over the sight of her gaining what she had lost in the first scene.

The second version also makes the most of the element of contrast between several strongly drawn characters and equally emphasizes the moral purpose of the piece. The fact that all the wicked characters perish and the noble persons are finally rewarded is hailed by spectators as "God's equal justice". The discomfiture of Edmund's double intrigue pleases them most. The later adaptation by the more learned Munshi proved too literary for the audience. There are here many well-balanced smart repartees, but they failed to meet with success. One may note as a typical example the rhythmical wit-combat between Lear, who is championing the cause of the poor, and Regan. The clever adapter, no doubt, laboured to secure a sensational curtain for each act, as he did his best to open each with a spectacle. The first tableau at the end of Act I reveals Regan repeatedly looking askance at Goneril and forbidding her from making any compromise; Lear wanting to tear his breast; Kent and Gloster trying to prevent the catastrophe. Towards the end of Act II, Goneril and Regan abuse Gloster profusely. A long rhythmic discussion on "fidelity" follows. Then an executioner is asked to kill Gloster, but is shot by Albany. A family quarrel ensues wherein Regan kills her husband and her devilish sister shoots Gloster. Two short scenes of battle follow in the typical Shakespearean fashion, with the addition of rhetorical songs. The act closes with a tableau showing Edmund arresting Lear and Cordelia. The play concludes with the spectacular Court scene where she offers the crown to her father, who passes it on to her with his blessings after joining her hand with that of France. The curtain falls as the dancing girls sing in jubilee.

(8) The swiftest and probably the last of the four great tragedies of Shakespeare, *Macbeth*,[14] achieved a success only

14. M. *Mānājirāva (Macbeth)*. By Professor S. M. Paranjpye, M.A., Shahunagar Company, Poona, 1896.

    G. *Mālavaketu (Macbeth)* or *Māyā-Prabhāva (Disillusion)*. By N. V. Thakkur, Deshi Natak Samaja, Bombay. Later, *Bedhārī Talavāra (Two-edged sword)*.

    B. (1) *Rudrapāla (Macbeth)*. By Haralal Ray, at the Great National Theatre, Calcutta, 1874.
       (2) *Macbeth*. By Girish Ghosh, at the Minerva Theatre, Calcutta, January 28, 1893.

surpassed by *Hamlet* and *Othello* on the Marathi stage. It also gained considerable popularity in the Gujarati theatre, although it did not succeed on the Bengali stage. It is recorded that out of the two Marathi versions presented to the Shahu Company, the one under consideration was selected, and that Dadasaheb Khaparde helped the production greatly by certain lessons in elocution. One of the secrets of the huge success of this play was the "wonderful acting" of Balabhau as Lady Macbeth in 'the sleep-walking scene'. When the troupe went to Bombay, on the night of its first production the tumultuous enthusiasm of the audience reached such a high pitch that they continued shouting "Once more!" (meaning repeat 'the sleep-walking scene'), declaring that they would not allow the play to continue until they were satisfied. Then the great Ganapatrao, who played Macbeth with distinction, came forward and lectured the audience: "This is not a music-hall, where you can encore a song as many times as you like. If you still persist in your demand, realize that such a consummate piece of acting cannot be repeated devoid of its context. Yes, I shall start the whole play again, and will need three more hours to reach this point. It is already one in the morning; but I have no objection if you get the necessary police sanction." The effect was instantaneous; the play proceeded.[15]

This production succeeded without any additional songs on account of great acting, for the Marathi stage could never afford the luxurious scenic devices and costumes of the Urdu and Gujarati theatres. To-day, however, such a faithful adaptation will hardly appeal in the same degree without the aid of songs. The version opens with a prayer in the orthodox fashion. Then the infernal trio is discovered in dark Hindu dress with beards. The Indian belief in the black arts lends itself to this portion of the theme. For the concluding couplet of I. i, a dismal chorus of the witches is

15. (Marathi) *Life of Ganapatrao*, p. 157.

substituted. Most of the metaphors of the epic scene which follows are preserved in their original beauty, as they have a universal appeal. Act II. iii presents a peculiar difficulty to the adapter; but he cleverly overcomes it. During that grim comic relief the 'Hell Porter' alludes to topical incidents regarding a farmer, an equivocator and an English tailor. A few contemporary Indian evils are substituted for these: (a) a hunter killing some poor persons, taking them to be wild animals; (b) a corrupt judge with his debased agent; (c) a moneylender forging documents and bribing false witnesses, etc. Also reference is made to the Pauranic notion that exact Nemesis overtakes such foul crimes—the wild hunter himself, after death, is at the mercy of the most ferocious animals in hell. This speech is doubled in length, but proves singularly effective.

All the dramatic irony for which the tragedy is famous is aptly preserved. As Hecate has no direct parallel in Hindu mythology, she is omitted, but the ghastly 'apparitions' and 'a show of eight kings', managed by a simple contrivance, are retained for spectacular effect.

Curiously enough, it has never occurred to the Urdu *kavi* to adapt this great tragedy; but the Gujarati stage mounted it on the general model furnished by the Urdu companies, though with a little better general tone. The adapter[16] quotes a didactic motto on 'greed for riches' which entirely misses the point of Shakespeare. In the preface it is stated that the English poet has only one *rasa* in a play and the Gujarati audience requires many *rasas*. Again, there are obvious 'defects' in Shakespeare on account of his historical material, the most notable being that regarding the prophecy to Banquo, which must be fulfilled in the play itself. In the imaginary Gujarati story he decides to 'improve'. This is done by placing the words "Thou shalt be king-maker" in the mouths of the agents of darkness; and ultimately it

16. This account is based on an earlier production which is printed in its entirety. Later on, the play was remodelled.

is Banquo (for Macduff is eliminated) who kills 'Belona's bridegroom' and crowns Malcolm.

The want of love-interest he supplies by an ingenious device which complicates the situation greatly. Macbeth's daughter, Mālatī, is desperately in love with Malcolm. When the royal guests arrive at Inverness, the ambitious lady not only takes the entire initiative of planning the murder, but takes her daughter in confidence and exhorts her to give up all idea of her beloved; she, however, is adamant, and secretly informs her lover, who is thus able to escape. She is not, on the other hand, able to save Duncan, who is shot by two hirelings in the course of a garden dinner. Later on, Malcolm is arrested and imprisoned for alleged patricide. Macbeth, instigated by the new 'queen', visits the prison in order to search for the place where a fabulous treasure has been buried. Its location is supposed to be known to Malcolm, who refuses to reveal the secret, and Macbeth leaves after uttering a mouthful of threats. Later on, at midnight, by a secret underground passage, Mālatī rescues her timid lover with the help of Banquo. Finally, their love culminates in their marriage and installation as king and queen.[17]

The third innovation is a farcical underplot relating to the caricature of certain contemporary theatrical practices, such as the maltreatment of *kavis* by managers and their amours with actresses. Songs make it even worse.

The fourth point 'gained on Shakespeare' is the heightening of pathetic appeal by including IV. i of *King John*. It follows closely the lines of the original here. The witches appear only in the first scene, which is combined with

17. "When the adaptation was over, they staged a pantomime— young boys (say between eight and twelve) performing the scenes of the same play all over again (dressed up and all), with slow music accompanying the performance. This mimic show took about twenty minutes. The dumb-show was a wonderful piece of dramatic device in the Elizabethan manner. Dr. C. J. Sisson was very much interested on that account" (C. R. Shah).

Shakespeare's I. iii, where they sing on the 'source of evil in man'. Later on, their equivocation is simply alluded to. In II. vii (Shakespeare's IV. ii), Macbeth, Lady Macbeth, and their soldiers arrive to murder the only son of Banquo (not Macduff). Ross intervenes, but he is shot dead by Lady Macbeth. Soldiers hold Lady Banquo fast, Macbeth shoots the boy, and then the poor mother swoons on the breast of Lady Macbeth, thus affording the tableau of the second act!

All that is best in Shakespeare—the epic narration of the bleeding soldier, the dagger scene, Banquo's ghost, the two magnificent soliloquies ("Seyton! I am sick at heart," and "She should have died hereafter"), and the rest—are altogether omitted. And yet it must be said in all fairness to the adapter that he makes it clear that all these changes are necessary in the present condition of the Gujarati theatre and that it will be a proud day when an exact translation of the original can be staged.

Both the Bengali versions are too literal to catch the imagination of the ordinary playgoers. The earlier one substitutes Hindu names, while the later retains the nomenclature of the original. The only noteworthy change in the earlier adaptation occurs in IV. i, where the Indian witches are revealed with the full paraphernalia of orthodox Hindu belief. The later adaptation was undertaken by one of the greatest actors and playwrights of India, Girish Ghosh; but he did so more as a challenge than out of affection for Shakespeare. The original is rendered in Bengali blank verse and prose almost word by word, with slight expansion here and there. Thus, at the end of I. i, more witches join and sing a chorus. A martial song is added at the end of V. iv for Malcolm's soldiers; and two more are substituted for the Shakespearean "Come away" and "Black spirits and white".

It is on record that the celebrated Girish Ghosh, however, made a sincere effort for the success of his close version.

He himself played Macbeth, the actress Tinkudi Lady Macbeth, and Mustafi the first witch and other minor parts. Dharamdas was the stage-manager. The scenery was painted by a European named Willard, and a Mr. Pim supplied the stage furniture. The editor of *The Englishman* observed: "A Bengali Thane of Cawdor is a living suggestion of incongruity; but the reality is an astonishing reproduction of the standard convention of the English stage." The production, though admired by scholars, had to be withdrawn after ten nights, as it failed to attract the ordinary playgoers.[18]

(9) The next tragedy, *Antony and Cleopatra*,[19] though staged in most parts of India, has not achieved any great success, partly owing to the fact that only a most consummate actress can do full justice to the rôle of 'the serpent of Old Nile'. Even as staged by the brilliant cast of the Shahu troupe it did not succeed in any great measure. That version is not available; but it appears that the union of three *rasas*—the erotic, the heroic and the pathetic—could not be achieved even by Ganapatrao. The audience failed to enter into the spirit of the play. From the general method of Professor Kelkar it is easy to surmise that he must have done his best to give a full Indian colour to the drama while remaining faithful to the spirit of the original. Another Marathi version seems to have been staged by a minor

18. (Bengali) *The Genius of Girish*, p. 71.
19. M. *(1) *Vīramaṇī āṇī Śṛṅgārasundarī* (*Antony and Cleopatra*). By Professor V. B. Kelkar, Shahunagar Company, Poona, 1893.
(2) *Śṛṅgāramañjarī*. By A. V. Barve, (?) a musical company, Amaravati, 1906.
U. (1) *Kālī Nāgana* (*The Black Serpent*). Produced by Mr. Joseph David for New Parsi Victoria Company, Bombay, 1906.
*(2) *Zan Mureeda* (*The Woman's Slave*). The Alexandra Company, Bombay, 1909.
B. **Cleopatra*. By Pramath Bhattacharya, at the Minerva Theatre, September 5, 1914.

musical company. For Rome and Egypt, the South and North of India are substituted. Octavius is King of the South; and his victorious general is wasting his opportunities in the embraces of the 'siren of Vindhyā'. Pompey, to serve his own end, intrigues against Antony, while Agrippa tries to help the General. Iras and Enobarbus are lovers. Charmian also has a lover. Octavia, like Olivia, has a Shakespearean fool as her companion. In IV. ii, Antony dreams of his new wife, praises 'Chaste Octavia!' and upbraids 'the serpent of old Nile', thus incensing the Queen. Act V develops on the lines of Shakespeare's IV. In Scene iv, Antony and Cleopatra both die; and in the final scene, as the curtain rings down, Octavia ascends the spectacular funeral pyre of her lord, as *satī*!

For still more startling changes and extraordinary liberties one must turn to the Urdu version, which had a fairly long run. On the title-page of a Benares publication of this adaptation it is stated (an instance of the utter carelessness of the perpetrators) that the "plot" is "from *Julius Cæsar*". The version is a curious medley, for Cleopatra, the wicked courtezan, dies, but Antony recovers from his wounds, repents of his folly, regains his throne, and is reconciled to his wife, brother, son, and Octavius! One may turn page after page and look in vain for either the genius of Cleopatra or of her 'man of men'. Her general resourcefulness is mostly retained, but her intellectual fascination and tragic grandeur have vanished. The traditional Moslem attitude to woman, of course, hindered the adapter, who seems to have been generally ignorant of English. The one aspect which he singles out and drives home is her vile nature, which she must expiate in the theatre. To impress the so-called moral is the principal aim of the adapter.

The Emperor of Rome is Antony. Neither Pompey nor Lepidus is mentioned. The antagonist is Augustus, ruling in Antony's absence. Fulvia does not die a natural death: she is killed by Antony in Egypt to propitiate his siren.

When Octavia goes to her brother, Cleopatra herself proceeds to Antony's camp and drags him away to Egypt. Antony has a brother and has also a son by Fulvia, who both escape from Augustus to a forest. Here comes a scene which is borrowed from the Hubert and Arthur episode. In the manner of Dryden's *All for Love* (which, of course, the adapter does not know), Octavia appears in Egypt, on the battlefield. In the last scene Cleopatra is discovered with a 'black serpent'. Augustus tells her about Antony's supposed death. She agrees to make love to him. They retire, and Antony enters, wounded, and upbraids her for disloyalty and she him for his past relations to wife, brother and son. Antony feels that the curse of Fulvia is on the point of being fulfilled. Octavia consoles him. Then arrive his brother and son. The tables are turned. Reconciliation follows; only Cleopatra, in sheer despair, applies the asp to her tongue and dies.

Another Urdu version which is more faithful to the original, and in which the actress Hira acted Cleopatra, is not available. In the Bengali translation the actress Tara played the heroine and Danibabu the hero; but it does not seem to have scored a popular success. It almost shared the fate of *Macbeth*, and for the same reasons.

(10) Since *Coriolanus* is not known to have been translated or adapted into any Indian vernacular, one may turn finally to *Timon of Athens*,[20] which was adapted into Marathi and was reckoned one of the major successes of the celebrated Shahu Company. Unfortunately, the version is not available. The title simply indicates a name which is known in Hindu mythology as an emblem of wrath and fierce passion. One can only say that the adaptation must have been generally faithful to the original and without songs; otherwise this troupe would not have produced it.

* * *

20. M. *Viśvāmitra (Timon).* The Shahunagar Company, Poona, 1905.

A review of the above versions indicates the fact that out of the ten Shakespearean tragedies (apart from the English chronicle plays) eight were staged in India; while out of the two remaining Roman tragedies *Julius Cæsar* was translated and adapted into Bengali and Marathi, though not produced. Only *Coriolanus* was left unrendered. Even more than in the field of comedy, the pride of place in tragedy belongs to the Marathi stage, as may be judged from the above survey. Out of the eight tragedies staged in India, the Poona companies not only produced seven, but even yielded two versions of certain tragedies, *Titus Andronicus* alone being omitted for its nauseating elements.

The Marathi stage deserves the greatest praise for different reasons. In the first place, all the prose versions are genuinely faithful to the spirit of the original and at the same time well adapted to the needs of the Hindu audience. The stage version of *Othello* set the highest standard for India. Secondly, they possess intrinsic literary merit, although some of the musical adaptations are naturally inferior. Thirdly, the Marathi theatre witnessed the greatest Shakespearean acting in India. For decades Ganapatrao and Bala Jog were names to be conjured with, the former being placed by an Indian authority, who visited England, superior to Sir Herbert Tree as Hamlet. The famous Indian actor argued that Antony's condition graphically resembled that of a bee sucking honey in the evening when the lotus gradually closes; but of this he is unaware. The intensity of his tragic passion culminates when he realizes that it is all too late. This goes to indicate that profound thought accompanied his interpretation of important rôles.

To the lasting glory of the successful Marathi company, it may be recorded that no great liberty is taken with the Shakespearean text, as was done in several European countries. For a complete contrast with this bright picture one may turn to the Urdu stage, which popularized most Shakespearean tragedies in its own characteristic style. As in the case of certain Restoration adaptations, the Urdu and the Gujarati *kavis* reveal an inordinate passion for balance in characterization. Like D'Avenant's Lady Macduff, Mr. Thakkur's Lady Banquo on the Bombay stage is presented as a complete contrast to Lady Macbeth. Times above number spectacular effects are sought, partly in the manner of Duncan's ghost seen by the wicked Queen of Scotland. What Jusserand says of Ducis's *Romeo and Juliet* is true of the Urdu productions, with a slight modification. "Piling up horrors upon horrors, instead of making people shudder, makes them laugh." Only on the Bombay stage these horrors are represented on the stage and not merely reported, as there are no classical canons to guide the *munshi*. In the typical French fashion also, confidants to the principal characters are provided. When one reads of the accusations against Otway's free version of *Romeo and Juliet* that he has made a "fearful hash of the deathless music of the lovers' speeches", one does not know how to condemn the utmost licence taken with the Shakespearean text on the Urdu stage. The fact that most of the finest speeches have been hopelessly garbled may be easily explained by the stark ignorance of the original displayed by almost all the *kavis*, but it can by no means be excused. They aimed at systematic creation of typical rather than of complex characters. They piteously failed to see life whole or a great character composed of mighty opposites. The obvious result of all this is that hardly any Urdu or Gujarati adaptation has any abiding worth.

The Bengali stage, it may be said to its credit, made the most laudable attempt to stage at least two great tragedies on the high English level with European scenery and costume, in literal Bengali versions. This great experiment was foredoomed to failure on the professional stage. If Girish Ghosh had obtained even a moderate success in terms of the box-office, he intended to produce other great Shakespearean dramas on the same scale. The professional theatre being what it is, however, it is difficult to see how a literal translation can succeed. The Marathi stage did wisely and well, for its faithful adaptations made the true Shakespeare familiar to thousands of playgoers and readers. Some further general observations regarding all the adaptations may be made at a later stage. It is convenient to turn here to a consideration of the stage versions of several non-Shakespearean comedies and tragedies.

CHAPTER IX

STAGE-VERSIONS OF NON-SHAKESPEAREAN PLAYS

THE predominant romantic tendency of the ancient Hindu drama received an immense impetus from the Shakespearean adaptations mentioned in the last two chapters. The stage versions of several Sanskrit classics and of Shakespearean comedies and tragedies ran side by side with conspicuous success on the Indian stage for decades. Once the tragic conclusion was accepted and the so-called 'stage-decencies' of the Hindu dramatic canon were violated, an enormous vista of theatrical adventure was opened before the Indian adapters in the nineteenth century. A great amount of English literature began to pour into India both in the educational institutions and outside in public and private libraries. The rapid circulation of cheap fiction and dramatic publications naturally fostered the inherent romantic bias of the nation.

The theatrical managers perceived the great opportunities before them and ransacked all popular sources with the help of their playwrights or *kavis*. In the course of their Shake-spearean productions, they had observed that farcical comedies such as *The Taming of the Shrew* and *The Merry Wives of Windsor* and melodramatic and rhetorical elements of great tragedies such as *Hamlet* could secure long and prosperous runs. They did not care in the least for fine comedy or high tragedy, subtle characterization or the finer essence of the great dramatist. Apart from their imme-diate objective of large commercial gains, their ignorance of English literature, in most cases, was responsible for their general and continual display of all the sensational elements of romance for the applause of unthinking audiences.

Almost all the playwrights rushed eagerly into the newly

opened field and seized whatever they could lay their hands on in the ancient myths, the epics, narrative verses, plays and novels. They had hardly any time to think or to study. Those who could not read the original English turned to any crude vernacular version of a plot or story, for which indeed they cared more than for anything else. In this great rush, the cultured Marathi writers did not fail to notice the growing needs of the reading public as well. The variety of material thus seized on may be gauged by the fact that we find popular dramas based on a Hebrew story (*Jayapāla*), an episode from the *Iliad* (*Minākṣī*), a tale of Spanish history (*Līlāvatī*) and the theme of *William Tell*.

If one turns to the inexhaustible mine of English fiction, it is interesting to observe that whilst the Marathi play-wrights devoted more attention to Sir Walter Scott (particularly *Woodstock* and *The Talisman*) and Marie Corelli (cf. *Thelma* and *The Temporal Power*), the Urdu *kavis* made the utmost use of the materials furnished by the popular novelist of questionable morals, G. Reynolds. Indeed there was no scruple there in seizing with avidity any sensational plot which furnished the opportunity for combining lust, murders, unnatural crimes and sense of mystery with a crowning revelation of an appalling intrigue.[1] If any striking element was wanting it was quickly supplied from some other source. Consequently it is not surprising that certain sensational plays based on stirring episodes from Hutchinson's *History of All Nations* gained huge popularity in Bombay. Similarly romantic and ironic situations, as in *Sohrab and Rustum* or painful separations of lovers and heroic self-sacrifice as in *Enoch Arden* found suitable expression on the Urdu stage. It must be remembered, however, that the tendency to sentimentalism and sensationalism is not confined to one province, for even in Bengal Lytton's *The Last Days of Pompeii* was successfully dramatized.

The English plays and foreign plays in English versions

1. Cf. such plays as *Khāki Putalā* (based on *Sorrows of Satan*).

which suited the requirements of the Indian theatre, were eagerly adapted after most of the Shakespearean comedies and tragedies had been produced in the several vernaculars. Some popular producers, such as Mr. Joseph David Penkar, indeed, mention in their prefaces that it is now high time to 'push forward' other great English dramatists, as the Elizabethan master had got more than his due. Out of the cheap series of English dramas (such as Dick's) many plays are selected and are adapted in part or *in toto* for a particular theatre; but, unfortunately, the actual obligations are seldom acknowledged. If in some cases the debt is mentioned, it is in a loose irresponsible manner as "from an English source", or "from an English play" or "from a popular English novel" and the like. This is due partly to the desire to conceal the fount of inspiration from rival producers. Again, in many cases, the versions are never published, at least in an authorized form. Thus it is rarely that full and frank acknowledgement is made by a conscientious adapter. There are even cases where the original plot is deliberately mangled to escape all detection.

It may be convenient now to select about ten or twelve typical non-Shakespearean comedies or farces and about the same number of non-Shakespearean tragedies or melodramas and to study their stage versions in some detail. Such a study will naturally facilitate a correct perspective of the direct influence of the British drama.

A. COMEDIES

Outside the Shakespearean comedy Molière has exercised the greatest direct and indirect influence on the Indian stage. Reserving the latter influence for a subsequent reference in the next chapter, it may be observed at once that the versions of the plays of the French dramatist are based in almost all cases on their English translations. Secondly, it should not be forgotten that most of these farces have been incorporated in more serious plays or have been acted as after-pieces, although, of course, amateur companies have repeatedly acted them independently. This can easily be explained by the fact that the professional theatres insist on long productions and demand not one but many 'sentiments' in quick succession. Nevertheless, as farcical interludes, several abridged and modified versions of Molière have been unsurpassed, his tendency to caricature tempting the player to overact and to excite uproarious laughter.

Out of the several comedies of Molière adapted into Marathi—*Tartuffe* or *The Impostor, The Mock-Doctor, The Citizen Turned Gentleman, The Miser* and *The Forced Marriage*, it is proposed to deal with the first three, for they are representative of the general mode of treatment.

(1) *Tartuffe* or *The Impostor*² in its excellent Marathi version appeared in a Poona periodical devoted to the cultivation of the vernacular drama. It is done in standard prose, rather too closely. The dialogue is in general a trifle expanded and the short scenes are combined for greater effect. It is interesting to notice that the argument of the piece has a striking effect on the Indian mind on account of many traditional stories of lovers posing as saints or 'impostors' and ultimately eloping with their willing brides (cf. *Subhadrā-Haraṇa*). The 'impostor' recites some appropriate imposing Marathi religious verses and, later on, several rhythmic satires. As the maidservant Dorine has a different status in Hindu society, the prominence given to her appears to the Indian mind just a trifle exaggerated.

(2) *The Mock-Doctor*³ appears in a most successful adaptation by the same eminent Marathi scholar. When every other argument fails, the farcical theatrical device, *Argumentum ad Baculum*, is most convincing to the audience.

2. M. *Dhūrta-vilasita (The Impostor)*. By H. N. Apte, as an Interlude, after 1890.

3. M. *Mārūn Muṭakūn Vaidya Buvā (A Physician in Spite of Himself)*. By H. N. Apte, The Shahu Company and others as an after-piece, Poona, 1890.

This version has been hailed as one of the most popular skits in India, when staged by the celebrated Shahu Company as an after-piece to serious plays. Even to-day it holds an important place in the repertory of the Maharashtra troupe. It is comparatively short and full of farcical characters, situations and witty remarks.

Its huge success on the stage is due mostly to the thorough Indian colour given to it by the genius of the adapter. Taking Molière's situations and the general development of his dialogue, Apte fits them naturally to the requirements of the Indian theatre. The typical Hindu family atmosphere is created by several changes, by a few additional speeches and by a judicious selection of names. The compression of the many short scenes in the original was, of course, necessary. Thus, in Act II, eight scenes are effectively combined. Sganarelle with a bottle on the stage would appear rather revolting to an Indian audience and accordingly his Brahmin prototype is seen with his pipe of strong narcotic (gāñjā) and tobacco. His vulgar behaviour to Jacqueline and the consequent indignation of Lucas have been aptly omitted. Here the nurse is an elderly lady of the family. Instead of the Apothecary, a disciple of 'the learned Doctor' suits Indian customs better, as all medical authorities are supposed to conduct their own schools. Some farcical verses at the end of Act I, an idiotic song given by the Mock-Doctor in II. ii, and an additional farcical song by him at the end prove exceedingly effective. The elopement is about to take place as in the original, but the uncle suddenly dies, leaving Leander a large estate, and everything ends merrily.

(3) The version of *The Citizen Turned Gentleman*[4] opens with a full acknowledgement and an apt quotation from Louis XIV: "Indeed, Molière, you have never yet done anything which has amused me more; and your piece is excellent." The publishers state that this fascinating play

4. M. *Rāva Bahādūra Parvatyā* (named after Mr. Jordan). By H. A. Talchekar, Maharashtra Company, Poona, 1900.

not only fully pleases but also instructs. The masterly preface by the adapter is worthy of careful perusal. He argues that a 'farce' here usually implies vulgarity and sheer buffoonery; but in the West (as a Barrister, he had been in Europe), even a farcical production maintains at least some dignity and decorum. Then he goes on to discuss the causes of the degradation of the Indian stage and advises all concerned to follow the models of certain foreign masters. As a student of French he was especially attracted by Molière. Then a tribute is paid to the genius of the French dramatist and especially to this comedy. "It has been popular throughout Europe, in England alone there being seven adaptations (quoted in the footnote) of this play."

The Marathi version opens in a manner different from that of the original. A servant, while dusting the European furniture in the drawing-room of the Rao Bahadur, mutters to himself: "My master has secured a Government title; but the consequence has been that he is going from bad to worse. He is wasting his time and money in a thousand follies and midnight revels", etc. In the second scene, the clownish hero is discovered at his toilet, with a photograph of an up-to-date English gentleman on his table. His aim is to ape the model in every detail. The comedy starts in right earnest from the arrival of a master-tailor on the scene. Then this free version runs more or less on parallel lines with the original. The interest of the piece is heightened by the problem of widow-remarriage, as Dorimene happens to be here a rich Hindu widow. The Rao Bahadur insists on marrying her, in spite of the fact that his wife is protesting against this height of stupidity. Thus the adaptation is turned into a contemporary Hindu social satire. On the whole, the spirit of the original finds expression in a suitable yet novel form.

When one turns from the profound influence of Molière on the Indian Comedy to that of Ben Jonson, it is not difficult to understand why the latter failed to make so deep a mark there. In the prologue to *Every Man in His Humour*, the author sets his face against all romantic excesses and decides to use only the 'deeds and language' which are actually employed by men. Consequently the reasons which endeared Shakespeare to the Indian mind served to alienate Jonson, with his artificial typical figures embodying the several 'humours'. *Epicœne, Or the Silent Woman*, "a singularly bright comedy in the midst of this darkness," is his only play known to have been adapted into Marathi; but no copy of the version is available.

(4) Restoration Comedy is represented on the Indian stage by the two-act prose Bengali version of Congreve's *The Double Dealers* (1693). Although this comedy has not the rich sparkle of the best of Congreve's work, the pathetic interest of the plot possibly appealed to the playwright, as it would give scope for developing the various *rasas*. On the first night Nrupendra Basu played Maskwell and the actress Niradsundari Lady Touchwood. From a glance at the dramatis personæ it is clear that the characters of Lord and Lady Froth and of Brisk are omitted. This omission clears the way for the playwright, for these persons are not organically related to the plot. Apart from the conventional female companions and singing-girls no new character is added.

The introductory song on 'The Two-headed Serpent' strikes the keynote of the tragi-comedy of intrigue. Act I carries the play to the end of Act IV in the original, where in Lady Touchwood's bedchamber her lord makes a more spectacular entry with a naked sword, Mellefont is completely humiliated and Maskwell exults in his wicked glory. A song on 'the wonderful world' closes the act.

Towards the conclusion of the play in the second act,

5. B. *Dumukho Sāpa* (*The Two-headed Serpent*). By Aparesh Mukherji, Star Theatre, Calcutta, 1920.
(His *The Mourning Bride* was rendered into Marathi but not acted.)

Lady Touchwood is completely baffled by a novel trick, whereby her lord, by means of ventriloquism, poses as Mellefont and takes 'the strumpet' to task. The didactic aim of Congreve expressed in such lines as "Let secret villainy from hence be warn'd" perfectly suits the Indian convention; but the adapter even goes a step beyond this in deference to Hindu ideals. Thus, after Careless condemns "the two double-headed serpents, the faithless friend and the dissolute wife", Lord Touchwood in a sudden fit of renunciation joins the hands of the lovers and settles his whole estate on his nephew. Sir Paul, also being aged and having a young and proud dictatorial wife, wishes to follow in his footsteps; but Lady Plyant is thoroughly converted and promises to obey her lord at every step. It may be noted that in the adaptation she is not vicious but only guilty of excessive pride and vanity. In accordance with the ancient Indian practice, the guilty couple are condemned to be led in procession through the town on a donkey's back. The final philosophical song sums up the moral.

(5) The two most brilliant eighteenth century English writers of Comedy, Goldsmith and Sheridan, are adequately represented on the Indian stage. As *The Good-natured Man* was not acted, although adapted into Marathi, one may proceed to discuss Goldsmith's greater work, *She Stoops to Conquer, or The Mistakes of a Night*[6] (1773). Even an ordinary adaptation of this famous comedy of manners, with a Shakespearean romantic atmosphere, was bound to be successful, whether produced independently or as an interlude. It was often given as a farcical skit after a serious performance. There is also another Marathi adaptation styled *Mistakes Due to Misunderstanding*, staged by the Shahu Company. Again, this farcical comedy was also occasionally exploited to serve as an additional farce—for instance, in an Urdu

6. M. *Ekā Rātricā Ghoṭāḷā* (*The Mistakes of a Night*). By D. N. Nerurkar, as an Interlude, after 1893.

version of *King Lear* (*The White Murder*). Thus in one form or another this comedy proved very popular. The version by Nerurkar is a literal translation with the original English names. This would naturally prove more acceptable to college amateurs and others who can fully appreciate European social manners. In fact the situations are so striking, the plot so skilfully contrived and the character of Tony Lumpkin so charmingly rendered that, as it is, it is capable of rousing hearty laughter.

(6) Even more than Goldsmith, his great successor, Sheridan, has been enormously popular throughout India. *The Rivals* (1775), the ballad-opera *The Duenna* (1775) and *The School for Scandal* (1777) have all been adapted and acted in India, whilst *St. Patrick's Day* was adapted though not produced in Marathi. A Marathi version of the first, it is true, failed on the Poona stage, for the simple reason, mentioned by the learned adapter, Mr. N. C. Kelkar, that the entire idea is altogether foreign to the Indian mind. The other two comedies, however, held the stage for a considerable period. *The Duenna*7 was first adapted into Marathi by V. T. Modak, after his collaboration in the stage version of *Pizarro* had been a most striking commercial success. The farcical ironical situations of this comedy created unbounded merriment in the theatre, as may be judged from the several English and Marathi Press opinions quoted in the first edition.

This prose version omits the "airs" and songs of the original but expands the three acts into five and gives to the play a complete Indian setting. As the Indian audience love longer productions this expansion seemed necessary if the play were to be given independently. After paying a

7. M. (1) *Praṇaya-vivāha* (*Love Marriage*). By V. T. Modak, The Shahunagar Company, Poona, 1902.
   (2) *Varavañcanā* (a musical comedy, *Husband Deceived*). By G. S. Tambe, Rangabodhecchu Company, Bombay, 1925.
   B. *Raṅgīlā* (*The Duenna*). By Janakinath Basu, The Minerva Theatre, Calcutta, 1915.

tribute to the dramatic genius of Sheridan, the adapter makes it clear that he not only wishes to please as much as possible but also to teach worldly wisdom. "Roars of laughter, clever puns, evolution of the *rasa* and masterly construction deserve supreme praise. Here is an Indian reflection of this delightful comedy with several modifications."

A characteristic Indian device starts the play with Lopez dressed as a mendicant singing devotional verses to the accompaniment of a cheap stringed instrument. Similarly, ·Don Antonio comes alone (not with Masqueraders) reciting pious verses. This device of exchanging messages with the beloved admirably suits the Indian theatre, as 'serenading' would look ridiculous. Many exquisite touches from Hindu mythology (cf. the reference to 'Aniruddha and Okhā') help the make-believe. Certain farcical scenes, as of the Duenna dressing and holding an interview with the fool Isaac, are greatly elaborated. Finally, Don Jerome gives a homily on worldly wisdom, as Isaac, reconciled to the inevitable, embraces his elderly blushing bride.

The second Marathi version is operatic and as such more in harmony with the spirit of the original. Unlike the earlier adaptation, again, this follows the original act by act and scene by scene—of course with an Indian background. This play is even to-day popular on the Indian stage with the actor Raghuvira Savakar in the rôle of the heroine. A few stage photographs form an interesting feature of the latest edition of this adaptation wherein 'the young, energetic and educated' actors of the comedy are praised.

The additional charm of the music has helped the production a great deal. It was not considered necessary to expand any scenes, since considerable time was certain to be spent in repeating the favourite songs whenever encored. The beautiful theatrical opening is in consonance with the spirit of the musical setting. The Marathi play of *Śākuntala* is just over. Lopez comes out of the theatre and hears the clock strike four near the house of Don Jerome. He repeats one of the haunting refrains from the musical play just witnessed. On account of the prejudice among the cultured classes against popular theatrical airs, Don Antonio, also in a singing mood in the early morning, is looked upon as a vagabond by the high-browed Jerome. Louisa makes apt musical rejoinders whilst her father is exasperated beyond all words. Most of the ideas are taken from the original songs, airs, duets, trios, etc., but they are freely rendered in the popular Marathi musical mode.

The Bengali prose adaptation in two acts, with a few songs, is styled "a wonderful operatic play". It is faithful in the main to the original, although the plot is greatly simplified towards the close by the omission of Sheridan's III. iv, v and vi, i.e. the Priory scenes in which Father Paul and the Friars are discovered drinking and then helping forward matrimonial relations. There is a change in II. iv (Sheridan's III. vii) when Ferdinand arrives sword in hand and challenges Antonio to a duel. Clare rushes in suddenly with the words: "Why attack your brother-in-law?" Ferdinand, utterly confused, murmurs: "What! You?" and then she garlands him (symbolic of love-marriage). In keeping with the usual Bengali custom, a confidante is provided for Lousia in the opening scene where she sings a love song in the early morning whilst her friends tease her (Lopez being omitted at the start).

(7) The most popular comedy of Sheridan, whose situations have been universally praised "as among the most perfect in the English theatre", *The School for Scandal*,[8] was successfully presented both in Bombay and in Calcutta. The Gujarati version, as the title page states, is "adapted to the Parsi social life". It may be noted here that the Parsis of Bombay have a peculiar genius for adapting English plays to their needs, *Charlie's Aunt* being a notable

8. G. *Nindākhānu* (*The School for Scandal*). By K. N. Kabraji, Victoria Theatrical Company, Bombay, 1895.

    B. *Asal o Nakal* (*Genuine and Imitation*). By Atula Krishna Mitra, The Minerva Theatre, Calcutta, November 22, 1912.

illustration of a huge success on their amateur stage.9
Sheridan's famous comedy is handled with great tact and
beauty. The Parsi characters are the prototypes of the
original, only Mrs. Candour's sister is added and Rowley is
permitted to take a little more active part, as it is he (not
Moses) who leads Mr. Premium to Charles. The Parsis
being among the pioneers in journalism in Bombay and
being often concerned in free social criticism in the Press,
the dialogue between Lady Sneerwell and Snake gains in
point.

The opening gives an exquisite picture of Parsi fashionable
society. There is a marriage festivity at the mansion of
Mrs. Candour's sister. It is late at night. Guests are dining
in batches and departing. In the corner of the stage, taking
advantage of the confusion, Mrs. Sneerwell and Snake are
hatching their plot. The one remarkable departure in the
scandalous discussion which follows is the position of Lady
Sneerwell, who does not cherish any secret passion for Charles
but who strains every nerve to secure his hand for her
daughter Dinā. This suits the Indian convention better.
Another meeting of the School for Scandal is held in the
Victoria Gardens, which again suit the requirements more
than the closet of Lady Sneerwell. Joseph goes out for a walk
with Maria. Just when he kneels in a corner of the garden
to entreat her, Lady Teazle appears on the scene and he in
utter confusion finds all sorts of excuses. II. ii (Sheridan's
III. i), in which Charles is indulging in riotous merriment
with his boon companions, is given a thoroughly modern
Indian colour by the presence of bottles of champagne
(now freely used in fashionable circles) and by an amorous
song by a favourite singing-girl. To avoid the evil of "dice",
the friends retire to the adjoining room for "ice cream".

The two most famous scenes—the Picture scene (IV. i)

9. "This very popular play was also recently staged by the Parsi
Theatrical Company (of the Madan Theatres Ltd.) at the Opera
House, Bombay. The adaptation was *Dilkipyās*, with Master
Mohan in the rôle of the Aunt" (C. R. Shah).

and the thrilling Screen scene (IV. iii)—are beautifully rendered. The place of the "little French milliner" is supplied by a Marathi washing-woman. 'The man of sentiment' is thoroughly exposed as "a guilty thing surprised". The conclusion of the piece is somewhat altered. Here Lady Teazle resigns her membership of the infamous School for Scandal. Sir Oliver indulges in a tirade against the scandal-mongers and Sir Peter drives away Mrs. Candour and others with curses on 'the blots to the fair name of the Parsi community'—"a tableau", as the curtain descends. There is neither prologue nor epilogue, but a few songs are added in the Parsi Gujarati dialect.

The Bengali stage version runs on different lines, as may be judged from the title which indicates the study of the characters of Charles and Joseph, but misses the entire structure of *The School for Scandal*. In fact, there is hardly any scandal in this adaptation, which is concerned with a plain intrigue by Lady Sneerwell and Joseph—for the one wishes to marry Charles for his beauty and the other Maria for her wealth. By way of farcical retribution it is suggested that Joseph should marry Lady Sneerwell! The concluding song hints at the moral of the piece to the effect that "there is no art to find the mind's construction in the face".

(8) Passing on to the adaptations of British plays of the first quarter of the nineteenth century, it may be observed that the conditions of the theatre in India resembled to a great extent those prevailing in England at that time and that the same reasons made W. T. Moncrieff's melodrama *The Jewess*[10] (1835) popular in western India. This 'romantic drama in three acts' is not to be confused with *Ivanhoe*, or *The Jewess*, 'a chivalrous play' of 1820, over the same

10. U. (1) *Karishmaē Qudrat, urfe, Apani yā Parāyi* (*The Wonder of Nature*, or *One's Own or Other's?*). By Munshi Talib, Victoria Company, Bombay, 1913.
(2) *Yāhūdiki Ladki* (*The Jew's Daughter*). By Aga Hashra, Khatau Alfred Company, Bombay, 1918.

signature. The play, which was successfully produced by
two Urdu companies, is indeed very moving, with at least
three powerful scenes: (1) II. ii where at midnight the lovers
meet in the pavilion, with the Jew behind; (2) II. iv, the
Banquet scene where Rachel brings the golden goblet to
her lover and screams, love turning into vengeance; and
(3) III. iv, the last scene when the Cardinal and the Jew are
dealt with. The characters of Prince Leopold and Rachel
are drawn with a masterly hand. The irony of the situation,
the disguises and the mysterious packet lend an exquisite
theatrical charm to the background of the Jewish persecution
by the Romans.

Both the Urdu adaptations were staged with Roman
scenery and costume, with several names changed and with
additional characters and farcical interludes. In the first
version, several Turkish characters are introduced without
any sense of propriety. For the humorous Englishman
Forrester making love to a Jewish and a Roman maid,
the usual type of Urdu farce is substituted. A number of
songs, some 'in the English tune', are sung. An unusual
feature is the use of detailed stage directions based on the
original. Leopold and Eudosia meet more frequently and
the delicacy of their relations in the original is sacrificed.
In all the important scenes, however, the original is fairly
closely followed, Eudosia finally joining the hands of Leopold
and Rachel.

The second adaptation takes many liberties with the
original and is less dignified. In the very first scene Eudosia
is discarded by the prince. In the next scene, a Roman youth
is going to outrage the modesty of 'the Jewess' when Leopold
intervenes in a Jewish disguise. A huge conflagration in the
Jewish locality, from which Rachel is saved by her foster-
father, closes the first act. There is an accident to the carriage
of Eudosia and it is through this and not for the purchase
of jewellery that she visits the house of Eleazer. After this,
the version runs more close to Moncrieff's. Curiously enough,

however, Rachel finally joins the hands of the Prince and Eudosia, herself renouncing the world.

(9) Even more popular were the plays of Lord Lytton. *The Lady of Lyons*[11] (1838), one of the most thrilling romantic dramas of the century, proved also immensely popular in India. Its 'cheap sentimentalism' and 'the introduction of spectacular elements' along with its 'genuine worth' helped to raise it to a huge commercial success. There is a Marathi version (*Mohanā*) extant, but it is not known to have been staged. A Gujarati popular play (*Vīṇā-Velī*) has a distinct echo of Lytton's. The Urdu adaptation, however, proved to be the greatest success. In this three-act version of *Love and Pride*, with the addition of a foolish farce and several songs, a Turkish setting with Moslem characters fits in easily. The celebrated beauty of Smyrna, Pauline, is deemed worthy of only a 'Nabob'. The richest man of the city, Beauseant, is refused and a poor gardener's son, Melnotte, is ushered in. They are hurriedly married. A procession passes on the stage. In the cottage, the passionate lover explains the situation and love at once yields to beauty's pride. Still, the very next day, the disillusioned father reclaims his daughter. After two years Melnotte returns as the general of the royal forces and everything ends quite simply as in the original, for the Moslem religion permits divorce and remarriage. In the novel farce, also, there is a parallel plot of disguise and deceit. All the finest elements of Lytton are, however, absent.

In the preface to the Bengali version, however, the adapter dwells on the central point of interest, the psychological conflict in the mind of Pauline. The new Indian society after the British contact is selected for the background. Three new characters have been added, viz. Beauseant's wife, a

11. U. *Dhūpa-Chāṁva (Sunlight and Shade)*. By Munshi Muradali, New Parsi Victoria Company, Bombay.
  B. *Śubha Dṛṣti (The Benign Look)*. By Aparesh Mukherji, The Minerva Theatre, Calcutta, December 6, 1915.

high priest and a procurer. The characters of Damas, Beauseant and Glavis (who happens to be a dissolute elder brother of Beauseant) are considerably modified. The widow takes a more prominent part in the play. Only Monsieur and Lady Deschappelles remain exactly as in the original. It is interesting to notice that many English expressions are freely used throughout. The play opens with Beauseant's outburst: "Nonsense! My wife? Who is my wife?" He discards his first wife Śāradā and runs after Pauline, who considers him unworthy of her hand.

Inspired by the photo of his beloved, Melnotte wins a cup in an English game. When he is rejected by Pauline he exclaims in the manner of Shylock: "Has a poor youth no soul?" etc. He is hailed as 'Prince Viśvanātha' and experiences the same inward conflict. But his dialogue after his civil marriage is somewhat in a different key, for he makes a bolder appeal to the proud beauty. The civil marriage certificate is returned, for no religious ceremony had taken place. The character of Śāradā, however, brings about a complete change in Pauline's life. She, a banished wife, stands as the incarnation of fidelity to her lord. Finally, she is reconciled to her erring lord Beauseant and her 'benign look' showers blessings on the happy Melnotte and Pauline.

(10) Lord Lytton's *Richelieu, or The Conspiracy*[12] (1839), was also successfully produced on the Marathi stage. The adapter, Mr. Kelkar, himself an eminent man of letters and a distinguished politician, seized the essentials of the original and perceived a close parallel between Richelieu and Mādhavācārya, the great ascetic, statesman and patriot of southern India. Vijayanagar preserved its independence for centuries against the Moslem invaders from the north. Lord Lytton's masterpiece with its powerful characterization of the Cardinal who was wedded to France and had a soft

12. M. *Amātya Mādhava (Minister Mādhava).* By N. C. Kelkar, Chittakarshaka Company, Bombay, January 1914.

corner in his heart for the beautiful orphan Julie is worthily represented on the Marathi stage by this model adaptation. The atmosphere from start to finish is genuinely Indian. No extra farce or song is added; only a few situations are partially developed for humorous purposes.

The weak king of the south (Louis XIII) is old. He has an intriguing foolish brother-in-law (Orleans) and a dissolute favourite (Baradas). To this crew of conspirators is added the young queen who plays into their hands. The conspiracy develops on parallel lines, but the Hindu ideals (from the tradition of Cāṇakya) and manners and customs are so ably preserved that one seldom feels that it is an adaptation at all. Lord Lytton's best scenes are carefully retained. Nothing important is sacrificed. Marion is raised to a higher level and marries François. Mauprat not only secures the hand of Julie but is also crowned, as the old king retires from the world, along with the Hindu Richelieu, after the motherland is saved from the foreign yoke.

(11) *The Silver King*[13] (1882) of H. A. Jones, written in collaboration with H. Herman and hailed by William Archer as "quite the best of modern English melodramas", which held the stage for forty years and which was acted thousands of times in many countries of Europe and America, was also a huge commercial success in the west of India. It "was constructed for that type of inner and outer stage which had been inherited from the theatre of the Restoration". Thus, these fifteen to seventeen scenes, shallow scenes alternating with deep scenes, suited the Indian conditions perfectly. The rapid onrush of the action, producing resounding theatrical effects in quick succession, and the stock characters, especially the dark villains and a long-suffering chaste heroine, fascinated the Indian play-

13. U. *The Silver King.* Anonymous, produced by Bandman Company, Gaiety Theatre, Bombay, 1907.
  G. *Pākzād Perin (The Chaste Perin,* named after Nellie Denver). By R. R. Sethna, Balliwala Company, Bombay, 1919.

goers. Despite this ideal suitability in almost every detail it is characteristic of the Urdu mode of adaptation that only the outline of the main plot is taken, whilst the dialogue is radically altered.

Moreover, even in this melodrama, a farcical element is added by the exploits of a briefless pleader whose advice is sought by the murderer Cripps (not 'the Spider'). Corkett and Leaker are removed to make room for the farce and the songs. The play opens at a gambling house (no 'Derby' being mentioned), when Denver loses everything. After Nellie and Jaikes return disappointed, the hero indulges in a long speech on the evils of gambling. Curiously enough, all the criminals are in love with the heroine. There is more of sentimental parting, for Cissy makes very tender appeals to her father. In the place of Detective Baxter, the 'Spider' happens to be also a police officer and makes a fanatical appeal to Nellie to yield to his desires. She, of course, refuses and protests in song. Here, at the end of Act I, 'the Spider' is thrown down by Jaikes. Nellie gags him, Cissy holds his hair and the criminal is revealed in utter helplessness, a tableau thus being formed.

In the last two acts the 'railway station' and 'the country inn' are both omitted. Only Denver is seen (after an interval of three years) soliloquising over his adventures and fabulous wealth. The interest is rather concentrated on the poverty, misery and chastity of the heroine. Instead of the quarrel over the booty at the wharf, the kidnapped Nellie is brought for immoral purposes and the little Cissy is threatened with death. Here Coombe interposes, discloses the mystery of the murder of Ware and 'the Mute' goes into raptures. A whistle is blown and the police arrive. The identity of the Silver King is carefully concealed till the very end and the play ends in merriment, drinking and 'an English dance by girls'.

The Parsi Gujarati version of this melodrama follows the Urdu version also with additional farcical scenes but treated in a more decorous manner. The adapter makes a confession in his preface. After quoting Sir Henry Irving and Beerbohm Tree on dramatic art, he mentions how he fell deeply in love with *The Silver King* after witnessing the Urdu version. But he says that he had no patience to wait till the original play was received from England and therefore he decided to follow the Urdu adaptation generally, although it must be said to his credit that the plot is fairly well adapted to the conditions of Parsi social life. At the start advantage is taken of the Parsi club life on the European model and Ware is depicted as an honourable gentleman. Great emphasis is laid on Nellie's constancy and on Jaikes's fidelity. The characters are the same as in the Urdu version.

(12) Finally, as a typical 'adaptation of an English play' one may select a Marathi production which in its prose version and with an addition of songs has held the stage from 1903, even to-day being in the repertory of several companies. This play,[14] as the scholar H. N. Apte noted in a foreword in 1916, does not depict the 'green-eyed monster' jealousy of *Othello* or even of *The Winter's Tale*. Here is a perfectly enjoyable comedy on the folly of unnecessary suspicion. In the manner of a typical character of Ben Jonson or Molière, the hero Phālgunarāva has the 'humour' of suspecting his sharp-tongued but innocent wife Kṛtikā. Their shrewd servant, Bhādavyā, warns his master from the start; but the latter is obdurate. The complication begins with the amorous intrigue between a rich youth, Āśvinaśeṭha, and a dancing-girl, Revatī. He gives her his photograph. Revatī, returning from a temple, faints and Phālgunarāva, in search of a clue regarding his wife's conduct, does her gentle services. This is observed by Kṛtikā from her window. So now she suspects her husband in turn and picks up the photograph of Āśvinaśeṭha, which is later detected by her husband, and so the fire is fanned. With this photograph

14. M. *Saṁśaya-Kallol* (a comedy on unfounded jealousy). By
   G. B. Dewal, Poona, 1903.

Phālgunarāva ultimately traces Āśvinaśeṭha, who on perceiving the photograph, begins to doubt the honesty of his beloved dancing-girl; and thus the confusion develops to a climax, after novel constructions are put on the harmless letters and subtle utterances between the two parties. Finally, of course, everything comes right. The interest here centres on the most perfectly interwoven threads of the plot. Looking over many plays in the "Dicks' Standard Plays Series", one discovers that this is a very happy and a fairly close adaptation of Arthur Murphy's *All in the Wrong*.

*　　*　　*

From the above notice of the several adaptations of Molière, Congreve, Goldsmith, Sheridan and the melodramatic productions of the nineteenth century, it is clear that, in the realm of Comedy, whatever is bordering on the farcical has often fascinated the Indian theatre. Characterization has seldom been a strong point with the Indian adapters, the thrills of melodrama proving the principal source of attraction. To add to these thrills all the situations and incidents of the original have in general been exploited to the fullest extent. The Marathi stage, true to its cultural traditions, has mostly maintained a fairly high level in its adaptations, as has also been noticed in its treatment of Shakespeare. The deep native love of music has to be gratified and consequently the addition of songs has been welcomed by playgoers. The Bengali theatre employs a smaller number but these are more significant. The Urdu playwright is usually concerned only with the outline of the original thrilling sensational plot and likes to add a novel farce even to a comedy.

B. TRAGEDIES

It is indeed surprising that in non-Shakespearean tragedy, Marlowe, whose one dominant passion, rant and bustle should have fitted the Urdu stage admirably, failed to attract the attention of the Indian playwrights. One wonders why the heroic struggle of his chief characters against over-whelming forces was not turned to useful account in the Indian theatre. Perhaps it was lack of feminine interest or of humour in him, but both could have been easily supplied by some resourceful adapters. One may suppose that it was partly due to ignorance and partly due to the accident that no stage-manager chanced to come across a copy of Marlowe. Among the Elizabethan dramatists who directly influenced the Indian stage are Beaumont and Fletcher, Massinger and Shirley, the choice of whose typical plays is not difficult to understand.

(1) A popular Urdu play[15] is stated to be adapted "with modifications from an English drama by Beaumont and Fletcher". The plot, however, seems to be so mutilated that hardly any exact parallel situation can be traced to the original. This tragi-comedy is of the usual blood-horror type, without any of the great relieving features of the Elizabethans.[16]

(2) The plot of *The Virgin Martyr*,[17] written in collabora-tion by Massinger and Dekker, abounding in torture, death and the patient sufferings of the saint, Dorothea, was turned into a musical tragi-comedy in three acts on the Urdu stage. An altogether new Moslem setting is given to this popular version. In the good old days, the Phœnicians at Tyre wor-shipped Osiris and other idols. The ship-wrecked Dorothea, her Angelo and a party of rich merchants are discovered at the port in the first scene. The general, Antoninus, is

15. U. *Zanjirē Gauhar* (*A Chain of Pearls*). By Abbas Ali, Victoria Company, Bombay, 1908.

16. The Urdu *kavi*, who never read the original and borrowed incidents from many sources, has mangled this loose version beyond recognition. Hints seem to have been taken from *The Maid's Tragedy* and *Thierry and Theodoret*.

17. U. *Hurē-Arab* (*The Arabian Damsel*). By Munshi M. Najan, Parsi Imperial Company, Bombay, 1913.

asked to subdue the foreigners. He falls in love with the
pious virgin at first sight. In the next scene, in the full
Court, in the presence of the arch-priest of Osiris, Theophilus,
the Emperor asks Princess Artemia to choose a bridegroom
for herself; but Antoninus refuses her offer. In the favourite
prison scene, the daughters of Theophilus are themselves
converted; but when threatened, they ultimately commit
suicide and are not killed by the bloodthirsty father. The
virgin saint is accused of being 'a sorceress'.

In the third act, the principal departures are noteworthy.
The arch-priest insists on executing the virgin in accordance
with an old law that those foreigners who refuse to worship
the idol of Osiris ought to be hanged; but as Theophilus
himself goes to kill her, he sees the ghosts of his daughters
and she is saved. This miracle converts Artemia herself.
Even the Emperor begins to lose his faith in the old religion.
Finally the priest accepts the challenge of confining the
virgin for twelve hours in a lions' den; and if she is untouched
he himself should undergo the terrible ordeal. The prosaic
reason is given that the lions spared her because they had
already been fed. In any case, Theophilus is sacrificed.
The virgin saint is appointed chief priestess and Artemia
marries Antoninus—a very simple arrangement indeed.
Regarding the farce, there is not much to choose
between the vulgar humours of Hircius and Spungius
on the one hand and of 'an effeminate nabob' on the
other.

(3) The "story of wild and criminal ambition centring
round Lorenzo" and ending with "a heap of tragedies", *The
Traitor*[18] (1631) of Shirley was skilfully adapted for the
Marathi stage. The special appeal of this tragedy to the
Hindu is the opportunity given here of dealing with the
disinterested love between brother and sister. Accordingly,
this version is styled *My Sister* and is dedicated to the

18. M. *Mājhī Bahīṇa* (*My Sister*). By Kirat, The Shahunagar
Company, Poona.

Hindu sisters whose traditional ideal is to follow in the footsteps of Amidea, Sciarrha's sister. In a short preface the playwright makes it clear that the play was first composed on the basis of *The Traitor*; but afterwards a few changes were made on the lines of its stage version, *Evadne*, or *The Statue* (1819), by R. Sheil. Possibly the actual title was suggested by the picture over the words 'Ha, My sister!' in Dicks' Standard Plays Series.

The Marathi version is a tragedy in five acts as in Shirley and not a tragi-comedy as in Sheil. Instead of Pisanio and Cosmo in the first scene, one sees Amidea and her confidante, a new character, talking. Amidea's situation follows the lines of the nineteenth-century adaptation. Pisanio's mind is poisoned by Lorenzo by means of the picture; but there is no dark agent like Sheil's Olivia. The traitor Lorenzo is aiming not only at the crown but also at the hand of Amidea, as in the later version. Again, as in Sheil, Amidea goes near the statue of her father (although the other statues are not mentioned), and entreats the king to spare her; but, as he persists in his vile demand, she wounds herself as in Shirley.

The humorous relief is supplied by developing the folly of Depazzi. A novel interest is added by the character of Rogero, who has a distinguished past and acts as a spy of the banished nobleman. Depazzi's sister, a widow, is chaste and refuses to yield to her foolish brother's advice to frequent the Court for his advancement. The masque, being out of harmony with the Hindu dramatic tradition, is rightly omitted. As the marriage procession of Pisanio passes by the house of Sciarrha, on its way to Oriana's palace, the enraged brother is no longer able to control himself and kills Pisanio. Florio does not disappear as in Sheil. The most powerful scene in which the brother finally kills his sister is admirably adapted; and so also the last painful scene is fairly closely followed.

(4) The early eighteenth century pseudo-classical tragedy

is seen represented on the Indian stage by Addison's *Cato*[19] (1714), which was selected for its intrinsic merits rather than on account of political prejudice. A Bengali version of the tragedy is also extant, but is not known to have been produced. At the beginning of the Marathi adaptation, a few appreciative extracts on *Cato* are quoted from Dr. Johnson, J. Hughes and Pope. A typical situation is selected from medieval India. For the Stoic republican Cato, Rāmadevarāva King of Devagiri (in south India), defying the great Emperor Allaudin, is substituted. He is one of the many Hindu kings who sacrificed themselves at the altar of their country and religion, although he is, no doubt, less intellectual than Cato. The place of Lucius and Sempronius, a contrast in characters, is furnished by two opposite types of the Hindu King's ministers.

Once this fundamental change is accepted, everything else fits in as desired by the adapter, for the glory of Hinduism and Independence supply the place of the Roman republican's sentiments, and love and sacrifice were the keynotes of Rajput chivalry no less than of the Roman character. On the lines of this novel framework, the original is faithfully followed, scene by scene, almost line by line. This extreme fidelity is perhaps responsible for a certain ring of artificiality. The prologue, the epilogue and the last speech being omitted, the Hindu ideal of absolution is held up at the end and a didactic touch crowns the piece.

(5) The romantic spectacular tragedy, Sheridan's *Pizarro*[20]

19. M. *Rāmadevarāva* (named after the hero). By S. M. Paranjpye, The Shahu Company, Poona, 1906.
20. M. (1) *Rāṇā Bhīmadeva* (named after Rolla). By V. R. Shiravalkar and V. T. Modak, The Shahunagar Company, Poona, 1890.
 *(2) *Āsurīlālasā* (*Devilish Ambition*). By Patwardhan, Aryasuboth Company, Poona, March 1, 1922.
 U. *Asīre-hirsa* (*The Slave of Ambition*). By Aga Hashra, The Parsi Company, Bombay, 1900.
 G. *Zālamjor* (*The Tyrant's Prowess*). By A. J. Khori, The Zorostrian Company, Bombay, 1876.

(1799), in which Kemble originally played Rolla and Mrs. Siddons, Elvira, and which proved an immense success on the English stage, has left a profound impression in the Indian theatre. This ingenious English adaptation of the original German play of Kotzebue has been hailed as a great commercial success on the Marathi, Urdu and Gujarati stages. With the possible exception of *Hamlet,* no other adaptation of a European drama has so fascinated playgoers. The preface to the Marathi version of *Rāṇā Bhīmadeva* states that "from 1890 to 1917, the play has been a unique success on the Marathi stage, as acted at Bombay, Poona, Satara, Baroda, Nagpur, etc.". The Urdu version made the fortune of the Parsi Company on the occasion of the Delhi Durbar of 1901. Although, in a continuous run, the prices were doubled, thousands had to be turned away.

The collaborators of the earlier popular Marathi version (the later is not available), however, do not take the trouble to acknowledge their obvious debt. After assimilating the spirit of the original, they fitted it admirably to their own stage conditions. In the course of their six-act prose version they pitched the first two acts and the last scene altogether in a different key. The most striking feature of this free version is that it is turned into a tragi-comedy with Rolla as the hero of the piece. The Hindu Elvira is depicted as a fair Rajput princess, Pizarro's prisoner of war (and not his mistress), destined to be finally rescued and married by the heroic and virtuous Rolla, who does not cherish any deep, secret passion for Cora but is simply misunderstood by her.

Full advantage being taken of the medieval Rajput chivalry, the situation is amply made clear in the first two acts. The Hindu Rolla happens to be a tributary chief of the Rajput king Ataliba. The Princess is taken prisoner by the Moslem antagonist, Pizarro, who is enamoured of her. She would prefer death to such a misalliance with Islam. Rolla and Alonzo, two towers of Rajput chivalry, make heroic efforts to save the Hindu kingdom. The latter deserted his former patron at the higher call of patriotism and humanity and this accounts for Pizarro's grudge against him. From the third act (Sheridan's second) there is an exact imitation of the original. The famous dungeon scene, with the touching interviews between Rolla and the sentinel and between Alonzo and Rolla, is exactly reproduced in powerful Marathi. Here, in the enemy's tent, Rolla and Elvira fall in love with each other.

A characteristic happy but artificial conclusion is provided in the last scene where the wounded Pizarro accepts the sovereignty of Ataliba and Rolla, who is not mortally wounded, marries Elvira, the sole heir to the crown. The curtain slowly descends as the Court bard recites heroic verses to the glory of the victorious king, 'defender of the Hindu faith', etc. The grandeur of Pizarro's character in the original disappears and the venerable Lascasas finds but a poor echo.

As the third Marathi version, a literal translation with European names, could not be produced, one may pass on to the popular Urdu adaptation. Although this is also turned into a tragi-comedy, it is on an inferior plane compared to the Marathi version. An additional farce is developed at the expense of two of Pizarro's guards, one of them making love unwittingly to his would-be daughter-in-law. At the start, Elvira is discovered in full splendour in the company of her female friends. Then to her great horror, she receives a bloody head of an old man (Orozembo) as a birthday present from Pizarro. Every spectacular device is not only seized on with avidity but is exaggerated. Thus, at the end of Act II, as Rolla heroically crosses the bridge with Cora's child, there is thunder, rain and lightning and the bridge crashes, with a picture of Pizarro's stupefied soldiers forming a sensational tableau.

In the last act, the mad Cora is seen marching with torches in both hands and believing her husband to be a ghost, and so on. The concluding scene, of course, is the most original. Pizarro, stupefied by the vision of Elvira at a critical moment, is on the point of committing suicide when his elder brother, Alonzo, stays him and the converted brother then offers the crown to Alonzo! Rolla is suitably rewarded; but the delicate relations between the two friends are twisted into those of King Alonzo and his general, Rolla.

Two Gujarati plays (*Satī Padminī* and *Vijaya-Kamalā*) show in their own way the influence of *Pizarro*. The version, however, which deserves attention is a Parsi adaptation and is older than the Marathi play discussed. The playwright simply describes it at the start as "from an English play with certain modifications". In the place of Spain and Peru, Turkey and India are substituted. The principal change is effected by a new character, Giraftār, Pizarro's noble sister, who passes as a near relative in male disguise. It is she who secretly helps Rolla at every critical moment, secures the release of the condemned Elvira and finally saves the life of her brother, by invoking mercy. She is, of course, married to her lover, Rolla, at the end. Another complication is developed by Pizarro's passion for Cora. Two foolish soldiers, one of the invading and the other of the Indian army, furnish fanciful material for an additional farce. Chorus girls sing songs in the palace to English tunes (e.g. one "in the tune of 'O sing we now right merrily'".) The last song sums up the argument of this tragi-comedy.

(6) Turning from this romantic melodrama to the high tragedy of Schiller, it is interesting to observe that his first great drama, *The Robbers*[21] (translated into English 1792), made a mark on the Marathi stage. This popular version, turned into a prose tragi-comedy in five acts, held the stage for more than three years. The scholar Paranjpye, who also adapted *Cato*, quotes, at the start, Schiller's own view of "a monster produced by the unnatural union of genius with thraldom", as well as various judgments by

21. M. *Bhīmarāva* (named after the hero, Charles). By S. M. Paranjpye, The Shahu Company, Poona, 1907.

Carlyle and others. Except for the usual concession to the taste of Indian playgoers at the end, the adapter follows the original closely, after making a few changes necessary to provide a medieval background. Basing his adaptation on the English translation in Bohn's edition, the playwright occasionally makes good use of the footnotes which indicate certain remarkable changes made in the German stage version.

The Indian background of outlaws or 'robbers' suited the purpose of the adapter. Even after the coming of the British many celebrated outlaws had been often praised for their deeds of chivalry and heroism. For Count Von Moor a mighty Indian landlord is substituted. Amelia could not be a near relation among high caste Hindus. Consequently, she is a ward in the chief's castle. All characters find their exact Indian prototypes. The family intrigue with the double object of securing the entire estate and of winning the hand of the heroine is as natural in India as in Germany. Despite the fact that some of the long speeches have been curtailed, the impression is created in the minds of the readers that often the adapter follows the original rather too literally and mechanically.

The last act is noteworthy. As in the acting German version, Francis attempts to throw himself into the fire, but is prevented by the robbers and taken alive. Schweitzer does not blow his brains out. In the course of the dialogue between Charles and the Old Moor (cut short) the father recognizes his son Charles and entreats him to forgive Francis who is thrown into the same dungeon. Charles and Amelia embrace lovingly and forgive the repentant Francis, who has experienced sudden conversion. Thus everything ends happily, with Charles drawing a moral for common action, not as 'robbers' against their own countrymen, but against the yoke of foreigners (Moslem tyrants). 'Emancipation of the motherland' resounds in the air as the curtain is lowered.

(7) Schiller's *William Tell* was translated into Marathi

but not staged; but the Marathi adaptation of his *Mary Stuart*[22] (translated into English, 1800) continued to be acted for some time. A very popular Urdu production, styled *The Lost Traveller*, was based on the life story of Mary Queen of Scots; but it has hardly anything to do with Schiller's masterpiece. In this Urdu play, Mary's amours with Bothwell are exhibited, Darnley's murder enacted, the Queen tried before Elizabeth and executed at the hands of the Duke of Norfolk. Turning to the genuine Marathi adaptation of the great tragedy, one finds that the spirit of reverence for the original is striking. A short account of the unfortunate Mary is given at the start. Then a glowing tribute is paid to Schiller, "the Æschylus of Germany". The adapter seems to have been at some pains to render the historical atmosphere exactly, although as the play was intended to be a stage version, Dixit had to give the necessary Indian colour to the story. The aim is to present two studies of feminine types in Elizabeth and Mary.

Two important changes were effected at once. The religious feud between the Catholics and the Protestants was dropped. Again, the suggested matrimonial alliance with France is discarded, and consequently, the French Ambassador and the Envoy do not appear. One new interesting character was added. This was Tanlon who, acting as a spy, found easy access to the Queen, took many liberties and overheard all that was necessary in the guise of the Court fool (as in Shakespeare's plays). He was killed by Shrewsbury when he attempted to murder the Queen. The love relations between Mortimer, who is favoured by the banished uncle of Mary, and the fair prisoner are even more romantic on the Marathi stage.

In the last act, the confession before Melvil being omitted, Mary is not fully cleared from the Babington plot. After disclosing her will and addressing her faithful servants, she

22. M. *Mahāmāyā* (named after Elizabeth, 'the Illusive Lady'). By K. H. Dixit.

says a simple prayer and resolutely ascends the steps of the scaffold. Then follows Leicester's outburst. Finally Elizabeth experiences a sense of utter loneliness as she utters the additional last words: "Alas! Have all now left me thus alone!" It is certainly true that the finer essence of the original was bound to be crushed, as the Indian prototypes could not inspire the same warmth, colour and beauty as the original characters.

(8) One more example may now be taken of romantic melodrama, not from a German source this time but from a French: "A most exciting play in which every speech, every word tells with tremendous force", *The Tower of Nesle*[23] by Alexander Dumas, *père*. From an English version (in Gowan's International Library) the sensational plot involving murders, incest, mystery and the like, caught the imagination of the Urdu producer. This romantic play 'in five acts and nine tableaux' could hardly fail on the Urdu stage. The didactic motto printed at the start is "Sin is sure to out in the end", and this is exemplified by the concrete story of Marguerite, Queen of Egypt.

The play has a novel opening. The banished Buridan conceals himself in a vault in Egypt and meditates revenge on his former mistress and present queen. Gaultier d'Aulnay is the general of the army. The Queen unwittingly makes love to her son, but he rejects her. It is from I. iv that the original outline is fairly closely followed. All the three wicked sisters are fully unmasked in the act of their diabolical crimes—a departure from the original. Thus, at the end of Act I, Buridan is seen below on the river; Philip, after his crime of incest, takes a rifle from Landry and shoots the two sisters, whilst Marguerite kills her son! Then Gaultier is bent on revenge for his poor brother. A novel interest is added by the presence of a princess of Egypt, the heir to the crown. Louis X here plays a more important

23. U. *Khûnē Jigar* (*The Heart's Blood*). By Munshi Maheshar, New Parsi Dramatic Company, Bombay, 1911.

rôle. Returning from travel he is ushered incognito into the presence of the Queen by her bawd. In a terrific fight which follows, all the important characters die except Gaultier, who marries the Princess, and Landry, who is appointed chief minister for his good deeds. A novel sensational farce of a doctor's daughters in love with their compounders, etc., and the usual songs are the common Urdu features of this tragi-comedy.

(9) A great French tragedy is, however, not unrepresented on the Indian stage, for Victor Hugo's *Hernani*[24] (1830) was produced in the Marathi theatre. It is indeed a heart-rending love story, the argument of which is beautifully summed up by Don Ricardo:

"Three gallants, one a bandit, his head due unto the scaffold; then a Duke, a King, adoring the same woman, all laid siege at the same time. The onset made—who won? It was the bandit."

The charm of powerful romantic poetry is everywhere present in the original, and the learned adapter tries his best to transfer this spirit to his standard Marathi prose.

The Indian playwright approaches Hugo with respect and affection, and, keeping as close as possible to the original, tries to adapt it to the world of medieval Indian chivalry with its passionate love and self-sacrifice, ancient feuds and heroic adventures. As in *The Robbers* this background easily adjusts itself to the story. As Don Ruy cannot marry his niece in the Indian version, he is made the elderly son of Dona Sol's maternal uncle. The principal change occurs in Act IV, where for "The Tomb, Aix-la-Chapelle, the vaults, which enclose the tomb of Charlemagne", very aptly, "a deserted garden at the end of the Hindu capital, an ancient dilapidated temple of the god Śiva and the Karālā Devī, an arch of triumph of Vikrama with an ancient inscription, an old underground passage", are substituted. A genuine

24. M. *Jayadhvaja* or *Asūyāgniśamana* (*The Extinction of the Fire of Jealousy*). By H. N. Apte, Shahu, Maharashtra and other Companies, Poona, 1911.

Hindu colour is given to the marriage celebration at the end, a rich scarf being supplied in the place of 'the Golden Fleece'. On the whole it is an excellent version in which full justice is done to the successive thrilling situations and also to the wonderful magnanimity of Don Carlos and to the tragical conflict in the souls of Hernani and his most faithful beloved.

(10) Approaching the modern period in the European drama, one may glance at a Bengali representation of Ibsen's *The Warriors of Helgeland*[25] (1857), one of the most powerful tragedies in all literature. Two Bengali versions of this are extant; but the earlier adaptation (*Vīra-Vikrama*) of 1915 is not known to have been staged. It is all in prose, without the aid of any songs. The later adaptation is described as "based on a play of the world-famous Ibsen"; but the exact piece is not mentioned. As usual, the glory and the chivalry of the Rajputs are selected as a convenient background. The scene is laid in Gujarat; and the action covers thirty-six hours till the full-moon night. The action is divided into three acts, the last with two scenes, thus keeping pace with the original four acts.

Only one new character is added—that of a Court bard who serves the purpose of a chorus and utters philosophical maxims. The funeral song by Ornulf which relieves his over-fraught heart is omitted; but a few suggestive songs are given, generally between acts. The least possible liberty is taken with the text. Degny also dies by the side of her husband, Ornulf and Gunnar being the only survivors of the tragedy. The concluding passage uttered in the presence of the bard is significant and not only admirably points to the two forms of the Hindu goddess but suggests the two characters, poles apart, of Degny and Hjordis, one the emblem of peace, beauty and grace, the other representing war, heroism and blind fury.

25. B. *Rākhī Bandhana* (*Tying the Sacred Knot*). By Aparesh Mukherji, The Star Theatre, Calcutta, 1921.

The long stage directions are mostly followed in great detail. The prose version gives place to Bengali blank verse when a character like Hjordis is inspired in her speech. The significance of the title is explained in the last act when she says, while darting her arrow at her true lover, that at one time when he killed the angry lion (not the 'white bear') she tied a sacred thread round him but it proved futile; but the blood-union which she is establishing now will certainly unite them for ever in heaven.

*　*　*

From the above notices of several tragedies it would appear that the Marathi stage once more leads in the field of genuine tragedy. In the first place the selection of such great plays as *The Robbers*, *Mary Stuart* and *Hernani* and the reverential approach with a view to production would do credit to any stage. Secondly there is no craze for the so-called artificial 'happy' ending as in the Urdu theatre. Thirdly, the Marathi adaptations are seldom divorced from literary qualities, as some gifted men of letters evinced an unusual affection for the dramatic form. It is true, however, that the more popular professional productions frequently show no interest in the inward struggle of such characters as Charles Von Moor, Mary Stuart, Don Roy de Silver and Ornulf, but concentrate more on the melodramatic elements of such plays as *Pizarro* for their commercial success. Nevertheless, it must be remembered that all that is best in Sheridan is better preserved in the Marathi version than elsewhere. Although *Richelieu* is not a tragedy, it maintains a wonderful tone of high seriousness throughout, and for its perfect adaptation one again turns to the gifted Marathi scholar. It is radiant with life and vitality on account of its being based on a brilliant chapter of genuine Indian history.

The Tower of Nesle, on the other hand, represents the type of popular tragedy in the Urdu theatre. Lust, murders, diabolical or unnatural crimes and a sense of mystery preserved to the last and such other elements appeal more to the playgoers of a different type. An Urdu playwright seldom cares for the spirit of the original. He is simply bent on the piling on of horror in a rhetorical style. Some of these adaptations are indeed clever, for they astutely seize on all the theatrical situations, incidents and farcical caricatures likely to make an appeal. Unfortunately, blood, revenge and horror are still taken to be the chief elements of tragedy. Even then, towards the conclusion, by the easy process of sudden conversions, wicked characters reform themselves and somehow things come out right. Again, the didactic aim is over-emphasized although the general atmosphere of the play is seldom healthy.

The Bengali stage, as in relation to Shakespeare, does not pay much attention to direct borrowings from foreign sources. Still it is true that one of Ibsen's great tragedies was produced at Calcutta. In fact, the genius of the great Bengali dramatists lies in a different direction, as one can easily perceive by turning from the direct influence to the indirect, subtle and more lasting influence of the British drama on the Indian theatre.

CHAPTER X

THE GENERAL INFLUENCE OF BRITISH DRAMA

It was while witnessing an amateur production of a Gujarati version of Dvijendralal Ray's *Sāhjāhān* that the profound Shakespearean influence, working subtly on the minds of the Bengali dramatists, was first truly appreciated by the present writer. The story of this play tells how the once mighty Moghul emperor, now old, weak, imprisoned, and with his mind hovering on the borders of lunacy, on account of the rank ingratitude of his tyrannical son, Aurungzeb, gives his "blessings" to his devoted daughter: "May you never, never beget children!" The raving utterances of the Indian sovereign are distinctly reminiscent of the furious denunciations of King Lear. It is indeed true that the situation is different from the one in which the English king hurls his curses on Goneril; indeed, the actual spirit of the scene is more like that of the 'Nunnery scene' in *Hamlet* in which the disillusioned prince admonishes Ophelia: "Get thee to a nunnery. Why wouldst thou be a breeder of sinners?" Thus, in all probability, when he wrote his scene the subtle influence of both these great tragedies was working subconsciously in the mind of the Bengali dramatist. This may serve as a typical instance, representative of a host of echoes heard from foreign models.

Here it is necessary to emphasize that this kind of foreign influence is altogether different from that which resulted in the adaptations of British plays discussed in the earlier chapters. Most of the best modern Indian dramatists are deeply read not only in the Sanskrit classics but also in the European masterpieces, the quintessence of which is assimilated by a constant process of reading, thinking and digesting. Naturally, therefore, in many original productions on the Indian stage, without any actual reference to foreign models, certain traits are revealed which may be traced back to these sources. However, it must be remembered that such an influence runs a curious, zigzag, subterranean course. On account of the subtle psychological process, it is often impossible to tell what has been consciously and what subconsciously introduced.

This deeper influence becomes noticeable only at a comparatively late stage. At the beginning of the Indian Renaissance there was enthusiasm and worship of ancient and foreign models, which led first to thoughtless imitations. Then literal translations and adaptations to Indian stage conditions followed. Then, in due course, original plays were produced which owed a certain obvious debt both to Sanskrit and to English masterpieces. It is extremely difficult to sift the native elements from the foreign ones for two reasons. Firstly, a talented playwright assimilates both so wonderfully that it is sometimes only by a vague echo that the original can be traced; and secondly, the inherent affinity between the Indian and Elizabethan romantic drama makes it a delicate problem to distinguish the one trait from the other. It often happens, indeed, that the traditional asset gains much in beauty and strength from a foreign source, as will be illustrated later on.

Before trying to examine this vast, varied and complicated field of the subtle foreign influence on the Indian stage, it is proposed to review the several modes of contact established between some of the best Indian playwrights, producers and actors on the one hand, and the European plays and productions on the other. The missionary services, the university education and English productions in Indian cities have been already noticed above. Even more powerful is the deep, abiding influence exerted on the minds of those who have visited Europe and who have been brought into personal contact with the best theatrical productions there. These may not inadequately be likened to the Elizabethan visitors to Italy, who returned fired with enthusiasm for the models they met with there.

One of the finest results of such a living contact with the West is exemplified in the work of Michael Madhusudan Datta, who created Bengali blank verse on Miltonic lines and wrote the first tragedy on a Shakespearean model. Writing to Gangooly about this tragedy of *Kissan Kumāri* (the material for which was supplied by Todd's Chronicles), he says: "As for Dhanadass, I never dreamt of making him the counterpart of Iago. The plot does not admit of such a character, even if I could invent it—which I gravely doubt! I wish Ballender to be serious and light, like the 'Bastard' in *King John*."[1] Again, "never 'strive' to be comic in a tragedy; but if an opportunity presents itself unsought to be gay, do not neglect it in the less important scenes, so as to have an agreeable variety. This I believe to be Shakespeare's plan". Admonishing his friends not to apply too severely the canons of Shakespearean criticism to his own plays, he wrote: "They perhaps forget that I write under very different circumstances. Our social and moral developments are of a different character. We are no doubt actuated by the same passions, but in us those passions assume a milder shape."

While filling his law terms at Gray's Inn, in 1864, Datta wrote to his friend: "I hope to be a capital sort of European scholar before I leave Europe. I am getting on well with French and Italian. I must commence German soon. Spanish and Portuguese will not be difficult after Latin, French and Italian. You cannot imagine what beautiful poetry there is in Italian. Tasso is really the Kālidāsa of Europe."[2] Pleased with some of Datta's Italian work in verse, King Victor Emanuel wrote to him: "It will be a ring which will connect the Orient with the Occident." It is not difficult to perceive that such a learned scholar, with a perfect mastery of the

1. Yogindranath Basu: *Maikal Madhusudan Dattera Jibana Carita*, Calcutta, 1908, p. 465.   2. Ibid., p. 552.

Hindu literature as well, and gifted with the power of creative expression, was bound to exert a most powerful influence on the Indian drama.

Another instance of personal contact with European life and thought is furnished by the greatest dramatist of Bengal, Dvijendralal Ray, who visited England in 1885. What he said regarding his *Lyrics of Ind* is significant: "The principal object in the composition of the following verses has been to harmonize the English and the Indian poetry as they ought to be harmonized." The same principle he followed in his dramatic endeavour. While in England, he made it a point to see all the principal theatres, and from his enthusiasm for them arose his desire to regenerate the Bengali stage.[3] After coming over to India, while in Government service, he used his best efforts to create a national drama for Bengal.

So far as the producers and actors are concerned it is noteworthy that the first Indian company to visit England was led by the gifted Parsi actor-playwright, K. M. Balliwala, from Bombay, in 1885. *The Sketch*,[4] commenting sympathetically on 'The Irving of India', wrote: "Mr. Balliwala brought his company of about twenty-five Parsee actors to the Indian and Colonial Exhibition. . . . As it made little impression on Londoners, it went home poorer in pocket but a great deal benefited in its professional accomplishments. . . . His Indian friends in Bombay presented him with a purse and an address of congratulations on the success of his efforts to 'raise the Indian stage to a higher state of perfection'." *The Tatler*[5] also paid a tribute to 'the most celebrated comic actor of India': "Mr. Balliwala is very enterprising, and made up his mind to visit England at the time of the last London Exhibition (1901).[6] He appeared

3. Dev Kumar Ray Chaudhari: *Dvijendra lāl*, p. 189.
4. No. III, March 13, 1895, p. 352.
5. Vol. V, No. 65, September 24, 1902.
6. It is unfortunate that at the Great Exhibition at Wembley, in 1927, Indian theatricals were poorly represented by some ignorant Tamil professionals.

at Portland Hall and performed first in Hindustani. His visit was a failure from a pecuniary point of view, but he learnt much."

The Indian Sporting and Dramatic News[7] recalled that "Mr. Balliwala has had the honour of playing by command before Her late Majesty Queen Victoria and His late Majesty King Edward VII. . . . He is the proud possessor of some thirty valuable medals from royalty and nobility all over the world". The primary object of these European tours was a desire to enlighten his actors and actresses on the technique of Western drama, and in this Balliwala greatly succeeded. Whilst the one direct result was the introduction of actresses on the Indian stage, the subtle influence on the mode of Indian productions and acting after these visits was unmistakable.

Modern thought and tendencies in drama, of which the fountain-source is Ibsen, appealed most to the late Mr. N. B. Vibhakar when he stayed in England for his legal studies, in 1910–1911. He saw a great number of plays, read a great deal about them, and wrote a series of articles on this subject. Later on he tried to embody most of the problems which gripped his imagination in a variety of Gujarati plays in Bombay. From the standpoint of modern technique, the recent European tour, especially to Russia, of the gifted artist Harindra Chattopadhyay, and the American visit of the celebrated actor Shishir Bahaduri, are fraught with the most interesting possibilities.

SHAKESPEARE

The subtle influence of Shakespeare has been profound in both the principal theatres of India, the distinguishing feature being that the Marathi stage is more conscious of it than the more original Bengali stage. In a characteristic preface to the historical Marathi tragedy of *Savāi Mādha-*

7. Calcutta, Vol. II, No. 7, February 16, 1913.

varāva, Mr. K. P. Khadilkar, a leading dramatist, confesses
that he was fascinated in his college days by *Hamlet* and
Othello after seeing them on the Marathi stage. The idea of
presenting characters of the nature of Hamlet and Iago in
the same play dominated his mind. While reading Khare's
sketch of Nana Phadanavis, he came across a character
which resembled a thoughtful but a passionate Hamlet; and
he created Iago in a selfish priest. Of course, he had to make
certain alterations to suit his purpose. Although the mind
of Mr. Khadilkar is consciously working on Shakespearean
lines to a certain extent, his material is altogether different,
and he does not aim at imitating scenes and passages from
the original. Only he has seized the idea, and the treatment
follows quite a natural course of its own.

    The ambitious design of Keśavaśāstrī (Iago) is made
partially clear in his very first soliloquy. With a view to
securing the post of private secretary, the Hindu Iago plays
several tricks and uses certain expressions which recall
Shakespeare. Pretending to conceal a forged letter of
'Bābāsāhib' (possibly a hint from Edmund's in *King Lear*),
which insinuates the illicit relations between Nānā and
Mādhavarāva's mother-in-law, Keśavaśāstrī says: "Mind
you, man's mind is suspicious by nature where women are
concerned. Therefore I tell you, my lord, if you act at all,
act after deliberation."[8] This recalls: "O, beware, my lord,
of jealousy." Yaśodā has the innocence and charm of
Ophelia. She, too, does not know what ails her Hamlet.
Mādhavarāva has fits of lunacy which gather in strength
and ultimately overpower him when he is persuaded to
believe that not only his wife but he himself is an illegitimate offspring of Nānā. Poor Ophelia tries to console him
and touches him gently, but with a mind intensely agitated
he exclaims: "Oh no, this touch of your hand is like the
combined sting of thousands of scorpions on one spot."[9]
This is reminiscent of Macbeth's "O, full of scorpions is my

8. Cf. *Savāi Mādhavarāva*, p. 52.   9. Ibid., p. 82.

mind, dear wife!" Finally it is reported that, in an un-
guarded moment, the hero throws himself from the top of
the palace, as Prince Arthur despairingly threw himself
from the Tower.

In another historical play of Mr. Khadilkar, *Bhaubamdakī*
(*Family Feud*), although no mention is made of the fact in
the preface, Ānandībāī is created after Lady Macbeth. It is
she who deliberately instigates her husband to kill their
nephew for securing the power and honour of the 'Peshva'.
She makes a slight alteration (*māravem* instead of *dharāvem*,
i.e. 'kill' for 'arrest' Nārāyaṇarāva) in the instructions to
the guard. Then by her beauty and charm, but more by
her dominant will power and resourcefulness, she compels
Rāghobā to acquiesce in the order. The deed is done. The
cause of truth and righteousness is championed by the
independent royal priest Rāmaśāstrī, a sort of Hindu
Macduff. After all means of winning him over have been
tried, he is roughly handled by the usurping Queen of
Poona. Her supreme ambition is that her children should
be kings.

After the murder, Ānandībāī enters with a bloodstained
dagger in her hands. Her husband is not easily reconciled.
The imaginative Rāghobā mutters: "Why do I hear the
piteous words, 'Uncle! Uncle!' all around me?" But she
inspires him with courage and fortitude by besmearing her
own forehead with the blood. After donning the royal
apparel of the Peshwa, he is again lost in a reverie with a
mirror in his hand. He raves: "Do you not see the face here
of my reproving father?" She promptly replies: "Where?
I see nothing. This is but the fantasy of your brain." Then
he says: "Ah! embrace me thus and I am a man again."
The hysterical fit comes on again, and he proclaims the foul
deed. This confession is overheard by a servant and leads
to the overthrow of the guilty pair. Although they do not
die at the end of the play, their souls are ruined and a wide
gulf created between Ānandībāī in utter despair and the

soul of Rāghobā haunted by the ghost of the murdered nephew.

It is also interesting to notice that in this play the two Hindu priests, Namakaśāstrī and Camakaśāstrī, inherit some of the salient qualities of Dogberry and Verges, for they seldom come to the point in their conversation and have a boring trick of frequent repetitions.

For even more subtle and artistically beautiful Shakespearean reminiscences one should turn to the great Bengali dramatist, Dvijendralal Ray. His *Sāhjāhān* is a powerful study in the relation between parent and offspring. The general setting for the play shows the fate of the mighty Moghul empire in the balance. The Emperor's third son, Aurungzeb, rebels against the authority of the old affectionate father and by his vile arts not only overthrows his three brothers but also imprisons his father and installs himself on the throne. The theme is altogether different from that of *King Lear*, but the spirit of the tragedy, the mode of treatment, and the occasional turns of speech and the expression of sentiments certainly recall the great English tragedy.

The Emperor is in his dotage. His fatal failing is his extremely affectionate nature, which is accentuated after the death of his queen. He defends the conduct of his sons by constantly pointing to the Taj Mahal and repeating: "These are motherless children, and I am so fond of them." This weakness, although accompanied by flashes of greatness, leads to his downfall.

As he hears of the most unnatural deeds of his son, he often utters, like Lear, "Oh, let me not be mad!" "O God, I shall go mad!" At the end of Act II he raves: "Oh Earthquake, arise with a terrible noise! Tear the bosom of this earth into a thousand pieces! Oh monster conflagration, come and consume this whole world into ashes! Oh devastating winds, dash those ashes on the face of the Creator!" This is clearly reminiscent of *King Lear's* famous storm scene. Even more striking, however, is Act V. iii, in which the aged king loses all control over his mind and his stormy passion is symbolically accompanied by "thunder, rain and lightning outside the castle in the dark night". He imagines that the dead body of his eldest son, Dara (butchered by Aurungzeb) is lying at his feet. He raves: "Who dare murder my Dara? Don't you see, I am Emperor Shah Jahan himself, guarding in person his body. . . ." Then his strength gives way: "Oh, oh, they have killed him! Look how the blood flows—nay, the whole house is steeped in it (*plunging both his hands in the imaginary blood*). What, still warm! Ah, it is reeking!" Then, after a moment: "Aurungzeb, do you stare and laugh in my face? Why, you still laugh! Wait, you fiend, I shall punish you; wait, you murderer! You ask for pardon? Never—oh, never." Then his attention is drawn to the fiery elements outside, and some of his words very closely follow these Shakespearean lines, III. ii:—

> Rumble thy bellyful! Spit, fire! spout, rain!
> Nor rain, wind, thunder, fire, are my daughters:
> I tax not you, you elements, with unkindness:
> I never gave you kingdom, call'd you children——"

The villain Aurungzeb also experiences an internal struggle as he marches boldy forward on his career of crimes. He hears strange, subtle noises and feels that he "shall sleep no more" in his royal bed. He sees the apparitions of his murdered relatives and knows remorse.

'The supreme philosopher of the East' is disguised as a Fool (Dildār) at the Moghul Court. He is partly designed after the pattern of Lear's Fool. The following dialogue is an instance to the point (I. ii):—

"*Dildar:* Is it true, my lord! that among certain wild animals parents devour their young ones?
Murad: Yes, what of that?
Dildar: But, there is no custom among them of children preying on their parents, is there?
Murad: No, there is none.
Dildar: Such a law God seems to have reserved only for mankind!"

P

Here the spirit of his satirical reflections is clearly based on Shakespeare's.

This play bears also another distinct impress of the English dramatist in II. v, in which the devoted daughter of the Emperor is checkmated in her noble efforts in full Court by the superior genius of her brother. The courtiers behave in the manner of the fickle crowd or the giddy multitude of *Julius Cæsar* or *Coriolanus*. Like Brutus, Jahānārā urges the claim of her father. She speaks many home-truths; and the courtiers are converted: "Long live Emperor Śāhjāhān!" Then, in the manner of the consummate actor Antony, Aurungzeb descends from the throne and by subtle insinuations carries his point admirably. The crowd is reconverted: "Long live Emperor Aurungzeb!" Poor Jahānārā confesses herself beaten.

One scene in this play is a partial echo of Schiller's *Mary Stuart*. Aurungzeb's signature to the death warrant of his eldest brother (IV. vi) is exploited with psychological skill in the manner of Elizabeth's signing Mary's execution order. He wavers, pauses, gives up the idea. Then changes his mind, somehow persuades himself that it is inevitable, desperately signs it, and then wishes it undone.

In the introduction to his other masterpiece, *Candragupta*, almost equally popular on the Bengali stage, Dvijendralal Ray makes it clear that his interpretation of Cāṇakya, 'the Indian Machiavel', follows European models. Thus the Indian Prime Minister is portrayed as "learned, intellectual and subtle". Drawing his information from Greek historical sources, the playwright artistically develops the plot of the political marriage between the Greek princess Helen and the Indian emperor Candragupta. The central figure, however, is the dominant personality of the Brahmin king-maker and minister. The original genius of the dramatist benefited greatly not only by the Sanskrit classic, *Mudrā-Rākṣasa*, but also by his profound study of English drama.

A few illustrations which recall Shakespearean passages may be noted here.

Candragupta's mind is deeply agitated on account of the gross insult given to his mother by his step-brother, the emperor Nanda. She was not 'Kṣatriya' by caste but 'Śudra', and the ruthless king dismissed her with the taunting words: "Get thee gone, thou low-born one!" Touched to the quick by the report, Candragupta soliloquizes (I. iv): "Low-born! Is a Śudra not a human being? Has he not hands and feet like a Kṣatriya? Has he no head? Has he no heart?" etc. These expressions obviously recall Shylock's "Hath not a Jew eyes?" etc. The Shakespearean passage has subtly influenced the mind of Ray.

The situation radically changes in III. vi, in which the 'low-born' Murā finds her stepson Nanda at her feet imploring mercy. She is adamant. Candraketu pleads thus: "Mercy is heaven-born like the Ganges; and her holy waters flow down to this mortal world. Everybody has a right to acquire merit by bathing in that sacred stream." This Oriental metaphor is beautifully developed from the Shakespearean "It droppeth as the gentle rain from heaven".

Immediately after the execution of Nanda, Murā turns to the executioner Kātyāyana: "I was a woman—foolish, weak, ignorant! But what have you done, oh Brahmin? How many times have you kissed this face? And with what devilish rapture are you now standing with the dead head? (*Here Kātyāyana drops the head.*)" One feels that Hamlet's reference to the skull of Yorick is partly at the back of the dramatist's mind.

The dramatic situation in IV. ii in *Candragupta* is partly reminiscent of Lytton's *Richelieu*. "Cāṇakya is depicted as a superman in every sense of the term. In political ambition he is unrelenting and ruthless, in religion he is an agnostic. He is so austere in his principles as to be almost egocentric, and yet he is never mean."[10] This great Brahmin reveals

10. Dr. Guha-Thakurta: *The Bengali Drama*, p. 166.

some of the traits of Richelieu, and in one particular scene
(IV. ii) the impression of Lytton gains in vividity, in which
the weak and foolish Candragupta tries to dismiss the
indispensable Cāṇakya and meets with the same unsur-
mountable difficulties as the vacillating Louis who dreamed
of humiliating the Cardinal.

The third great drama of Ray, comparable to the above
two in lofty conception and beauty of expression, is *Nur-
jāhān*, named after the beautiful queen of the Moghul
emperor Jahangir. Her character is created by means of a
few exquisite touches and suggestions in the manner of
Shakespeare. Her deep internal conflict, often expressed in
soliloquies, between duty to her first loving husband and
ambition to become the Empress of India, is delineated with
a masterly skill, Ray's very significant lyrics providing an
appropriate background. In II. iii, she is standing before a
looking-glass and is lost in a reverie as she talks to herself
in words beginning with "Was this the face?" which easily
recall Marlowe's famous lines. Even more striking is the great
Temptation scene, in which, by careful stage-directions, her
entire stage business is indicated. She stands at the window
of her chamber in the royal palace alone at midnight and
broods on her destiny: "What is it to be the Queen of
India?" She has still not decided whether she should accept
the crown or not, although her husband has been murdered
four years before.

Her precocious daughter by her first husband is created
partly on the lines of Macduff's son. She is indeed in many
respects a true sister to her Shakespearean brother. She
stands nobly for the honour and pride of the family and
refuses to submit to the dictation of intruders. Her intense
affection for her lost father turns her mother's thoughts to
introspection. Later on, the bold girl stands before the
emperor himself and remains undaunted to the last.

It is no use, one feels, multiplying instances of this kind,
for they can be traced in many places. One or two peculiar

Shakespearean devices frequently used by Ray and others may, however, be noted. Nemesis proceeding from supernatural sources is repeatedly emphasized. This Shakespearean trait is indeed used as a stock device by many playwrights. In Ray's *Mebār Patan* (*The Fall of Mewad*) the guilty soul of Sagarsinh is ill at ease. He has betrayed the cause of Hinduism. He is terribly afraid of even the least noise at night in the forest and in the fortress of Chitor. His innocent grandson cannot sleep because of his screams: "Oh, my lord!" Boy Aruna: "What is the matter, grandfather?" "Oh, that Ghost!" "There is no ghost here, is there?" (*Pointing with a finger*) "There, look there!" and so on.

Another device is of a disguise on the stage which is revealed only at the end (cf. Kent). This may be well illustrated from Khadilkar's *Premadhvaja* (named after the hero and partly based on Scott's *Talisman*), in which the emperor Akbar is cleverly disguised as a physician and effectively helps the genuine lovers. Ray also uses this device with great advantage in *Mebār Patan* (III. iii), in which Arunasinh appears as an ambassador in the Jodhpur Royal Court. Such a device naturally leads to frequent ironical situations and remarks. Some of the most striking instances of romantic disguises of the type of Viola and Imogen are to be found in the Gujarati playwright Vibhakar, the presence of boys dressed as girls on the Gujarati stage adding a peculiar charm.

This and other devices such as that of mistaken identity are, however, of minor importance compared with the great lead which Shakespeare gave to the tragic form on the Indian stage. The first tragedy to be acted in India was Dinabandhu Mitra's *Nīla Darpaṇa*[11] (dealing with the problem of indigo planters in India). It is a domestic tragedy in which the entire native family is wiped out by the tyranny and greed of the European planters. The technique is Shakespearean. One of the favourite social tragedies

11. It is translated into English by Long.

on the Marathi stage, *Ekaja Pyālā* (*Only a Glass of Wine*), follows the same technique, the crisis being reached in the middle of the third act; in this, the pleader, after his name is struck off from the roll of the local court, during a crucial relapse to the drink habit, extorts a solemn oath from his wife. In the fourth act he unwittingly kills his only child, himself dying at the end. Ray and Khadilkar[12] in most of their plays usually follow the Shakespeare technique. For instance, the crisis is reached in *Candragupta*, III. vi, in which, despite the king's orders, the powerful minister and the enraged Murā force the hands of Kātyāyana to kill Nanda.

If one bears in mind the ancient and medieval Indian drama, one cannot fail to perceive the following remarkable changes in the modern plays to-day: (*a*) Many plays now open with only a prayer or without any ceremony whatsoever, and proceed straight with the business of the plot (cf. Khadilkar and Ray). Thus the ancient Indian mode of prologue has fallen into disuse or decay. Modern audiences usually smile at the relics of ancient *Sūtradhāra* and *Natī* sometimes still introduced by the orthodox playwrights. (*b*) Unlike the practice of the ancient drama, many short explanatory scenes (in which generally minor characters figure) are introduced in the manner of Shakespeare. This process is greatly facilitated by the use of alternate scenes. (*c*) These many scenes are grouped in five acts in the European manner. The ancient mode of seven or ten acts has completely disappeared. The five-act Shakespearean technique has proved immensely attractive both on the Bengali and the Marathi stage. On the Gujarati-Urdu stage, however, the modern English tendency of three acts is usually welcomed. (*d*) The melodramatic elements involving

---

12. It is not suggested that the several stages in the evolution of the plot are peculiar to Shakespeare; but in the case of both these dramatists the treatment of their material was strongly influenced by their constant study of this English poet.

murders, lust, sensational escapes and unnatural deeds have been borrowed profusely by the Gujarati-Urdu stage from the Elizabethan drama. (*e*) The concluding prayer or epilogue has now disappeared in many cases.

In the field of comedy Shakespeare's influence has been pronounced in various ways. Falstaff's amours are cleverly reflected in the relations of Jaladhar and Jagadambā in Dinabandhu's *Nabīn Tapasvinī*. The Shakespearean wit-combat has influenced several intellectual dramatists, who frequently pun on vernacular words to excite merriment.

The Chronicle plays, too, especially *Henry V*, have exercised a most lasting influence on the Indian stage. Shakespeare pointed the way towards the glorification of great national heroes and of the motherland. The soil being thus admirably prepared by the English example, the patriotic sentiment at the beginning of the century assumed an attractive form on the stage. Great nation-builders like Pratap and Shivaji were treated with even greater reverence and sentimental pride than Henry V had been by Shakespeare.

As Mrs. Besant has rightly pointed out, the virtues of public spirit, patriotism and the like grew directly out of the Western ideal of free and independent man. "Personal dignity, self-respect, the sense of honour, of justice, and all the allied virtues, have also their root in this ideal of the strong and free man."[13] It is a militant ideal and breeds leaders of action rather than saints. This ideal has been expressed vigorously on the Indian stage and its ultimate source is Shakespearean.

THE COMEDY OF MANNERS

The realistic comedy of manners was also an introduction from the West. Jonson, Molière and the Restoration comedy were all eagerly read and imitated by Indian writers of light

13. *The Hindu Ideals*, Benares, 1904, p. 17.

comedy. The dramatists started to observe contemporary life shrewdly and satirized the follies and foibles of Indians aping European ways and manners. This was altogether a novel type introduced on the Bengali stage, the ancient romantic traits being replaced by realistic methods. On the Gujarati stage a play of this type, *The Barrister*, had a particular success. The newly returned barrister from England makes a fool of himself by teaching his wife the use of European high-heeled shoes and of the terms of English etiquette. He also invites much ridicule on himself in his new relations to the several members of his family.

The treatment of the same theme, by the great Bengali dramatist, Amritlal Bose, is more pointed and artistic. In his very popular farcical comedy *Bābu* (*The Man of Fashion*), the treatment deserves careful analysis. The chief character habitually uses many English phrases and words, even when others reply in chaste Bengali. His oddities are precisely similar to those of the French fops such as Sir Fopling Flutter ridiculed on the English stage. Even when he comes to see his brother-in-law, Babu sends his visiting-card (this is ridiculous in Hindu society). He enters with "Hallo, Good morning, How do you do?" and uses such slang as "By all the devils". Again, he is "too busy", "out on a social mission", and "can't attend to political affairs". He stands on European etiquette in all his replies, and everybody smiles at his folly. He becomes unnecessarily formal and curt, and, like Chaucer's lawyer, poses as busier than he is. In another scene he passes scathing remarks on time-honoured Hindu customs and conventions without adducing any logical arguments or adopting a persuasive attitude. He utters many philosophical English sentences which are, of course, Greek and Latin to his poor devoted wife. He ultimately forces her to give up the veil and takes her out for a walk in the Eden gardens. Here the folly of his platitudes and his cowardice are mercilessly exposed by the gifted satirist. An English sailor comes there singing "Drink to me," etc., and accosts the Bābu's wife: "Fine woman indeed; come on, my rosebud." The Bābu tremblingly utters: "Now—sir—don't interfere—with—our—lady." Then he runs away for succour while the woman kneels to the sailor!

In another popular comedy Amritlal Bose ridicules the excesses of a doctor, Mr, Simh, recently returned from England. He comes to see (cf. *Bibāh Bibhrāt* (*The Marriage Dilemma*), I. ii) a lady friend, Mrs. Karforma, interested in the study of physics. The doctor goes into raptures over the English life: "Oh, you will be a curiosity there! . . . Tea there, dinner here, Picnic abroad, Yachting, Skating, Riding, Driving, Sight-seeing, Crystal Palace to-day, Vaux-hall to-morrow, holidays every day! And presents! Rings, Brooches, Dresses à la Paris", etc. He boasts about his degrees and is generally held up to ridicule both in his private and in his professional life.

This social satire is not, however, confined only to one class. Throughout India the younger dramatists tear off the mask from the pedantic, hypocritical, orthodox, out-of-date people. Among vegetarian circles, two habits usually associated with the West, drinking and meat-eating, have often formed the objects of ridicule on the stage. The great social evils of India, such as child-marriage, the miserable condition of the Hindu widow and the dowry system, have also been treated in a light, satirical manner. The novel idea of treating glaring social evils as serious problems worthy of trenchant analysis on the stage came only with the very latest theatrical movements in Europe.

MODERN TENDENCIES

The tradition of the Sanskrit drama, of which the keynote was harmony between good and evil, right and wrong, and wherein the truth of the grim reality of life was obscured by artificial happy endings and divine interventions at critical moments, received, perhaps, its greatest shock from the earnest European manner of tackling actual problems of the complicated social organ of our modern civilization. Original thinkers and artists, such as Ibsen and Shaw, who put an end to the epoch of short-sighted optimism and exposed the snobbery and hypocrisy of the pseudo-respectable classes, here exerted a profound influence on the minds of the younger school of Indian playwrights.

The conditions and problems of Europe and India being widely different, it was not advisable for the Indian dramatists to practise at this stage Shaw's iconoclasm or to wield his two-edged weapon in facing such problems as the sex-war. Nor is the knowledge of science sufficiently advanced for producing successfully such plays as *Damaged Goods* in order to illustrate how the social taboo acts strongly even against the most innocent. In these circumstances, the modern Indian playwrights have to proceed with extreme caution. It is almost impossible for them to discard the partially romantic settings and the use of songs on the popular stage.

If one takes two typical playwrights from western India, the methods pursued will be fairly well illustrated. An altogether modern note was heard on the Gujarati professional stage when, in the play of *Gautam Buddha*, the late Mr. Vibhakar[14] dealt with the problem of the down-trodden agriculturists in a serious under-plot.

In this play, a Hindu missionary dedicates himself to the cause of the amelioration of these 'pious, honest and industrious' millions, and rises in protest against the blood-sucking landowners. Instead of the playwright shedding conventional sentimental tears, the magnitude and significance of the problem are ably stressed.

The opening scene of *Megha-Mālinī* (named after the

14. The writer had the opportunity of examining in Bombay some of the MS. copies of the plays of the late Mr. Vibhakar and of Mr. Jaman among others.

lovers) is designed after the pattern of I. i in Hauptmann's
The Weavers. The labourers of the Bhāgyanagar Textile
Mills are shown singing national songs. Then the mill agent
and his cashier enter. The poor workers are unfairly and
even hard-heartedly treated, much in the same manner as
Pjeifer and his tool treat Becker and his companions. After
many romantic adventures of the First Weaver's daughter,
Śobhanā, this play, which bears a partial impress of *Man
and Superman* as well, ends on a characteristic modern note:
"Truly speaking, man is not sinful, mean or detestable by
nature; but sin, impiety and lack of culture are really the
products of our chaotic social condition. Therefore, let us
crush it and level down false barriers between the high and
the low."

It is characteristic of the nature of the transitional stage
in the Indian theatre to-day that, whilst Vibhakar draws
his inspiration from modern plays, as well as from Tolstoy
and Victor Hugo, in his discussion of the problems of labour
and capital and the like, he also makes a use of the dramatic
devices of a play within a play and of Olivia falling in love
with Viola-Cesario (cf. *Madhu-Baṁsarī* (named after the
lovers). In one popular play, *Sneha-Saritā* (named after the
lovers), the heroine is discovered, in the first scene, to have
returned from England and to be urging the right of women
to practise at the bar. A league is established for the
regeneration of women. The under-plot of this piece reveals
the influence of Pinero's *His House in Order.* In his last
play this dramatist discussed the problem of a multi-
millionaire's life, partly based on his study of Andrew
Carnegie.

Many modern problems, though seriously intended, are
thus confused with many melodramatic devices on the
Gujarati-Urdu stage. On the Marathi stage, on the other
hand, Mr. Varerkar is trying his best to tackle several social
questions in the manner of his acknowedged master, G. B.
Shaw. Like John Tanner, many of his characters are "talking,

talking, talking", and doing little on the stage. The credit of looking squarely at the several glaring evils of Indian society to-day and of expressing his opinions boldly belongs to him. No other playwright in India has so far shown such remarkable courage on the popular stage.

He satirizes the legal profession in one play, confronts the problem of caste-ostracism in another, of conversion in a third, of prostitution in a fourth, and of the dowry system in a fifth. If one analyses one of his typical plays, *Sattece Gulām (The Slaves of Power)*, 1922, for example, it is easy to trace his ideals and his models. In this work, Nalinī is an unconventional maiden who finds herself in the hands of her lawyer, who is interpreting her father's will; but she is a typical modern woman and refuses to submit to the 'slavery' of her lawyer, who tries all means to secure her hand. In I. i her personality is revealed in the following dialogue:—

"*Nalinī:* If necessary, I shall slave in order to maintain myself. I am not a cripple.
Ramā: Slavery? Slavery or marriage?
Nalinī: Marriage! excuse me, but is marriage a necessary condition of life?
Ramā: What a foolish question!
Nalinī: And, supposing I do not marry?
Ramā: How can you do without it? A girl must marry.
Nalinī: And supposing the husband dies immediately after the marriage, what then? What is the girl to do?"

It must be remembered that the idea of a free, independent life for a woman is altogether revolutionary for the Indian society of to-day. The pleader Keropant is stripped of his pretence of service and revealed in his true colours. Vaikunth is partly fashioned after John Tanner, and his remarks throughout the play are full of the author's satirical criticism of contemporary life. II. iii is partly modelled on the opening scene of *Man and Superman*. The playwright reveals also traces of a certain influence of *The Devil's Disciple* in this play.

The same note of woman as 'a slave' of any authority who can wield power over her is also struck in the case of a young widow, Revā, who complains that the Hindu widow has to suffer a thousand insults from so many with whom she comes in contact. The so-called 'servant of the country' is also fully exposed.

The sincerity of this dramatist's passion for the reform of the modern stage may be realized from the fact that he took the actors of his company to witness the productions of English companies visiting Bombay, including those of Mr. Picthall and Mr. Holloway, and that he sought the help of English producers (e.g. Lewis Perman) in order that some of the weaknesses of the Indian theatre might be remedied by their assistance.

Although he has been forced to introduce songs in his dramas, he is setting a praiseworthy example by curtailing the number of these. His prose is direct and forcible, though critics have found it uninspiring. The prejudice, however, against all his modern methods is so strong that so far he has not achieved conspicuous success in directing the stage along new lines. Perhaps this may be due to the fact that, although he is talented and industrious, he lacks genius. He has neither the transparent seriousness of the greater masters nor any depth of purpose below his wit and satire.

In addition to the general tendencies which may be traced to the influence of the Western theatre and which have been dealt with above, two other things deserve to be noted. In the Western drama of modern times an ideal or a movement in life is often deliberately symbolized in one figure, and this feature has already found its way to the Indian stage. Thus the study of Shelley on the one hand, and of Ibsen on the other, led the playwright Ray to the conception of such characters as Mānasī. As the playwright makes it explicit in his preface to *Nebār Patan* (*The Fall of Newad*), he aimed at creating three idealistic types of womanhood: (*a*) Kalyāṇī as the embodiment of wifely devotion even to a husband who was a convert to Islam; (*b*) Satyavatī as the emblem of nationalism above all inter-communal strife; and (*c*) Mā-nasī, the soul of love for mankind and of regeneration of the world, irrespective of all differences of race, class and creed.

Secondly, the idea of heredity has come to influence strongly some of the Indian playwrights. The reading of such plays as *Ghosts* and *The Wild Duck* created a powerful impression on their minds. Several successful plays of a Gujarati dramatist (Mr. Jaman, for example) often harp on this subject. Thus, in *Emāṁ Śuṁ* (*What does it Matter?*), a rich landowner is seen agonized at the sight of his son characteristically repeating his own follies and vices. It may be true that the literary merit here is not great, but the tendency itself merits attention.

Gradually, however, the dignity of drama as literature and as a fine art is being generally recognized, not merely by way of imitation of European models, but also on account of the fuller realization of the inherent worth of theatrical art. This is to be seen even in the altered form of modern theatrical play-bills and programmes. In the course of the last decade or so, plays published in Bengali and Marathi endeavour to acknowledge obligation to all the important artists connected with the production. In some cases a full list of the more important characters in the *première* are printed there. The stage-manager (the producer), the musicians, the scene-painter and the general manager are also named. This is altogether a modern feature, and so far has not been accepted by all companies.

Quite apart from purely theatrical matters, there are two tendencies in modern Indian literature which deserve to be mentioned here because of their influence on the popular stage. It has been noted above that mythological themes have always proved popular in India, and many young dramatists have turned to these, but, in doing so, have modified the ancient methods of treatment. A new interpretation of character and motive is thus introduced, and greater emphasis is laid on the human element in these mythological tales. In many cases a profound logical and philosophical interpretation is provided for ancient epical events and personages. In such an attitude of the novelist or the dramatist the Western influence has its share.

G. M. Tripathi's novel, a Gujarati masterpiece, *Sarasvatīcandra*, parts of which have been dramatized, is the product of an original thinker who has gained immensely from English literature. To him Hanumāna becomes the incarnation of the ideal of selfless service and Arjuna that of refined strength and of beauty of character.

On a slightly lower plane, perhaps, is the modern intellectual and partly humorous manner of dealing with extremely popular mythological heroes and heroines, such as Kṛṣṇa, Arjuna, Nārada, Satyabhāmā, and Rukmiṇī in Mr. N. C. Kelkar's witty play *Kṛṣṇārjuna Yuddha* (*The Fight between Kṛṣṇa and Arjuna*). Here the human element is particularly stressed, although the attitude of reverence for the august figures is retained. Only a student of British drama could have attained the polish and refinement of treatment that this playwright brings to bear on his material.

CHAPTER XI

RETROSPECT

WHAT Stanislavsky[1] describes as the chaotic condition of
the Russian stage before the founding of the Moscow Art
Theatre is generally true of the present Indian scene: "We
protested against the customary manner of acting, against
theatricality, against bathos, against declamation, against
over-acting, against the bad manner of production, against
the habitual scenery, against the star system which spoiled
the ensemble, against the light and farcical repertoire. . . .
The best theatres were monopolized by a group of little-
gifted dramatists who wrote their empty plays for the benefit
of this or that actor and often at his order and under his
direction, or took plays from the German or the French
and adapted them for the Russian stage and to Russian
life, signing themselves as the adapters of the original writer
with the postscript 'subject taken from ——'."

Stanislavsky's efforts to improve these conditions may
not inaptly be likened to those of Professor Shishir Bahaduri.
In founding the "Nāṭya-Mandira" Professor Bahaduri is
aiming at the reform of the Calcutta stage, and Mr. Charan
Ray co-operates with him in this laudable attempt by
designing and painting suitable realistic scenery. The chief
aim of this new movement is to encourage original productions, real, artistic, scenic truth on the model of modern
European stagecraft, and natural, restrained acting which
should express as much by vivid personality and facial
gesture as by speech, intonation and voice. It must be confessed, however, that Mr. Bahaduri has so far not met with
any considerable success comparable to that of the Moscow
Art Theatre.

That there are certain inherent difficulties in the path of

1. *My Life in Art*, London, 1924, p. 330.

progress may be realized from the attitude of the various Indian theatres to the European drama noticed above. For a proper appreciation of the exact nature of the direct and of the indirect influence of British drama on the Indian stage, treated at some length in the foregoing chapters, it is necessary to bear in mind the complete general background provided by the ancient and medieval theatres of India on the one hand, and the changing political, religious, social and economic conditions in the country during the nineteenth century on the other. In the course of Part I (the first four chapters) the religious basis of the Sanskrit drama, its essentially idealistic, poetic and romantic atmosphere, its intimate treatment of external nature, its great variety of characters, and its peculiar form of prose dialogue interspersed with recitative or musical verses, have been noted. Its characteristic contribution of the *rasa* theory has been also illustrated.

Several parallels have been instituted between the ancient Indian stage and the Elizabethan theatre, both on the architectural and on the histrionic sides. Certain dramatic devices, such as those of mistaken identity and of pathetic fallacy, and a few stage conventions have been noted as common to both the theatres. So far as the medieval stage is concerned, a few points of affinity with the European 'Mystery and Morality' plays have also been mentioned. In order to complete the picture of the suitable soil existing for the germination of the seed of the European influence, typical characters, situations and poetic sentiments in the Sanskrit drama, recalling corresponding examples from Shakespeare, have been referred to. The presence of the internal conflict, of the note of fatalism, and of the touch of the supernatural have been dwelt upon as among the common features of the ancient Hindu and of the Elizabethan dramas.

In the course of Part II, the rise of the European theatres, mostly amateur in character, in the three great cities of

India—Calcutta, Bombay and Madras—has been outlined, with a description of the manner in which this new movement, along with the influence of University education, affected the origin and the development of the modern Indian theatres. The dignity of the new amateur acting by professors, civilians and business men, the changed status of women actors, the varied nature of the productions from the highest to the lowest, the early Victorian scenic apparatus and the living contact with perhaps the richest dramatic literature of the world are emphasized as of momentous importance in the formation and growth of the new movement of the theatre in India (Chapter V).

These new vernacular theatres rapidly turned into purely commercial concerns. The chaotic nature of the present condition of the Gujarati-Urdu, Marathi and Bengali theatres is dealt with in Chapter VI. Here the question naturally arises: Why has the Western influence so far not produced satisfactory results in the several Indian theatres of to-day? It is indeed true that Shakespeare has been loved, admired and acted throughout the country as no other dramatist has ever been. On the Marathi stage alone, thirteen out of the seventeen Shakespearean comedies and eight out of the ten tragedies have been acted, some of these, notably *The Taming of the Shrew* and *Hamlet*, being constantly in the repertory of the Shahu company. Great Shakespearean actors have arisen, such as Balliwala, Ganapatrao and Jog. Apart, too, from the singular reverence displayed towards the great English poet, several other European masterpieces, including *The Robbers* and *Hernani*, have held many sections of the Indian stage for a considerable period. An important contribution to Indian productions has been made by the subtle influence of Shakespearean technique, characters, situations, devices and ideas in the field of the new mythological and historical drama on the one hand, and by the partial imitation of the models furnished by Ibsen and Shaw in the recently opened vein of social problem plays on the other.

CHARACTERISTICS OF THE ALTERED VERSIONS

Some general observations may be made here regarding the characteristics of the altered Indian versions of foreign plays.

(1) In the conditions peculiar to India only plays fully adapted to the Indian life have succeeded on the professional stage. Although experiments in literal translation, such as those of *Macbeth* and *Othello*, were given a fair trial, they failed. The task of adaptation, it is noteworthy, was greatly facilitated on account of the rich Indian tradition of romantic drama, although, in spite of the age-long monarchical system, several drastic changes had to be introduced by way of concession to the existing social prejudices and dramatic conventions. Even while making the necessary changes several scholarly adapters, in order to emphasize their attitude of reverence to Shakespeare, made it clear in their prefaces that the glory of the version belonged to the original but the shortcomings were their own.

(2) There being no question of pseudo-classical bias in India, the unities of time and place never troubled the minds of the adapters, whilst the unity of action was generally observed in the Shakespearean sense in all the major Marathi and Bengali versions. The inherent romantic impulse of the nation never prevented the mixture of 'genres'. Thus comic elements could freely be introduced in tragedy and *vice versa*. Only it may be observed that the Urdu *kavi* often went to the absurd length of confining roaring farce to certain scenes of an adaptation, reserving the pathetic extravagance to others. The decencies of the stage were frequently violated without any compunction, especially in the Gujarati-Urdu theatre.

(3) Except the first-rate stage versions of the celebrated Shahu company, almost all the adaptations of foreign plays were converted into operatic versions on account of the traditional love of music and song among the Indians. It is,

however, noteworthy that such songs were sparingly used and more artistically introduced by the Bengali adapters, and, although frequently thrust into many Marathi versions, were there rarely debasing in character, while the utmost liberty in this direction was taken by the Urdu stage.

(4) Even more than songs, the use of gorgeous scenery and clever manipulation of machinery appealed to the Urdu playgoers. Thus, the interest of an adaptation was often centred more on brilliant spectacle, on striking revue effects, and on pageantry of costume than on the play itself. This tendency is no doubt responsible for the ruthless mangling of some foreign models and for the utter loss of adequate characterization. Economic considerations, on the other hand, aided the Marathi and the Bengali adapters.

(5) On account of the national taste, the greatest emphasis was usually laid on the emotional side ('heart interest') in the altered versions. The sentimental appeal of such scenes as those of 'Arthur and Hubert' and of the 'Sentinel and Rolla' was indeed extraordinary throughout India. Pathetic situations in Shakespeare and others appealed deeply to the emotional nature of the playgoers. Intellectuality was generally neglected.

(6) Of all such characters, the suffering ideal wife (a sort of patient Griselda), in harmony with the tradition of Sītā and Śakuntalā, always aroused unbounded enthusiasm among the audience. This love of constancy and fortitude was responsible for the warm reception of such characters as Desdemona, Imogen, Cora and Dona Sol. There were perhaps more tears of sympathy shed over such figures than over any others. Therefore it is no wonder that in some of the altered versions such favourite sentimental heroines were presented in more striking situations and exposed to even greater misfortunes than are to be met with in the originals in order that their virtue might shine the more. The peculiar preoccupation of the Indian mind in this respect might not inappropriately be illustrated by a refer-

ence to the titles of many adaptations which are named after the idealistic heroines of those plays.

(7) The motive of moral reformation generally went hand in hand with this striking sentimental appeal. Consequently in most of the adaptations some sort of ethical significance was usually engrafted on the original tale. Many rhetorical speeches directly preaching a didactic message were applauded and similar interpolated songs were repeatedly encored. This glorification of virtue was often accompanied by Hindu philosophical sentiments based on the ideas of pre-birth and *Karma*.

(8) In certain cases, however, a sort of poetic justice was introduced to impress on the audience the final reward of virtue (the installation and marriage of Malcolm and the daughter of Macbeth, with the help of Banquo, might serve as an example). Many inferior adapters were accordingly not able to resist the tendency of an improvised 'happy' close in their versions of tragedies, as in the treatment of *Romeo and Juliet* and *King Lear*. The Urdu *kavis* went even farther; they desired to show the torture of the villain, whose agony on the stage might give full scope for ironical laughter.

(9) While the stock tricks of the stage, such as horror, suspense, surprise, disguise and mistaken identity, were exploited by the Urdu stage, the Marathi and the Bengali adapters concentrated more on characterization and on the study of the human mind. One of the chief defects of the Urdu stage was the artificial sharp division between comic and tragic figures, both endowed with certain stock qualities. Virtue or vice, as embodied in several figures, was there so grossly exaggerated that the characters became mere puppets. Thus Macbeth and Pizarro could have no redeeming qualities nor Ophelia and Cora any weaknesses. Although such stock persons may be found in the Marathi and Bengali versions, there was at any rate an attempt made in these to provide fitting expression of personality.

(10) Another weakness of the more popular stage was the low moral standard of the altered versions. Vulgarity and obscenity were the besetting sins of the farcical interludes in serious plays. Perhaps no other single weakness has alienated the sympathy of the intelligent middle class of India more than this.

(11) The tendency to make political capital out of the stage versions, by introducing Mr. Gandhi, the spinning-wheel, etc., was not confined only to the Gujarati-Urdu theatre. By means of varied covert suggestions, sometimes even of an improvised nature, the evils of foreign domination and the message of freedom and of national regeneration were emphasized whenever an opportunity presented itself in the adaptations. Whereas, however, the Urdu stage was crude and vociferous in its expression of these sentiments, the more advanced theatres preferred to employ subtle insinuations which were plain to intelligent members of the audience.

(12) Although the Indian mind was very quick to seize upon the striking points of plot, construction, situation and incident, the two highest peaks of Shakespearean greatness, the perfect mastery of character and the sublimity of poetry, generally remained unconquered by most of the popular adapters. A few gifted Marathi adapters, such as those of *Hamlet* and of *Othello*, were able to approach very close to the original in the first respect, but even they could not transfer all the poetic beauties to their vernacular.

(13) So far as the medium of expression was concerned, the blank verse and heroic couplets of the original gave way to ordinary prose (with the occasional use of dialect), except in the case of a few Bengali experiments. The interpolated songs were supposed to supply the place of rhythmic beauty.

(14) As it has been suggested in some quarters, owing to varied reasons, the vogue of Shakespeare has declined in India since 1912. The fact is that in the peculiar conditions of the popular theatres in India to-day, the vein of direct

borrowings is worked out.[2] Consequently, adaptations of non-Shakespearean plays are more frequently tried to introduce novelty and variety. These versions are also altered for the needs of the varied vernacular theatres.

(15) The truth is that a new and distinct stage of development in the theatre is now being rapidly reached. Foreign dramatic pieces undergo such a subtle process of assimilation that in the completely altered versions of this type they can hardly be recognized at all. Thus many successful original Indian productions now reveal the indirect and more artistically beautiful impress of great foreign models.

(16) Finally, these Shakespearean and non-Shakespearean adaptations have not only strengthened the repertory of Indian theatres but have given impetus to the whole dramatic activity in India, and have also pointed the way to the refinement, modification and enrichment of the ancient and medieval tradition of the theatre there.

THE INDIAN SCENE

When all is said, however, the painful fact (noted at the beginning of the chapter) remains that the modern vernacular theatres of India are much behind the general European standard of dramaturgy and production. The problem before the student, therefore, is to account for the existing deplorable conditions in these Indian theatres in the light of such immense Western inspiration and guidance and of an increasing flow of good dramatic models from Europe and America. In other words, one may ask: How far has the direct and the indirect British influence been really salutary in its effect on the Indian stage?

Here perhaps it may not be inopportune to contrast briefly the influence of Western models on India with the influence of the alien models on sixteenth-century England.

2. Cf. Appendix C, where more than two hundred translations of and adaptations from Shakespeare are noted.

The Elizabethan age received tremendous impetus from the Renaissance, from the Reformation, and from the exploration of the New World. Its great national form of expression, the drama, was permeated by Italian influence, which, however, could not dominate over the English mind. The strong and free English nation, whilst assimilating all the foreign influences, not only stamped its own native genius on continental gold, but also developed its own robust tradition to counteract alien forces. This golden age of the drama followed a period of unprecedented national glory in the field of action, adventure and intellectual progress. Unfortunately, during the Indian Renaissance in the mid-nineteenth century, neither of the two above peculiar features existed.

After the decay of the Moghul empire, India had fallen into a state of utter political confusion. It was not until 1857 that the country settled down to a period of peaceful development. As Mr. E. Wingfield-Stratford[3] argues: "The opening up of the country by railways, telegraphs, post and newspapers had knit India together as never before in the course of her history. And not least important was the fact that England had supplied her with a common language for political purposes." At the same time, as the author reminds us, all the evils of an elaborate and complicated bureaucracy are "immeasurably strengthened when the bureaucracy is alien in race and sympathy to the people under whom it functions". The British civilians, as a rule, "came to form a close and jealously race-conscious caste, isolated from the life of the country".

In this political atmosphere, the new system of education created a curious class of Indian intelligentsia. "Many of the new type of educated Indians desired nothing better than to model themselves on the pattern of the West. When the whole of the immense influence wielded by the Government was exerted on behalf of Westernization, the danger

3. *The History of British Civilization*, London, 1914, pp. 1047–1049.

was great indeed." The tendency "to crush out imagination and individuality" was the outcome of this new political and educational machinery. When the national genius is completely overawed by a foreign domination, the so-called 'inferiority complex' or 'slave mentality' follows. The 'Rajas' (landowners) of Bengal were the rich privileged classes to whom the invitations to European theatres in Calcutta were often extended. These in turn organized luxurious productions almost exclusively on Western models, and their powerful influence gave a decisive bias to the Indian theatres.

It must not be forgotten, however, that even more than this spirit of spurious imitation due to political inferiority, the inherent Hindu religious or philosophical attitude to life greatly handicapped dramatic productivity. Emancipation of the drama from the medieval religions and the establishment of a fundamental human basis was the crying need during the Indian Renaissance. The purely human basis would have led to the salvation of the theatre; but, unfortunately, medieval superstitions and the doctrine of predestination and the notes of asceticism and pessimism retained still a great control over the new literary forces. This persistent philosophical attitude was greatly responsible for arresting the evolution of the Bengali *yātrā* to the full stature of a great national drama. As Dr. S. K. De[4] clearly points out: "The Hindu's deep-rooted pessimism with regard to this world and unlimited optimism with regard to the next had produced a stoical resignation, an epicurean indifference, and a mystical hope and faith which paralysed personal action, suppressed the growth of external life, and replaced originality by submission."

The third handicap to the proper development of the Indian drama proceeded from the essential social framework, which, although it preserved the Hindu society intact for

4. *Bengali Literature in the Nineteenth Century*, Calcutta, 1919, p. 446.

thousands of years, led it to decay. Through a variety of causes, many degrading evils grew up, including those of child marriages, of diverse dowry systems, and of caste ostracism. As these were bound to be reflected on the new stage even more powerfully than on the medieval stage, they naturally, in the hands of light satirists and inferior carica- turists, assumed merely sordid or farcical forms. Moreover, the barrier of class, which has become now artificially rigid, prevented the recognition of the true worth and quality of even the best actors on the professional stage. The actors are thus often recruited from the lower classes and seldom acquire any status in Indian society. The case is even worse in relation to actresses. The ancient tradition having died out during the Mohammedan supremacy, only dancing girls are seen in female rôles, or else boys perform those parts. Again, due to the 'purdah' evil, women of the higher class are largely conspicuous by their absence in the theatres; and so it is not to be wondered at that the atmosphere on both sides of the curtain sometimes becomes tainted with vulgarity and vice.

The fourth difficulty, the economic deterioration of India, is perhaps most responsible for the present state of affairs in the theatre. Despite the wealth of a few millionaires in Bombay, the majority of the population lives in abject poverty. Whilst the limited number of rich merchants patronize the stalls, the cultured middle class avoids the theatre as a place not sufficiently respectable for them. Thus the main source of the income of the commercial manager of a Gujarati-Urdu company depends largely on the new monied classes and on the pit and gallery receipts. The official figure of the average income of an Indian being £7 a year, one can imagine the power of his purse for theatrical entertainment.

To this grinding poverty must be added the standing handicap of illiteracy. The cosmopolitan audience of Bombay, drawn from several parts of India, can hardly be expected to understand the literary quality or poetic beauty of dramatic dialogue. It is no matter for surprise, therefore, that these playgoers demand only the spectacular effects which modern European stagecraft can produce in the theatre.

Along with this love of spectacle, they demand also sensational thrills, with which they are now fully familiar in the cheap cinema shows. In the course of the last two years, however, the Western influence of the 'talkies' has proved even a greater menace to the theatre proper.[5] Consequently, most of the members of the audience in a typical industrial centre demand for their eightpence or shilling something better and longer than a cinema programme. The commercial manager in these circumstances has to provide a most varied fare in the course of an entertainment of nearly five hours. He solicits the help not only of song, music and transformation scenes, but also of farcical situations, of acrobatics and stage combats. The presence of young boys in Bombay and of young girls in Calcutta is exploited often for the purpose of typical revue effects in the manner of a variety theatre. All these items, good in their place and degree, mar altogether the dignity and beauty of the legitimate theatre. The root of all this utmost

5. "The popular vogue of the 'talkies' in India—in Hindi, Marathi, Gujarati and other vernaculars, produced by the Indian film companies—has undermined the importance of the dramatic companies. These 'talkies' follow the same technique and can make their shows spectacular; besides, the entertainment they provide is not very expensive. They can afford to pay higher salaries to the actors and actresses; and so the modern tendency is to attract the good actors and singers of the theatres in Bombay and make them act and sing for the screen. So many well-known actors—Ashrafkhan, Bhagwandas, Patwardhan and others—have left or are about to leave the stage and sign contracts with the film producers. These great actors and singers are thus found to lower down their standard of music and acting and make it suited to the cosmopolitan crowd that flock the cinemas in Bombay" (C. R. Shah). (This observation is more or less true of all the theatres of the world to-day.)

confusion and bewilderment in the theatre is, we may not doubt, largely economic.[6]

There is one other factor which deserves to be taken into account. It is the influence of one vernacular theatre on the other. The commercial companies of Bombay employ the medium of the Hindi-Urdu vernacular, which is most widely understood throughout India, and they are, therefore, able to travel to all parts of the country and to exert both good and bad influences—good in the sense that they give a stimulus to the art of powerful acting and to the appreciation of wonderful scenic effects and of brilliance of costumes, and bad in the sense that they confuse their dramas by presenting a mass of variety items in one 'play'. Such a vitiating influence may be illustrated with reference to the Urdu theatre at Calcutta. The standard Bengali stage is doing an excellent service to the cause of dramatic art in that city. Nevertheless, the rival Urdu stage, by means of its revolving stage, its clever comedians, and its introduction of Anglo-Indian girls on the stage for revue performances in the midst of patched-up plays, exerts a debasing influence on the morale of the more legitimate theatre.

In the midst of this extremely confused state of affairs in the theatre one cannot, of course, expect the best of results from the influence of the British drama. In the first place, some of the elements of 'Westernization', often thoughtlessly imitated by advanced Indians, were strongly resented by orthodox Indian society. The Western life reflected in the European productions in India was perfectly natural in its place, but, foolishly aped on the Indian stage, it was bound to be thoroughly denationalizing. Thus, for instance, in ordinary sex-relationship, embracing and kissing, even in the presence of others, is considered harmless in

6. It is true that the Elizabethan audience also was not wealthy and was largely illiterate. Nevertheless, the fact remains that the modern Indian playgoers are politically, socially and economically quite differently situated.

the West. Everyday terms of endearment like 'dearest' and
'darling', and the addressing by Christian name of husband
by wife and *vice versa*, accepted as conventional in Europe,
jarred a great deal on the orthodox Indian notions of propriety and decorum. Duśyanta in Kālidāsa advances near
the lips of his beloved but does not kiss her on the stage.
A social stage decency like this is respected by most cultured
Indians even to-day. The popular playwrights, however,
borrowed the many European social conventions from the
British drama on the Indian stage and denationalized the
whole atmosphere, and thus estranged the orthodox
classes.

Another degenerating factor proceeded from the modern
drink evil often mirrored on the stage in riotous scenes of
drunkenness. Many such situations from the European
drama were exploited fully, especially by the Urdu commercial managers. A number of Westernized gallants freely
indulging in champagne and beef-eating were utilized partly
for satirical purposes and partly to show the pitiable plight
to which the Eastern culture was reduced in modern times.
Similarly, several European modes of dress and of habits of
life which were considered to be opposed to the Indian
ideals, being thoughtlessly reflected on the stage, alienated
the sympathies of certain classes. Horse-racing, gambling
and many similar vices, representative of the actual Bombay
and Calcutta Indian life, profoundly influenced by the
European example, were also seized upon by the imitative
Indian theatres.

Perhaps even more debasing in its effects was the problem
of sexual morality as it finds expression in the European
drama. The conventional intrigue between a lover and a
married woman in many French plays and in Restoration
comedies, being freely followed on the Indian stage, often
revolted the feelings of those who attached importance to
the ennobling influence of the theatre. Light and frivolous
sex-relations on the stage exploited for farcical purposes

have been generally resented by many serious students of the drama.

In addition to the above follies and foibles due to the heedless imitation of the European social fashions, customs and conventions, there is another thing to be considered. The European companies in India naturally devoted more attention to the inferior species of drama, such as musical comedy and pantomime for purposes of pure enjoyment, than to high opera or great tragedy. And a society in a degraded frame of mind generally welcomes and follows the lower models. The result was that most of the elements of the musical comedy and the pantomime have taken a firm root in the soil of the Indian theatre. It is not difficult to realize that the very essence of higher drama is crushed out when transformation scenes, dazzling costumes, variety of songs, dance and ballet dominate the minds of the playgoers and producers.

All these difficulties and defects were inevitable, if one dispassionately considers the entire chain of circumstances. Still, the fact remains that, put in the balance, the numerous benefits derived by the Indian theatres outweigh all the above-mentioned shortcomings. Perhaps one of the greatest services rendered by the living contact with the British drama was the impregnation of new life and vitality to the modern Indian productions by providing them with a purely human basis instead of the outworn religious and doctrinaire settings. The perfect mastery of mundane realities revealed by Shakespeare has done incalculable good. He boldly brought the message of fully recognizing the actual facts of life and of facing its manifold problems squarely. The Indian dramatists realized that it was no use shutting their eyes and their ears to concrete evils and dark passions. The perpetual struggle between the higher and the lower forces within the human soul was studied and expressed with a conviction and sincerity almost unknown to the ancient masters.

That Shakespeare gained such an immense hold over the Indian mind throughout the country was unquestionably the result of his romantic method of treatment already noticed. After winning over the hearts of Indians, Shakespeare led them to regard tragedy as the highest form of dramatic endeavour. The use of this great dramatic form opened unprecedented possibilities before the quick-witted Indian mind. That the inferior Urdu playwrights, who could hardly read Shakespeare in the original, concentrated solely on the melodramatic thrills and forgot the acute internal conflict in the soul of the great tragic heroes was no fault of Shakespeare's; and their activities, as has been shown, may be balanced with higher endeavours elsewhere to capture the true spirit of Shakespeare's work.

This internal conflict, which was partly foreshadowed by the Sanskrit drama, developed with altogether a new force, fire and beauty in such modern Marathi and Bengali writers of historical tragedy as Khadilkar and Ray. Many social tragedies, directly constructed on the Shakespearean model, employed most of the English poet's devices with extraordinary effect. Whilst for the inartistic and extensive use of songs on the Marathi stage he was not at all responsible, the credit for their restricted use on the Bengali stage largely belongs to him.

In the field of comedy, also, Shakespeare exerted an ennobling influence. For the vulgar medieval farces, fine comedy, partly on the ancient Indian model, was substituted.

Another memorable service rendered by him was the restoration of the medieval play to the dignity of literature, which it had once enjoyed in ancient India. That the drama was a great literary form of human expression had been forgotten for centuries. With the introduction of Shakespeare's plays came a reawakened realization that drama was not merely a thing of thrills and laughter; and many Indian dramatists now endeavour to aim at appealing both to a reading public and to spectators in the theatre.

On account of the insistence on mundane realities, on the tragic conflict, and on drama as a form of literature, stress is being now laid on character often conceived in Shakespearean terms. It can easily be proved that whilst the third-class *kavis* have generally made capital out of the plots, situations and incidents furnished by European dramatists, the better playwrights have adopted the Shakespearean mode of construction and stage technique even in original plays, and the best dramatists have concentrated most on the Shakespearean art of characterization. For the vehicle of expression, the English blank verse was followed as a model by some Bengali playwrights, but was ultimately given up in favour of rhythmic prose.

Other great European dramatists have also wielded immense influence on the Indian mind more or less on the same lines as the English poet has done. The outstanding romantic impulse given by him to the new movement in India naturally fed the native stream, which in turn was amplified by many other romantic productions on the model of foreign masters. In recent times the tendency to ultra-romanticism was partly checked by the study of Ibsen and his followers. Some playwrights were persuaded to come to grips with the actual social problems of modern India. Others, no doubt, preferred to build on the fundamental human passions, on the model of Shakespeare; but they began to treat historical material for the purpose of rousing the nation from sleep and lethargy. Thus the national movement sought and obtained the help of the theatre for the necessary propaganda among the playgoers. These two aspects—of social reform and of patriotic message—gave a decided didactic turn to most of the new type of productions.

Whilst the new ideas of Ibsen have profoundly impressed several characters of Ray, certain enthusiasts, such as Mr. Varerkar, are making a strenuous effort to introduce the modern stage technique of Shaw in India. They desire to abolish the multiplicity of scenes now existing in the Indian theatre. They are tired of the old conventional painted scenery. They attempt to free their plays from the excessive use of songs. They aim definitely at realistic conversation by discarding the declamation, long rhetorical speeches, as well as asides, soliloquies, and the like. So far the new tendency has not been able to banish the Shakespearean dramatic technique, but the effort, however, deserves to be noticed.

In the sphere of amateur experiments, there are to-day two genuine progressive movements: on the one hand, that of several clubs, such as the 'Sugun Vilas Sabha' of Madras, to improve the entire level of productions in the country by means of refining the actual practices on the stage; and, on the other, that of gifted pioneers who have nothing to do with the professional stage and aim at poetic and symbolic productions. Both these groups, however, draw their inspiration in their own way partly from foreign models, methods and stagecraft.

PROSPECT

India to-day is undoubtedly passing through an acute stage of transition. As Sir C. P. Ramswami Iyer[7] truly observes: "In the ceaseless and inevitable conflicts of cultures and civilizations we have assimilated many of the inutilities of the West, and its shams, and superimposed them over the already complicated psychology of the double life of our own environment. The divorce between the real and the ideal, precept and practice, the Philistine life indoors and the swaggering life abroad that is characteristic of much modern life, is peculiarly a feature of the mixed culture of Europe and India." This double life is distressingly reflected

7. "Social Drama and Its Scope", in the periodical *Shama'a*, II, January 2, 1922, p. 68.

in the modern Indian theatres. It is hoped by many, however, that a greater and a higher Renaissance will follow in the course of time, after political, intellectual and moral emancipation is achieved.

Another genuine Renaissance, such as is envisaged here, will certainly welcome all that is best in international art. The process of assimilation will be more complete and the nation will be able to stamp its genius on all its borrowings. So far, the Indian theatre is in a state of utter confusion, since the country does not know its own mind and has not yet reached the proper period of self-unfolding. It simply borrows crudely and imitates. Signs of hope, however, are still to be found, and it is certain that there has been a certain steady though slow progress in the Indian theatre throughout the course of the last century. In the Bengali and Marathi theatres especially, mythological plays on a religious basis have mostly given place to historical and social plays on a human basis. The modern scientific and rationalistic attitude has also affected the stage to some extent, as new and human interpretation is given to mythological characters. And the notes of social, economic, religious and political reformation are distinctly to be heard.

What India really needs just now is an independent development of the legitimate drama on a three-dimensional stage[8] and a thoroughly Indian Ibsen or Shaw who would tackle contemporary problems with the earnestness and artistic appeal of those writers. At present, unfortunately, stage conditions are in such a state of chaos and uncertainty that such a dramatist, were he to arise, would have much pioneer work to do before he came to a true period of creation. As things are, neither author nor audience knows whether a play is written for a platform or for a picture-frame stage. The modern stage has no apron and makes use of European stagecraft, and yet all the seventeenth-century

8. Bengal has just started the experiment with a considerable success.

dramatic devices are still practised. The system of back-cloth and of several wings on grooves and sky-borders painted in perspective with the use of shutters continues to persist. This is a relic of the early nineteenth century and needs complete remodelling. The present chaos in costume and lighting, too, would have to give place to something better and more carefully conceived.

In all or most of these directions the light of inspiration will have to be shed by amateurs. The educated classes will have to form many more dramatic societies and produce plays earnestly throughout the country. Such would certainly create a more wholesome atmosphere. Plays then would be written for the new technique. The success of this new movement must, however, greatly depend on the educated women of good families coming forward to help the national dramatic revival. Once the full dignity of the art is realized by the country, there is indeed a very great future for India in the Renaissance of the theatre.

It is premature to outline any scheme of a national theatre for India in the manner of Mr. Granville Barker's English attempt. It is equally premature to advise the professional theatre to profit by the advice and guidance of great modern masters of stagecraft such as Reinhardt, Gordon Craig and Appia, as Dr. Guha-Thakurta seems to do. Before these great experiments can be profitably employed on the Indian stage numerous changes will certainly be necessary.

In all future efforts for the development of her theatre, India will assuredly need the generous co-operation of the Western drama and theatre. Even when she develops her own national theatre[9] of a distinct type she will gain immensely by constant contact with the finest European models, even although greater benefit will be derived from

9. Mr. Grant Anderson quite recently made an effort in this direction, in Bombay, with a troupe of Indian artistes; but, so far, he has not succeeded.

a subtle process of assimilating than by the mere adapting and imitating of ideas. But, whatever course the stage takes in the future, there is absolute certainty about one thing: the Indian theatres will always maintain their reverence and affection for Shakespeare, and will yield to none in their love for the dramatist they consider as belonging to all nations. Thus, although the contact between the East and the West in the field of the theatre has already borne remarkable fruit, one believes that it is indeed yet capable of bearing even more and richer.

APPENDIX A

A FEW IMPORTANT EXTRACTS

I. TRAGEDY IN SANSKRIT DRAMA

(1) *Dr. S. K. De's Notes to this work:*

The Sanskrit Drama does not entirely exclude tragedy; but what it really does is that it excludes the direct representing of death as an incident, and insists on a happy ending. It recognizes some form of tragedy in its pathetic sentiment (*karuṇa rasa*) and during separation in love (*vipralambha śṛṅgāra*); and tragic interest is almost central in some plays. In the *Mṛcchakaṭika* and *Śākuntala*, for instance, the tragedy does not indeed occur at the end, but it occurs in the middle, and in *Uttara-rāma-carita*, where the tragic interest prevails throughout, it occurs in an intensive form at the beginning of the play. The theorists appear to maintain that there is no tragedy in the mere fact of death, which in itself may be disgusting, horrible or debasing and thus produce a hiatus in the æsthetic pleasure. Tragedy, in their opinion, either precedes or follows the fact of death, which need not be actually represented but the effect of which may be utilized for evoking the pathetic. It may be noted, however, that we have at least one instance where this injunction is obeyed in the letter indeed but not in spirit; for Vasantasenā's apparent murder occurs on the stage.

(2) *Dr. S. K. Belvelkar's Notes to the* Kāvyādarśa *of Daṇḍin* (I. 17.):

In epic poetry as in drama there was in India a general feeling against a tragic ending. And yet we find the *Ūrubhaṅga* of Bhāsa and the *Hammīramahākāvya* of Nayacandrasūri as instances to the contrary. However, the normal objection to tragic ending seems to have been based on the fact that, while poetic justice requires that the hero's fate be deserved and not arbitrary, if the hero who meets such a fate is at the same time to win the sympathy of the audience, the poet would thereby be doing something detrimental to the moral interests of men. The Greek idea of Nemesis overtaking a person when his virtues practised to excess turn into vices, or the modern psychological idea that

every emotion—no matter of what kind or character—leaves
the man all the better and the soberer for it, does not seem to
have been properly grasped by Indian formulators of poetic
theory.

II. Moral Purpose in Sanskrit Drama

Dr. S. K. De's Notes:

Sanskrit Drama is seldom didactic in the ordinary sense,
although it is fully alive to the great problems of life and destiny;
nor does its implicit purpose interfere with the higher purpose
of dramatic art. Ideal heroic characters are indeed presented,
but this is because the conception of the Sanskrit Drama is
fundamentally different. It is idealistic and romantic, and therefore often ignores realities of action or character. The object is
not to mirror life by a direct portrayal of action or character,
but to delineate *rasa* or sentiment, be it heroic, amatory, quietistic;
and action and character are subsidiary or contributory to this
purpose of evoking certain sentiments in the audience. Hence
the sentimental or poetic envelopment, which was conducive to
idealistic creation at the expense of action and characterization.
The analogy is to be found in the Indian painting or sculpture
which avoids crude realism of bones and muscles, and concentrates exclusively on the spiritual expression. This, of course,
does not mean that reality was entirely banished, or that the
characters were devoid of the milk of human kindness. Cārudatta,
for instance, is not a mere paragon of virtue, but a perfect man
of the world whose great virtues were softened by an equally
great touch of humanity. The greater Sanskrit dramatists with
their inherent artistic sense always rose superior to mere drama-
turgic conceptions, but it must be admitted that they regarded,
both in theory and practice, the drama as a division of poetry,
and the conceptions were essentially poetic. On this point I have
written elsewhere: "Both theory and practice laid down that the
drama or *Rūpaka* was a subdivision of the *Kāvya* or poetry in
general, and that the main interest of the drama was not (as in
Western plays) so much in the action or characterization as in
the delineation of sentiment. Thus the drama came to possess
an atmosphere of sentiment and poetry, which in the lesser
dramatists overshadowed all that was dramatic in it." It is for
this reason that sentimental verses preponderate and form the
more essential part of the drama, the prose merely acting as

connecting link or as a means of carrying forward the story. As there is thus a fundamental difference in the conception of the drama, the Sanskrit plays, judged by modern or Western standards, would not all be regarded as dramas in the strict sense, but rather as dramatic poems. It is not surprising, therefore, that a modern critic would regard only *Mudrārākṣasa*, in the whole range of Sanskrit dramatic literature, as a drama proper. But this is an extreme view, for the authors of *Śākuntala* and of *Mṛcchakaṭika* knew very well that they were writing dramas and not merely a set of elegant poetical extracts.

III. THE RISE OF THE MODERN BENGALI THEATRE

This thesis was submitted in July 1931. Since then several important articles on the "Early History of the Bengali Theatre" have appeared, e.g. three articles by Mr. Brajendra Nath Banerji in *The Modern Review* for October, November and December 1931. A few supplementary notes drawn from these may prove interesting:

(1) A new *yātrā*, *Nanda-vidāya* was performed twice in March 1849 at the house of the author, Ramchand Mookerjee of Jorasanko, and again on April 14, at the residence of Srikrishna Sinha of Jorasanko. "The most revolutionary departure in its performance was the acting of the women's parts by young girls" (*Sambad Bhaskar, March 30 and April 17*, 1849).

(2) A Bengali actor named Vaishnav Charan Addy twice acted the part of Othello with great credit at the Sans Souci Theatre on August 17 and September 12, 1848.

(3) The dramatic enthusiast, Babu Nabin Chandra Bose, set up a private theatre at his own house in Shambazar, on the site of the present Shambazar Tram Depot, about the year 1833 and staged four or five Bengali dramas in it every year. *The Hindu Pioneer* (October 22, 1835) pays a tribute to these: "These are native performances, by people entirely Hindus, after the English fashion, in the vernacular language of their country; and what elates us with joy, as it should do all the friends of Indian improvement, is that the fair sex of Bengal are always seen on the stage, as the female parts are almost exclusively performed by Hindu women."

(4) Of all the schools or college dramatic clubs, the David Hare Academy (established in 1851 at Burtola) set the example of the performance of a complete play in English by a school; cf. the notice for *The Merchant of Venice* in the *Sambad Prabhakar*, a vernacular daily, on February 10, 1853. Mr. Clinger, Head Master of the English Department of the Calcutta Madressa, trained the students. This academy also staged *Julius Cæsar* in 1853.

(5) The example of the David Hare Academy was followed by the rival institution—The Oriental Seminary. The school organized a regular theatre (The Oriental Theatre) and produced Shakespeare. Under the guidance of Mr. Clinger, *Othello* was staged on September 26, 1853. The performance of *The Merchant of Venice* is remarkable for the last appearance of Mrs. Creig on the Calcutta stage, for she acted as Portia with the Hindu amateurs on March 17, 1854. The last piece to be staged in this Oriental Theatre was *Henry IV* on February 15, 1855.

(6) The next dramatic club to present Shakespeare plays was more ambitious and not attached to any particular educational institution. It was Jorasanko Theatre, which was housed in the Jorasanko residence of Pyari Mohan Basu, a nephew of Nobin Chandra Basu, the patron of the Bengali Theatre. *Julius Cæsar* was staged on May 3, 1854: "The residence was illuminated by lamps and decorated with pictures and other beautiful objects pleasing the eye. The beauty of the stage, particularly, can hardly be described" (*Sambad Prabhakar*, May 5, 1854).

(7) The 'sixties were rich in a variety of amateur theatres, such as "Bawbazar Banga-Natyalaya" established by Chunilal Basu and Baldeb Dhar. "This was the age of intense but to a very great extent ephemeral dramatic activity. Almost the sole occupation of the idle rich of Calcutta was to start amateur theatres." The most important of these, perhaps, was the Baghbazar Society of Nagendra Banerjee, Girish Ghosh, Radha Madhab Kar, Ardhendu Mustafi and others in 1868. This theatre was soon converted into a public theatre, selling tickets for its performances. Girish Ghosh was against the idea and left the society. However, the famous actor Amritlal Bose joined the Baghbazar troupe and on December 7, 1872, the first professional Bengali theatre was inaugurated at Jorasanko.

* * *

(More recently, several important articles on the History of the Bengali stage, by Mr. Hemendra Das Gupta, have appeared in the columns of the Daily national newspaper, *The Amrita Bazar Patrika* of Calcutta. The writer thanks Mr. G. L. Mehta for kindly drawing his attention to these.)

APPENDIX B

AMATEUR EXPERIMENTS

ONE of the most remarkable results of the influence of British drama in India was the immense impetus given to amateur acting. For the first time in India, members of high-class families began to cultivate the art of the theatre for its own sake. They came to realize the essential dignity and worth of acting. The most noteworthy instance of this is furnished by the "Sugun Vilas Sabha" of Madras, which is the most flourishing and the best organized amateur club in India. The aim of this society is to raise the entire level of professional productions throughout India by setting the best example in the direction of the legitimate theatre. Some of the highest Indian officials and national leaders are taking a living interest in the association, which has now about 1,500 members and which produces about forty plays and variety shows every year[1] in five languages.

Mr. P. Sambanda, the soul of this great organization, writes: "The members of the Sabha besides putting in the form of prose drama classical Indian stories, like *Hariścandra*, etc., have also adapted or translated great gems of Sanskrit drama like *Śākuntala* etc., and have also translated several works of the greatest of world's dramatists—Shakespeare. Some of Molière's works have been adapted from the English translations. Several original dramas have been written by its members, mostly of the romantic type. . . . Of late years the Sabha has attempted to open a new line, by writing and staging dramas of present social life among Indians, following in the wake of great Western writers like Ibsen, Oscar Wilde, and others."[2]

Although they have not yet been able to introduce women on the amateur stage, in all other respects they are deeply influenced by the European amateur productions in Madras. Serious plays have been produced and acted with dignity and restraint. Melodramatic extravagances have been avoided and the use of songs is generally harmonized with the spirit of the plays. The presence of the most respectable members of society

1. Cf. *The Report of 'The Sabha'* for 1928.
2. *The Suguna Vilas Sabha Souvenir*, Madras, 1929. (Exact quotation from its preface.)

as possible, an absolutely natural background is preferred. The
on the stage exerted a profound influence on the minds of thinking
playgoers. The society aims at introducing new methods of scenic
display in the highly modern theatre which it is at present
planning to build.

In Western India the Gujarati amateur experiments have
recently received an excellent impetus from the greatest living
novelist of Gujarat, Mr. K. M. Munshi, who boldly follows the
Shavian technique, has a shrewd sense of the theatre and is
now publishing a series of lively plays. One of these, a social
comedy, *Kākānī Śaśī*, has already enjoyed immense popularity,
notably as produced by the Bhavnagar College amateurs. His
accomplished wife, Mrs. Lilavati Munshi, particularly excels in
the art of writing one-act plays. Another noteworthy success
is *Śaṅkita Hṛdaya* by the popular and gifted novelist Mr. R. V.
Desai. It is also interesting to note that such patrons of fine
arts as Sir Chinubhai Madhavlal II, Bart., and Seth Ambalal
Sarabhai of Ahmedabad and Seth Karsandas Vissanji Khimji
of Bombay, are making admirable efforts to raise the level of
private performances in Gujarat.

DR. TAGORE'S PLAYS

As contrasted with the great Madras experiment in amateur
acting, one may note Dr. Tagore's symbolical productions at his
international University of Shantiniketan. The Tagore family
has been deeply interested in the theatrical movement for genera-
tions. It has produced poets, musicians, thinkers and painters,
and many of these have turned their attention to the drama.
The central courtyard of their palatial buildings has often been
utilized for theatrical experiments, the verandah with a huge
flight of steps being used as a stage. The poet writes a play;
a friend sets his enchanting lyrics to music; a brother designs
the simple but symbolic scenery and many members of that
gifted family, men and women, take part in the production, the
poet himself supervising the whole.

What the original genius of the poet with a message of his
own to the world has gained from Eurcpean example and especially from the Irish Stage Society will never be determined.
However, that by a subtle process of perfect assimilation his
mind has thus been enriched can hardly be gainsaid. He generally
loves to produce his poetical plays on the occasion of the spring
or the rainy season festivals. In an open-air production, as far

thread of the plot is very thin, the progress of the play being suggested by a number of exquisite songs. As an instance of his symbolic plays, *The King of the Dark Chamber*, with its twenty to twenty-two songs, may be mentioned. Although there is little scenery, the poet often provides a feast of colours by means of luxurious costumes. For musical purposes only the *Dilruba* (an Indian stringed instrument) is utilized. All artificiality of voice and of gesture is banned.

He has written exquisite plays for the children's autumnal festival, and impressive pieces, such as *The Dancing Girl's Worship*,3 for an exclusive cast of women. He has made attempts at realistic plays (e.g. *The King and the Queen*); but he is at his best in such characteristic allegorical pieces as *Muktadhārā*, in the preface to which he explains his symbolic purpose. His *Post Office* has been a universal favourite. It has been staged with considerable success in several parts of India and of Europe. Mr. Chandravadan Mehta, a gifted Gujarati amateur, has produced several plays of Tagore among others, in Bombay, with the aid of the students of the Elphinstone College and of the Fellowship School. It must be confessed, however, that although Tagore's dramas have appealed widely to the reading public, his productions have so far aroused little enthusiasm among playgoers in general.

OTHER POETIC PRODUCTIONS

The names of James H. Cousins and Harindra Chattopadhyay must be recalled in connection with some of the finest amateur experiments in India during recent times. The dominant influence on these two verse-playwrights is exercised by W. B. Yeats and the Irish Literary Society. As A. E. Morgan points out: "The splendid object of Mr. Yeats, in 1892, was to 'spread a tradition of life that makes neither great wealth nor great poverty, that makes the arts a national expression of life, that permits every common man to understand good art and high thinking and to have the fine manners these things can give'. . . . Mr. Yeats is

3. This was beautifully produced, at Calcutta, in the original Bengali, by the girls of Shantiniketan, at the time of the Tagore septuagenary, in 1932, at Tagore House. It was also exquisitely produced in Gujarati, quite recently, by the girls of the Fellowship School, Bombay, with Miss Taru Kara as the heroine, and also by the girls of the 'Mahilā Vidyālaya', Bhavnagar, with Miss Shridevi Oza in the title-rôle.

first and last a poet, and his drama is always subject to the poetic influence which commands his whole work. It is not merely that the greater part of his drama is written in verse: the essence of his work is poetic, inspired by the lyrical sense and impregnated with symbolical and mystical fancy".[4]

The same high quest for beauty is the leading theme of the visionaries in India. Mr. Cousins' *The Sword of Dermot*, for instance, creates the same type of poetic illusion as was created by Mr. Gordon Bottomley's *Ardvorlich's Wife*. The poetic and symbolic setting and the rhythmic verses appeal strongly to the heart and imagination of the audience.

Mr. Harindra Chattopadhyay, a poet of considerable merit, belongs to one of the most gifted and advanced families of India, one of his sisters being the celebrated poetess Sarojini Naidu. His stay at Cambridge and visits to Europe developed his poetic genius. His great ambition is to make his art a national expression of Indian life. As he believes in English as the international language, his voice is English; but his message is thoroughly Indian. The highest teachings of Christianity have coloured his mind and yet he is fully representative of Indian nationalism. He has published numerous English poems and verse-plays. Even more striking is the fact that he himself is a consummate actor and producer, his accomplished wife, Mrs. Kamaladevi Chatto-padhyay, and brothers and sisters, including Miss Mrunalinidevi, acting with him. Plays such as *Tukārām* or *Puṇḍalik* (Indian Saints) may be mentioned as typical of his genius and method.

"His dramatic work is either definitely religious, or is over-shadowed with consciousness of the Divine and Eternal. . . . His themes are constantly those of the religious poets of the Indian race."[5] As a leader of the Shama'a players, he recently produced *Abu Hussain* with great success, natural acting, sugges-tive setting and English songs set to Indian music being its noteworthy features.

Finally, it may be added that Indian Amateur Dramatic Associations, such as the one at Bangalore, are doing several important services to the country by trying to keep abreast of international developments in dramatic art and by organizing lectures and conferences for the purpose of securing a great national revival in the drama and the theatre.

4. *Tendencies of Modern English Drama*, 1924, p. 139.
5. *Shama'a*, Vol. VII, Nos. 3–4, July–October, Madras, 1927, p. 208.

APPENDIX C

A LIST OF SHAKESPEARE TRANSLATIONS AND ADAPTATIONS

(i) Those marked "EX" are examined above in this work.
(ii) Those marked "T" are mere translations.
(iii) Those marked "(*)" are either not printed or out of print.
(iv) Those marked "(G)" are mentioned by Dr. S. C. Gupta in his unpublished thesis, *Shakespeare in India*, London, 1924. His spellings have been generally preserved.
(v) For abbreviations of Indian vernaculars, see *A Note on Transliteration and Abbreviations*.

A. COMEDIES

PLAY		VERSION	REMARKS
1. *Love's Labour's Lost*	U.	*Yavon ki Mihmat Barbad*, by Muhammad Sulaiman, 1899	(G) T
2. *The Comedy of Errors*	G₁.	*Jodiyā Bhāiyo*, by N. R. Ranina, Bombay, 1865	(G) T
	B₁.	*Bhramajāla*, by Venimadhav Ghosh, 1873	(G). The correct title is *Bhrama Kautuka*
	M₁.	*Mhatarya Vyaparyachi Goshta*, by R. V. Oka, 1875	(G)
	M₂.	*Bhrāntikṛta Camatkāra*, by R. B. Jathar and B. R. Pradhan, 1877	(G) EX
	H₁.	*Bhramajalaka*, by Ratnachandra, Allahabad, 1879	(G)
	B₂.	*Bhrāntivilāsa* (based on Vidyasagar's story), Calcutta, 1888	Staged. (*)
	U₁.	*Bhūla-bhūlaiyān*, by Firoz Shah Khan, 1896	(G) T
	G₂.	*Rāmā-Ratana*, by N. K. Vaidya, 1903	Staged. (*)
	H₂.	*Bhūla-bhūlaiyān*, by Lala Sitaram, 1905	(G) T. (Sitaram's Hindi Shakespeare† mentioned as Urdu translation.)

† The writer thanks Professor C. R. Shah for drawing his attention to this series.
Mr. Lala Sitaram, B.A., wrote in 1915: "I propose to publish Hindi versions of all the thirty-seven plays of Shakespeare." This series is not obviously meant for production. "Each play contains the preface with the usual bardolatry." So far about ten versions seem to have appeared. They are usually free and in simple language.

PLAY		VERSION	REMARKS
2. The Comedy of Errors (cont.)	Ta.	Vibhrama Vihāram, by A. Venkatacharyar, 1905–6	(G) T
	U₂.	Gorakhadhandā, by Narayan Betab, 1912	(G) EX
	U₃.	Bhūl-bhulaiyān, by Abdul Karim, 1913	(G)
3. Two Gentlemen of Verona	M.	Kāntipurcā Don Gṛhastha, 1880	Staged. (*)
	K.	Kusumakare, by M. R. Annaji Rau, 1897	(G). Prose adaptation
	Ta.	Suguna-Sukesar, or Friendship and Love, by S. Ramaswami Aiyangar, 1899	(G)
4. A Midsummer Night's Dream	M₁.	Madhuyāminī Svapna, by K. N. Athale	Not staged
	M₂.	Veṣaviparyāsa, by K. P. Godgol	(*)
	M₃.	Sītā, 1889	(G)
	Ta.	A Midsummer Night's Dream, by S. Narayana Swami Ayar, 1902	(G) T
	U.	'Ali-Jam'i ul fat, by Muhammad Azhur, 1903	(G)
	B.	Jahānārā, by Satiśacandra Chattopadhyay, 1904	(G) EX
	M₄.	Premamakaranda, by A. N. Ukadive, 1904	(G) EX
5. The Merchant of Venice	B₁.	Bhānumatī-cittavilāsa, by Harachandra Ghosh, 1853	(G)
	M₁.	Strīnaya-cāturya, by A. V. Patkar, 1871	(G)
	H₁.	Venice-nagarkā byāparī, by Arya, Benares, 1888	(G) T
	K.	Panchalu-Parinayam, by A. Anandarao, 1890	(G) T
	G₁.	Strīnyāyakalā, by Narsidas Vanamalidas, Bombay, 1893	(G)
	U₁.	Chand Shah i Sud-Khwar, Anonymous, 1895	(G) T
	B₂.	Suvalatā, by Pyarilal Mukhopadhyay, 1897	(G)
	S.	Husna en Dildar, by Qualij Beg Faridam Beg, 1897	(G)
	U₂.	Venice Ke Saudagar, by Ashig husain, 1898	(G) T
	U₃.	Dil farośa, by Aga Hashra, 1900	(G) EX
	M₂.	Pranaya Mudrā, by V. S. Gurjar, 1904	EX
	Ta₁.	Venis-Varttakan, by S. V. Kallpiram Pillai, 1904	(G) T
	G₂.	Jagata Simha (or, A Pound of Flesh), 1904	(*). Partly based on a Bengali novel

A LIST OF SHAKESPEARE TRANSLATIONS AND ADAPTATIONS—*continued*

PLAY		VERSION	REMARKS
5. The Merchant of Venice (cont.)	Te.	Venicpura Varta Kodantham, by Tallaprageda Surya-narayanrao, 1906	(G) T
	H₂.	Ek Aurat Ki Vakilat, by Krishna Hasrat, Benares, 1908	(G)
	M₃.	Mohanācī Añguthī, by D. G. Limaye, 1909	(G)
	M₄.	Venice Nagarcā Vyāparī, by K. B. Belsare, 1910	(G) T
	B₃.	Saudāgar, by Bhupendra Bandopadhyay	(G) EX
	B₄.	Merchant of Venice, by Mon Mohan Roy	(G) EX
	G₃.	Vibudha Vijaya (a free version)	Staged. (*)
	Ta₂.	Vanikar Vanikam, by P. Sambanda	(Sugun Vilas Sabha Amateurs—Madras)
	M₅.	Saudāgar, by M. Agashe	(*)
6 The Taming of the Shrew	M₁.	Trāṭikā, by V. B. Kelkar, 1892	(G)
	M₂.	Caṇḍāve Ratna (the same with songs added)	EX
	M₃.	Karkaśā-damana, by Patankar	EX
	Ta.	Vigata Sundari, by Kandusami Pillai, 1906	(G)
7. The Merry Wives of Windsor	M.	Caturgaḍhcā Vinodi Striyāñi, by P. G. Limaye, 1905	(G)
	B.	Nabina Tapasvinī, by Dinbandhu Mitra	EX
8 As You Like I	H₁.	Manabhavana, by Gopinath of Jaipur, 1897	(G) T
	B.	Ananga-Rāgiṇī, by Manada Prasada Vasu, 1897	(G)
	U.	Dilpazir, by Charandas, 1901	(G)
	M.	Premagumphā, by V. S. Patavardhan, 1908	EX
	Te.	Sri Sarojini, by T. V. Venkatachalamu, 1910	(G)
	Ta.	Vidame, by P. Sambanda	EX
	H₂.	Apani Apani Ruci, by Lala Sitaram	T

PLAY	VERSION	REMARKS
9. *Twelfth Night*	B. *Suśilā-Candraketu*, by Kantichandra Vidyasagar, Calcutta, 1872	Prose romance
	U. *Bhālabhālaiyām*, by Munshi Mehadi Hasan, 1905	EX
	M₁. *Bhramavilāsa*, by B. H. Pandit, 1910	EX
	M₂. *Priyārādhana*, by Navalkar	(*)
	M₃. *Twelfth Night*, by F X. Douglas, 1911	(T) (in Kokanī dialect)
10. *Much Ado About Nothing*	M₁. *Rajacā Gaja*	Not staged
	M₂. *Virodhābhāsa*, by P. V. Sahastrabuddhe	(*)
	U. *Dam i Muhabbat*, by Lala Sitaram, 1907	(G) T
	H. *Manmohan kā Jāl*, by Lala Sitaram	T
11. *All's Well That Ends Well*	M₁. *Vallabhānunaya*, by V. M. Mahajani, 1880	Not staged
	G. *Vaidya Kanyā*, by Narayana Hemchandra, Ahmedabad, 1895	(G)
	K. *Satimaṇi Vijaya*, by B. Somanath Ayya, 1897	(G). Translated from Telegu
	U. *Husna-ārā*, Parsi Company, Bombay, 1900	(*)
	Te. *Saundarya Satimaṇi*, by Bhave Narayanudu, 1904	(G). An adaptation in seven acts from Telegu translation of Lamb's *Tales* by K. Veeresa Lingam Pantulu
12. *Measure for Measure*	M₂. *Priyārādhana*, by V. S. Patavardhana, 1912	(G) EX
	U. *Shaheedē Nāz*, by Aga Hashra, 1905	EX
	G. *Measure for Measure*, by N. P. Dave, Bhavnagar, 1906	(G) T
	M₁. *Samānaśāsana*, Poona, 1909	(G) EX
	B. *Vinimaya*, by Birendra Nath Ray, 1909	(G) EX
	M₂. *Sumati-Vijaya*, by H. N. Apte, Poona, 1911	Not staged
	H. *Bagulā Bhagata*, by Lala Sitaram	T

A LIST OF SHAKESPEARE TRANSLATIONS AND ADAPTATIONS—continued

PLAY		VERSION	REMARKS
13. Cymbeline	B₁.	Suśilā Vīrasena, 1868	(G)
	B₂.	Kusumakumārī, by Candra-Kali Ghosh, 1874	EX
	M.	Tara, by V. M. Mahajani, Poona, 1879	(G) EX
	G₁.	Ramanasundarī, by G. K. Delvadekar, Bombay, 1895	(G)
	Ta₁.	Sara-Sangī, by T. R. Sarasalochana Chetti, 1897	(G)
	Te.	Susena-Vijayam, by Hamimantu Rau, 1898	(G)
	U₁.	Zulme-nā-ravā, Bombay, 1899	(*)
	U₂.	Mīthā-Zahara, by Munshi Mustafa Saiyadalli, 1900	EX
	G₂.	Cāmparāja Hāmdo, by V. A. Cza, 1900	EX
	U₃.	Cymbeline, by M. 'Abdul Aziz, 1902	(G)
	K.	Jayasimha Rājā Caritam, by C. M. Nanjappa, 1907	(G)
	Ta₂.	Simhalamānadha, by P Sambanda, 1910	(*)
14. The Winter's Tale	B₁.	Madanamañjarī, 1876	(G)
	M₁.	Vikalpavimocana, by Nevalkar, Poona, 1894	EX
	G.	Candrahasa, by V. A. Oza, Bombay, 1894	EX
	M₂.	Samsaya Sambrama, by G. C. Deva, 1895	(G)
	U.	Murdeedā Shak, by Munshi Hasan, 1898 (By Muhammad Shah, 1900)	(*)
	B₂.	Tamālini, by Dhanadacharan Mitra, 1914	(G)
	M₃.	Mohavilasita, by V. M. Mahajani	(G) Not staged
15. The Tempest	M₁.	Tempest, by N. J. Kirtane, 1875	(G) T
	U.	Ferdinand-o-Miranda, by M. Shafi 'al-din Khan, 1896	(G) T. Part only
	B₁.	Nalini-Vasanta, by Hemachandra Bandopadhyay, 1900	(G)
	M₂.	Tuphān, by K. B. Belsare, 1903	EX
	Te.	Tempest, by Paramahamsa Vidyananda Svami, 1907	(*)
	B₂.	Jhanjhā, by Nagendraprasad Sarvadhikari, 1913	(G) T
	H.	Jamgala mem Mamgala, by Lala Sitaram	(G) T

PLAY	VERSION	REMARKS
16. Pericles	U. Khudā-dāda, by Munshi Karimuddin, 1891	Staged. (*)
	M₁. Sudhanvā	Not staged
	M₂. Pratāpamuktā, by B. R. Patil	(*)
	Te. Raghudeva Rajeeyam, by Bhava-Narayanudu, 1899	(G)

B. ENGLISH HISTORICAL PLAYS

PLAY	VERSION	REMARKS
17. Richard III	M₁. Jayājirāo, by B. R. Nanal, 1891	(G)
	U. Saide-Havasa, by Aga Hashra, 1906	EX
	(By Aga Muhammad, 1909)	(G)
	M₂. Rājā Rākṣasa, by H. H. Dixit	Not staged
	M₃. Richard III, by H. B. Atre	Not staged. T
	H. Rājā Richard, by Lala Sitaram	T
	M. Kapidhvaja	EX
18. King John		
19. Henry V	M. Pañcam Henry, by K. B. Belsare	Not staged. T
20. Henry VIII	M. Rājā Raghunāth Rāo, by H. B. Atre, 1904	(G) T

C. TRAGEDIES

PLAY	VERSION	REMARKS
21. Titus Andronicus	U₁. Junūnē Vafā, by A. B. Latif Sad, 1910	EX
22. Romeo and Juliet	B₁. Charumukha Chittahara, by Harachandra Ghosh, 1864	(G)
	G. Romeo and Juliet, by Dosabhai Randeria, 1876	(G) T
	B₂. Ajaya Sinha-Vilasavati, by Yogendra Ghosh, 1878	(G)
	M₁. Pratāparāva āni Manjulā, staged in Poona, 1882	(*)
	M₂. Sasikala-Ratnapāla, by Kanitkar, staged in 1882	(*)
	K. Ramavarma-Lilavathi, by Anand Rav, 1889	(G) T
	B₃. Romeo and Juliet, by Hemchandra Bandopadhyay, 1895	(G)
	U₂. Bazmē Fānī, by Mehar Hasan, 1897	EX
	(By Muhammad Shah, 1900)	(G)

A LIST OF SHAKESPEARE TRANSLATIONS AND ADAPTATIONS—continued

PLAY		VERSION	REMARKS
22. Romeo and Juliet (cont.)	H.	Romeo and Juliet, by Gopinath of Jaipur, Premalila, 1898	(G) T
	M₃.	Sālinī, by K. V. Karmarkar, 1901	(G) EX
	U₃.	Gulnar Faroz, by Mehdi Hasan Khan, 1902	(G)
	U₄.	Firozliga o Gulmarsiyar, by Nazir Beg, 1905	(G)
	M₄.	Tārā-vilāsa by Dattatraya Mantakeskar, 1908	(G)
	U₅.	Gulsaz i Firoz, by J. L. Seth, 1908	(G)
	Ta₁.	Ramyanum Jolidaiyam, by S. V. Srinivasaiar, 1908	(G)
	M₅.	Mohana-Tārā, by K. R. Chapakhane, 1908	EX
	M₆.	Premacha Kalasa, by K. B. Belsare, 1908	(G) T
	Ta₂.	Ramaṇa-Jvalitā, by P. S. Duraiswami Iyengar.	Staged by Shashi Vilas Sabha (amateurs), Madras. (*)
	M₇.	Romaketu-V jaya, by V. G. Vistar	(*)
23. Julius Cæsar	M₁.	Vijaya Sinha, by K. G. Natu, 1872	(G)
	M₂.	Julius Cæsar, by R. T. Pavanskar, 1883	Not staged
	B.	Julius Cæsar, by Jyotindranath Thakura, 1907	(G) T
	M₃.	Julius Cæsar, by K. B. Belsare, 1912	(G) T
24. Hamlet	B₁.	Amarasimha, by Parmatha Natha Vasu, 1874	(G)
	M₁.	Vikāravilasita, by G. G. Agarkar, 1883	EX
	M₂.	Himmata-bahādura, by A. S. Barve, 1890	Not staged
	M₃.	Vīrasena, by G. V. Kanitkar, 1890	Not staged
	B₂.	Chandranath, by Siddhesvara Gupta, 1894	(G) T
	B₃.	Hamlet, by Chandiprasad Ghosh, 1894	(G) T
	B₄.	Hamlet, by Mon Mohan Ray	(G) T
	U₁.	Jahangir, by Umrao Ali, 1895	EX
	B₅.	Harivāja, by Amrarendranath Datta, 1897	(G) T
	U₂.	Khānē-nāhaq, by Munshi Mehdi Hasan, 1898	(G) EX

PLAY		VERSION	REMARKS
24. Hamlet *(cont.)*	U₃.	*Hamlet*, by Muhammad Afzal Khan, 1902	(G)
	U₄.	*Wagi'ah i Jahangir i Nashad*, by Nazer Beg, 1902	(G)
	Ta.	*Amalāditya*, by P. Sambanda, 1911	(G) EX
	H.	*Hamlet*, by Lala Sitaram	T
	M₄.	*Puṣpasena Rājaputra*	A special adaptation for boys
25. Othello	G₁.	*Kashivrajnom Karasthana*, by N. R. Ranina, 1866	(G) T
	M₁.	*Othello*, by M. G. Shastri, 1867	(G) T
	B₁.	*Bhīmasinha*, by Tarinicharan Pal, 1875	(G) EX
	M₂.	*Jhumjāvarāva*, by G. B. Dewal, 1880	(G) EX
	Te₁.	*Jayadratha*, by Padmanabha Razu, 1894	(G)
	B₂.	*Othello*, by Kaliprasanna Chattopadhyay, 1894	(G)
	U₁.	*Ja'far*, by Ahmed Husain Khan, 1895	(G) T
	K.	*Surasena-Caritra*, by Basappa Shastri and C. Subarao, 1895	(G) T
	U₂.	*Shaheedē vajā*, by Munshi Mehdi Hasan, 1898	EX
	Ta₁.	*Othello*, 1902. (Shakespeare Series for Tamil Homes)	(G) T
	G₂.	*Saubhāgya-Sundari*, (Part), 1903	EX
	B₃.	*Rudrasena*, by Nanilal Bandopadhyay, 1906	(G)
	Ta₂.	*Yuddhalolam*, by P. S. Durai Ayengar, 1911	(G) EX
	U₃.	*Othello*, by Gopal Goil, 1911	(G) T
	Punj.	*Othello*, by Jivan Singha, 1911	(G) T
	M₃.	*Ajitasinha*, by Mr. Kolhatkar	Not staged
	U₄.	*Shēr-Dil*, by Najar Dehlvi, 1918	EX
	B₄.	*Othello*, by Devendranath Basu, 1919	Staged. (*)
	Te₂.	*Pulindra Suśilam*, by C. Srinivasa Rau	(G) T
26. King Lear	M₁.	*Atipīdacarita*, by S. M. Ranade, c. 1880	(G) EX
	U₁.	*Lear*, by Lala Sitaram, 1893	(G) T
	K.	*Hemchandra Raja Vilas*, by M. S. Puttana, 1899	(G) T
	B.	*King Lear*, by Yatindra Mohan Ghosh, 1902	(G) T

A LIST OF SHAKESPEARE TRANSLATIONS AND ADAPTATIONS—continued

PLAY	VERSION	REMARKS
26. King Lear (cont.)	H₁. Snehapariksa, by Badrinarayan, 1903	(G) T
	U₂. Hāra-Jīta, by Munshi Murad Alli, 1905	EX
	U₃. Safed Khūn, by Aga Hasshra, 1906	(G) EX
	Te. Lear, by Paramahamsa Vidyananda Swami, 1907	(G) T
	M₂. Kanyāpariksana, by G. S. Gore	(*)
	H₂. Raja Lear, by Lala Sitaram	T
27. Macbeth	B₁. Rudrapāla, by Haralal Ray, 1874	(G) EX
	B₂. Macbeth, by Tarknath Mukhopadhyay, 1875	(G) T
	B₃. Macbeth, by Girish Ghosh, 1893	(G) EX
	K. Pratap-Rudra-Deva, by M. L. Sri Kranthesa Ganda, 1895	(G)
	Te. Macbeth, by O. S. R. Krishnama, 1895	(G) T
	M₁. Mānājīrāva, by S. M. Paranjpye, 1896	EX
	G. Mālavaketu (later Bedhāri Talavāra), by N. V. Thakur	EX
	M₂. Dākinīvilāsa, by L. N. Joshi	(*)
	Ta. Magapati, by P. Sambanda	T. Not staged
28. Antony and Cleopatra	M₁. Vivamani āni Śṛṅgārasundarī, by V. B. Kelkar, 1893	Staged. (*)
	M₂. Śṛṅgāramañjarī, by A. V. Barve, 1906	(G) EX
	U₁. Kāli Nāgana, Bombay, 1906	EX
	U₂. Zan Mureeda, Bombay, 1909	Staged. (*)
	B. Cleopatra, by Pramath Bhattacharya, 1914	. (*)
29. Timon of Athens	M₁. Viśvāmitra, Poona, 1905	Staged. (*)
	M₂. Bhārivasu, by S. Kanitkar	(*)

INDEX